The Other Side of Paradise

Staceyann Chin

A Memoir

SCRIBNER   *New York London Toronto Sydney*

SCRIBNER

A Division of Simon & Schuster, Inc.
1230 Avenue of the Americas
New York, NY 10020

The names and characteristics of some individuals
in this book have been changed.

First Scribner hardcover edition April 2009

SCRIBNER and design are trademarks of
The Gale Group, Inc., used under license
by Simon & Schuster, Inc., the publisher of this work.

For information about special discounts for bulk purchases,
please contact Simon & Schuster Special Sales at
1-866-506-1949 or business@simonandschuster.com.

The Simon & Schuster Speakers Bureau can bring authors to your
live event. For more information or to book an event contact the
Simon & Schuster Speakers Bureau at 866-248-3049 or visit our
website at www.simonspeakers.com.

Text set in Baskerville MT

Manufactured in the United States of America

10 9 8 7 6 5 4 3 2 1

Library of Congress Control Number: 2008034022

ISBN-13: 978-0-7432-9290-0
ISBN-10:   0-7432-9290-1

Selections of Kamau Brathwaite's *The Arrivants: A New World Trilogy*
(Oxford University Press) have been reprinted courtesy of the author.

For Bernice, who stayed

The Other Side of Paradise

Prologue

The front of the car was not designed for having sex. And Hazel did not want to think about the wet that would be left on the smooth leather seats afterward. What kind of man would bring her here for an intimate evening? He was a man of means. He could afford a hotel room. What did he take her for? She was not a whore. She was just a girl who needed a little help, that's all. She needed his help, but she didn't have to put up with this. It was time for her to go home. She reached out for the metal lever, but he leaned across her and pushed her hand away.

He was upset that she wanted to leave. Then he was cajoling. They hadn't even had a chance to talk, he said. Finally, she agreed to stay. But she let him know that she was not going to have sex with him in a car parked on the road somewhere. She was not that kind of girl. He seemed hurt by the suggestion that that was all he was after. Montego Bay is a tourist city. If he didn't want to spend time talking to her, he would have taken her to one of the numerous hotels filled with Americans having vacation sex, he said. He asked about the romance novels he saw her reading all the time. He listened attentively when she told him how difficult it was to find a good job if you didn't come from a rich family. Suddenly she was sorry that she had mistrusted him. She sighed and fiddled with the hem of her navy blue linen skirt. He wasn't at all like she had imagined.

Hazel forced herself to relax. She smiled and leaned against his chest. She told him that she wanted to make something of herself.

Why shouldn't a girl from Lottery have nice things like the women living in those big houses in Montego Bay?

He had his limitations, but he wanted to give those things to her, he told her. His hand caressed the curve of her shoulders. She tried to pull away from him. She reached for the door again, but he held both her arms and eased her slowly toward him. She braced her palms hard against his chest as he placed the tiniest of kisses on her neck. She shouldn't let him do this to her. She was better than this. Better than his pale hand on her breast, his red lips against her throat. Her soft "no" was swallowed as breath when he pushed the small of her back into the jutting door handle and placed his mouth over hers. She was better than this, she thought. She deserved a whole lot better than this.

This story is the only one I have imagined that holds all the irrefutable facts while leaving room for my existence. My mother, the man she swears is my father, and the people who knew them then have very different accounts of what happened or didn't happen between them. In each version my mother is young and beautiful and basking in the attention of the Chinese man she says is my father. Everyone agrees that they met at a bar. My mother has admitted that she thought the witty Chinese gentleman interesting, that even though he was short, he had a way with words and was unafraid to speak his mind. The men who frequented the bar say that the two of them enjoyed being in each other's company. After that the details get sketchy.

My mother was raised in the country, but three years living in Montego Bay had made her city-smart. Poor, young, and a single mother, she nursed a penchant for distinguished older men with money. The Chinese man she met in the bar was a fairly well-off married man with a reputation for liking young pretty girls. She insists that she did not know he had a wife. He recalls laying all his cards on the table. Other versions of the story suggest they are both omitting things. People say she spent a lot of time with him. She said it was only one date. Both of them recall an interaction in a parked car. An unspecified number of months later, my mother gives birth to me, half black, half Chinese. This is the loose skeleton upon which I have hung the beginning of my own life.

The event of my birth, however, comes vividly to life. My grandmother's frame settles into her chair when she describes the week she spent cleaning every inch of the Lottery Police Station in preparation for the Christmas holidays. "Every one of them police officers was kind to me, so me wanted to make things nice for them. So me was just working and working and working every day. But the day before Christmas, the police chief come directly to me and tell me, 'Miss Bernice, you take care of us all year, please put down the broom. Go home and take care of your own sweeping. This is the season for family, go home and be with yours.' Those days me could hear a little better, so me catch most of what him say."

She laughs when she remembers his words: "Sometimes a woman needs to feel her own dust sticking to her sweating face."

At twenty-three, my mother spent her evenings out and about. That Christmas Eve she got home a little after midnight. As soon as my mother stepped in, she started complaining about a pain in her stomach. Grandma always pauses dramatically here. She rubs her chin and mentions that she had been nursing a slight suspicion that my mother was with child. But since Hazel was good at secrets, she wasn't entirely sure.

She watched my mother drop her bag on the veranda and head toward the outhouse. But before she got to the door she doubled over, panting. The way she was holding her belly made Grandma ask her if she was pregnant. She shook her head no. But Grandma knew she was lying. So she held on to her and told her to stoop and do whatever she had to do right there. "Stacey, I wish you coulda see her! Your mother is such a prideful woman. She tell me no, that she is not a wild animal to be using the floor as a bathroom. She was so vex with me, but I wouldn't let her out. She had to bend down right there on the floor. In no time, you was born. Your mother look on her wristwatch and tell me that since it is after one o'clock, your birthday is Christmas day proper. Same day as Christ Jesus of Nazareth."

Grandma says that I was smaller than any baby she had ever seen. But I had all my fingers and toes, so she quickly cut my umbilical cord and wrapped me in my two-year-old brother's baby blanket. My mother told people I was that small because I was premature. But Grandma secretly believed that it was because Hazel, in an effort to hide her pregnancy, used strips of cloth to flatten her belly during the pregnancy. When Grandma tried to hand me to my mother, Hazel took one look at my face and said she was too tired. Then she fell asleep.

People had to be careful when they held me. The neighbors all thought I was going to die. Miss Cherry, the local expert on premature births, said I wouldn't live for more than a week. Three of her six children were dead on account of being born before their time.

"A baby that born too early need to be inside a glass thing they call a incubator!" she pronounced. "A baby born more than two months premature can't live without that machine. And this baby look like it born about three months before time. If it live, it will be a miracle or a mistake."

Grandma pauses here to remind me that God does not make mistakes. For when I opened my mouth to cry, everyone had to admit that a baby with that much lung capacity did not sound like a baby that was destined to die. "Stacey, the whole of Lottery could hear you bawling! And when me was cleaning the blood off your face, you was fighting me like a little bull. Me just tell everybody fi keep them mouth shut because this little girl here going to live and live and live till the good Lord see it fit to call her back home."

There are days when I yearn to know exactly what happened to spark the very beginning of me. But in the absence of the most basic facts, I have had to create my own story and, in many ways, set my own course. The story that follows is the journey I remember. It tickles me to think that from my very first breath, everyone expected me to stop breathing. Against the odds, I surprised everybody. And I must admit that in some of the moments of my life so far, no one has been more taken aback by my own breath than me.

Part I

Suffer the Children

Everything good always happens to my big brother, Delano. He starts school for the first time tomorrow. He is the one with the father in Montego Bay. He is the one who is a boy. And he is the one who gets to wear a full suit of khaki tomorrow morning. The only things that we share are our deaf grandmother and a mother who has run away and left us.

Grandma presses the face of the iron onto the damp clothes and the smell of fresh rain on dry dust fills the small room. His new school uniforms are just back from the tailor. She smoothes the wrinkles from the khakis as she mutters a word of prayer. "Lord, I beg you, deliver me from the heat inside this house. Jesus, watch over these children mother. Keep her safe in your bosom." She wipes the sweat from her shining forehead and turns to me. "Stacey, the Good Book tell us, *In every thing give thanks, for this is the will of God in Christ Jesus concerning you.* Father God, bless these children and keep them, make your face shine upon them. Lord, you know they need food to sustain them, shoes . . ."

Grandma prays all day long. I say amen when she is done, but I know that many of the prayers won't be answered. God works in such mysterious ways that you never know which prayer he will answer. When I pray, I just ask for one thing. That way God can't pick and choose what to give me. He has to give me the one thing I ask for.

When each crease is as sharp as a knife, Grandma drapes the khaki suit over the back of the wooden chair. Then she runs the iron swiftly over my only church dress. When the iron is stored safely away, I jump to the floor and race to find my brother.

Unawares, he corners invisible thieves and shouts orders with his gun at waist level. I tap him on the shoulder. "Delano, everything is ready for you first day at school tomorrow."

He presses the imaginary trigger, delivering a round into my belly.

"Delano! You listening?"

"Stacey, me shoot you already! You dead! You can't talk anymore, because you dead!"

"Delano, how me must be dead if me wasn't playing no police-and-thief with you? You hear what me say 'bout you clothes them?"

"Everybody have clothes—that is nutten fi talk 'bout! Now you is the thief and me is the police. Brapbrapbrap! Me just shoot you so you haffi dead!"

I fall to the floor and close my eyes tight, wishing it were me going to school tomorrow. I don't want to be dying here on the floor. I want to be starting a new life with pencils and books and new clothes made especially for me.

Grandma pokes her head out to the veranda. "But Lawd Jesus! Stacey, get up off that floor! And come inside here right now!"

Two plastic teacups of hot mint tea sweetened with condensed milk sit on the table. Delano blows into his before he sips. I take a sip and burn my tongue. I look to Delano for help. He sucks his teeth and reaches over for my cup. "Stacey, you have to blow on it like this, and take a little at a time. If it still too hot, give me back and me will blow it, all right? But don't take all night fi drink it. Remember that Grandma have to wash the cup them before we go to bed."

Nighttime in Lottery is both magical and scary. There are no street-lights. By sundown everything is so black and quiet I worry that I won't ever see or hear anything ever again. I drain the cup and follow Grandma out into the soft darkness of the yard. Under the moonlight, the backyard does not look like the one I know. The cool night breeze makes the leaves of the banana trees wave about like strange night-praying people. The bigger trees look like duppies. Duppies are the unsaved souls of dead people. Grandma says that we shouldn't be afraid of duppies. "The Bible tell you that a duppy can't do anything to a child of God."

I am still afraid because Delano says that there are some really terrible people who live for the Devil when they are alive. They kill other people and blaspheme and behave like the lawless people of Sodom and

Gomorrah. When these children of the Devil die, they are so unwilling to pass over into the eternal fires of hell that they stay here on earth and walk about at night, frightening anybody who happens to see them. The mango tree looks like a big fat devil-duppy waving at me. But then I hear Grandma singing. I can't see her in the dark, but her clear, sweet voice floats across the pitch-black yard.

Rock of Ages, cleft for me,
Let me hide myself in thee;
Let the water and the blood,
From thy wounded side which flowed,
Be of sin the double cure;
Save from wrath and make me pure.

When we get back inside, we find Delano sitting on the just-ironed clothes. Everything is squashed between his back and the chair. Grandma grabs him. "Delano, get up from there! You nuh see the press clothes them behind you? You want fi look like crush callaloo tomorrow?"

Delano sighs and throws his body onto the bed. Grandma smoothes out the clothes and lays them flat on the table. "Only God know why you would sit down on the clothes me just fix up for you! Delano, you getting too big for dat kinda behavior! You is a big boy now, near five year old—and going to school! You have to do better than that, man!"

I want to hit Delano in the head for messing up his clothes. I am not big enough, but if I could, I would sit on him and twist his arm until he says that he is happy to be going to school tomorrow. He just sits there on the edge of the bed picking at his toes. I touch Grandma's arm and carefully mouth to her, "I wouldn't do that to my school clothes, Grandma. I would do better than that."

"Stacey, me wasn't talking to you. Now kneel down there so oonu can say oonu prayers."

Morning arrives with Grandma shaking the sleep out of our droopy eyes. The two of us strip naked and pad out to the dew-covered back-yard. Delano tosses a pebble at the stray fowl drinking from the zinc pan filled with water. Delano puts salt on our toothbrushes. Shivering, I push the brush back and forth across my front teeth. I hate brushing my teeth. The hard bristles bruise my mouth and the salt burns the cuts. I reach down to rinse out my toothbrush, but Delano grabs it and adds some more salt. "Brush the back one them! You want to have rotten teeth?"

Roosters crow as Grandma thoroughly lathers us from neck to toes. Her hands move quickly as she washes the suds from our shivering bodies. I am happy when she finally wraps us into one warm, squirming, toweled bundle. We sit with our feet dangling from the bed, eating one slice of hard-dough bread, half a boiled egg, and a cup of fever-grass tea.

Delano looks like a big boy in his khaki suit. I am so jealous I want to yank off his brown and white shoes with the tan laces. Grandma wets his hair and parts it down the middle. Then she combs the sections neatly behind his ears. His head glistens in the sun. Because my hair is not as straight and pretty as Delano's, Grandma has to use Vaseline when she braids it. Delano gets a long pencil, which Grandma has sharpened with the kitchen knife. I want a pencil too, and my own khaki uniform.

On our way to the schoolhouse we pass Marse Jeb's yard, the police station where Grandma works, the big church with the pretty glass windows, and Marse George's yam grounds. The school is a bright blue house with two tiny windows in the front. A tall woman, whom Grandma calls Miss Sis, meets us on the steps. When she reaches for Delano, he shrinks from her and hides behind Grandma. She stoops and smiles at him. That all her teeth are the same exact size scares me. I join Delano behind Grandma's skirt. Miss Sis pokes her head around Grandma's legs and smiles again.

Her voice is soft and kind. "Lawd, Miss Bernice, he looks like a little gentleman! I am pleased to have him here. He looks like he will do well. And this is the little sister! She is as pretty as a willy penny!"

Grandma gently pushes Delano forward. "Delano, I beg yuh, please behave yourself. Do not give Miss Sis any trouble. I will come back for you this evening."

Miss Sis takes Delano by the hand. Grandma and I begin to move down the steps. I look back at Delano standing there, lips trembling, eyes filling with tears. I don't want him to stand there by himself crying. I pull away from Grandma, run up the steps, and grab his hand away from Miss Sis. "Let him go! Is not your brother! Him is mine!"

Grandma tries to pull me off him, but I stick both hands into the waist of his pants and sink my teeth into his leg. Both of us are screaming and holding on to each other. Grandma is so ashamed she can't even look at us. "Miss Sis, is not so me raise them, you know! As there is a God up in heaven, I never see them behave like this at all, at all!"

Miss Sis places her face directly in front of Grandma's. "Miss B, look at me face so you can hear me. It is quite all right, is normal, especially if is only the two of them. Tell you what—as long as she can say when she need to use the bathroom she can stay with him."

Delano squeezes my hand and we both stop crying to listen.

"Oh, yes, Miss Sis! She can talk plain, plain as day! I never see a little girl talk so much from me born! Her mouth is bigger than the whole of Montego Bay and Lottery put together. That would be a blessing, ma'am, but me only have the money for the boy. Me can't pay for both of them with the little I get from the boy father."

"Don't worry about that, Miss Bernice, money is not everything. Just pay for the boy. If and when you have a little more, you can give it to me then."

"Lord, Miss Sis, this is truly a blessing to me! Thank you very much, ma'am. The Lord will bless yuh more and more for your kindness to the poor and needy."

"One hand wash the other, Miss Bernice, one hand wash the other."

Miss Sis ushers us into the blue house. A table and two long benches almost fill the room. The walls are covered with round red things that sort of look like tomatoes. Miss Sis informs us that there are nine other children in the school. The boys sit on one bench while the girls sit on the other. I don't want to sit so far from Delano, but I am afraid to say so lest Miss Sis sends me back home.

Miss Sis goes to the blackboard and makes a mark. She says the mark is the letter *A*. "And what word begins with the letter *A*, children?"

Nobody says anything.

"Don't worry, children. It is normal to forget. Can someone point out an apple in this room?"

I look around. Nothing on the walls looks like an apple to me. The other children look equally bewildered. Finally Miss Sis smiles and points to one of the red tomato things on the wall. "This is an apple, children. And *A* is for apple—repeat after me, *A* is for apple."

Confused, I face the tomato-looking picture and say with the other children, "*A* is for apple."

"Good, and now we will do some writing."

Miss Sis says she is here to help each of us to learn to write our own name. "Boys and girls, everything we learn, we learn through constant and diligent practice!"

In our books, she makes dots and encourages us to connect them. When I am done connecting, she holds my face and kisses me. She smells like Vicks VapoRub and thyme. I feel very special when she asks me if I have any questions about the lesson.

"Yes, Miss Sis. Is why you tell the children that the tomato them is apple?"

She smiles. "Stacey, I know that those things look like tomatoes to you, but they are apples. Not like our apples, these apples are American apples. You ever hear of a place called America?"

The smell of thyme on her breath makes me think about brown-stewed chicken. I inch closer to Miss Sis. "Grandma say America is where the banana boat go?"

"Yes, Jamaica exports banana to America on the banana boat. Very good, Stacey! You have a good memory for things! Now, let us see what we can do about teaching you to write those things down."

Delano makes up games for us to play. He tells me where to stand and what to do and how long to do it. Because he makes the rules, he is always in charge. On Saturday morning while Grandma does housework we play Superman on the veranda. The rules of Superman are simple. I sit square in the middle of a cloth foot-wipe. Delano grabs the two front corners and shouts, "Ready, Stacey? You ready to fly?"

Ready or not, I say, "Yes, Delano, I am ready to fly."

The object of the game is to slide me from one end of the veranda to the other. Delano takes a breath and rapidly propels me forward. He trips and I end up hitting my head. I try hard not to cry. As long as I remain dry-eyed, Delano is gentle with me. So I button my lips and brush off my dress. He hurries over. "You all right, Stacey? You can go again?"

"Yes, Delano! Me fine!"

"All right! This time we going to go really fast. But don't worry, this time I go take good care of you."

He takes my hand and sets me on the foot-wipe. Beneath the surface of the polished wood, my reflection is alive with excitement. Delano's voice is pitched high with his own enthusiasm. "All right, Stacey. We go do better this time. Just make sure you hold on good!"

He dashes forward and we are off. I am trying my best not to fall off the square of yellow cloth. My brother slides me across the slippery wood. The maroon-red floor is a rushing blur, and inside my head my eyes are spinning like tops. Suddenly Delano flies into the veranda rail. I sail pilotless into the wall ahead. My right knee jerks up, smacking my forehead. It feels like my head has opened up. I am sure my forehead is bleeding. I spit flat into my hand and rub the sore spot above my eye. There is no blood, but now there is too much spit on my face. I wipe the slimy excess all over my neck. I check to see how Delano is doing. He is also wiping globules of sticky saliva from his forehead. We burst out laughing. We laugh and laugh and laugh until our stomachs hurt. I have to think about Jesus dying on the bloody cross before I can stop.

Finally, I roll over and brush the tiny pieces of red floor polish from my legs. Delano drags himself upright. "All right, Stacey, hurry up and get back on!"

I am exhausted from the flying and too much laughing. And my head hurts. A big round coco is already forming on my bruised forehead. The raised bump throbs against my fingers. I don't feel like flying anymore. "No, Delano, me finish!"

"What you mean, you finish? Me not done yet! Just wipe off you bottom and get back on the mat, man!"

"But, Delano, me don't want to play anymore." I don't know why I am arguing with him. I know I will eventually have to do what he wants.

"If you play one more time, we can finish after that. One more time, Stacey, then after that you can do anything you want!"

It feels good to just lie down on the cool floor. Through the slats of the railing, I see strips of the blue sky. Then Miss Sylvie is coming in her big, broad flower hat. In the bright hot sunlight her white dress makes her look like a duppy floating upside down toward me. But I know it is not a duppy. It is only Miss Sylvie going to church. She goes on Saturdays because she's a Seventh-Day Adventist.

She holds down her hat with one hand and waves to us with the other. "Good mornin, children! Good mornin!"

I don't want to play Superman anymore. I want to stay right where I am and watch Miss Sylvie as she calls out a greeting to Marse George, who is approaching from the other direction. He waves back with his gleaming wet machete. Miss Sylvie gets smaller and smaller as she walks farther and farther away. Marse George is getting bigger and bigger. Grandma says that men who work the ground from sunup till sundown have all of God's good blessing on them. Marse George might have God's blessing, but he does not have one tooth in his head. When you look inside his mouth all you see is his tongue and the little ball hanging down from the back of his throat. I think I would rather have all my teeth than all God's blessing. At least with teeth I can eat sugarcane.

Marse George spends his days planting fields and fields of white yam. He also has two big fat cows that give fresh milk. Every day he brings a bottle of milk and gives it to Grandma for free. He raises the empty quart bottle in greeting. "Howdy! Howdy, tell Miss Bernice I say howdy! Tell her I will pass back with a fresh bottle when me done milk them cows!"

Because Grandma can't hear what he is saying from so far away, Delano tells her what is said. She listens and then smiles and waves back. "All right! All right, sah! Me will be right inside here, just make one of them come inside and call me!"

I stick my arms through the openings in the railing and shout, "Mornin, Marse George! Mornin, Marse George!"

"Mornin, little miss! Good mornin to you too!"

Marse George waves at Miss Cherry, who passes every morning to fetch water from the public standing pipe. Beads of sweat glisten on her large nose as she straightens her dress, wipes her face, and adjusts the waistband of her skirt. Not once does she reach up to steady the five-gallon kerosene pan full of water on her head. I marvel that the pan does not fall with all that movement.

"Morning, children! Make me come inside the yard so you Granny can see to hear what me saying."

Miss Cherry lowers her face to Grandma's. "Lord, Miss Bernice! You two granny them look especially white and pretty this morning. Keep them outta the sun, you don't want fi spoil up them skin—especially the little girl!"

"Thank you, Miss Cherry! How is Marse Jeb this week?"

"Lawks, Miss Bernice, him so-so. But God won't give we more than we can bear. We just have to praise his name and hope for the best."

"You talk truth deh, Miss Cherry! You just keep on bathing him in that fever grass, and put him before the Lord in prayer, and leave him there!"

"Yes, Miss Bernice, but you must call them in from off the veranda. That little girl going to turn black in the hot, hot sun!"

"Thank you, Miss Cherry. But the room is too small fi keep them coop-up inside. The sun not doing them anything, and everything that happen is the Lord's will."

"But remember, Miss Bernice, God help those who help themself. The color them have is only because them mother have sense. Hazel have enough sense to make sure to give them fathers with clean white skin. You have to take care of them until she ready to come and take them to America. Is Canada or America she gone?"

"Is Canada, ma'am, but—"

"I am sure that things is just like them is in Jamaica. A clean complexion will take them very far in them life—much farther than them other tar-black pickney them who born here and going to dead right in Lottery."

"Well, only God know what in store fi these two children, Miss Cherry, only the Father know."

"True words, Miss Bernice, true words! But I will tell Jeb you ask after him! See you fi church tomorrow, God willing."

As Miss Cherry disappears around the bend, I touch Grandma's arm. "Grandma, why Miss Cherry don't want we fi get black?"

"Stacey"—there is a sharp note in her voice—"Stacey, is not everything good fi eat good fi talk."

"But, Grandma—"

"Stacey, stop asking me that foolishness and keep yourself outta big people business!"

"But, Grandma, me was sitting right here when she was talking 'bout we! I wasn't listening to anything that is not my business!"

"Stacey, put your bottom on that cloth before I make your backside red with something else! You believe you hire any washerwoman to rub any red polish out of them clothes?"

I know that Delano will tell me, so I adjust my bottom and whisper to him with my mouth turned away from Grandma. "Delano, is true say we white?"

"Well, Stacey, we are not white like real white people. But we father is Chiney, so we not Black. You understand?" I nod and he continues. "But you know that I am more whiter than you, right?"

"How come?"

"Because my hair is straight and yours is rough and tough like Grandma."

"My hair lie down just as flat like yours when Grandma put castor oil and water in it!"

"Stacey, listen to me, you not as white as me—feel my hair, it don't need no castor oil, just a little water make it lie down flat."

"Delano, the two of we look just the same. The two of we is Chiney Royal—that mean say the two of we is white."

"Yes, the two of we is Chiney Royal, but my hair is nicer and me skin is whiter, so me more Chiney Royal than you."

I am tired of Delano acting like he is better than me. So what if he has nicer hair or whiter skin? It does not mean anything. And when I look at him I don't think we look that much different from one another. Delano picks up the foot-wipe and flaps it loudly in the air. He lays it flat onto the floor again.

"But, Stacey, you still better off than them other Black children. You can feel good about that. Now, come sit down and let me pull you."

I cross my arms and smugly ask the first question. "Delano, if you whiter than me, that mean that me is blacker than you, right?"

"Yes, Stacey, that is true."

"And our mother is Black, right?"

"Is what kind of stupid question you asking me? Everybody know that our mother is Black!"

"Okay, that must mean say me must look more like Mummy than you, right?"

Delano does not answer. He roughly pushes me onto the cloth and tells me to hold on before I fall and break my stupid Black neck.

"You ready to fly again?"

I begin to cry.

"Come, man, Stacey. Don't bother with that."

He roughly grabs both my hands and raises them above my head. "Who am I?"

I sniffle and whine. "Superman."

"And who are you?"

I know all the answers. "Superwoman."

"So what that mean, Stacey? Come, man, tell me what it mean." Delano is now pumping my arms up and down and shouting, "Come, nuh, say what that mean, Stacey. Tell me, tell me what that mean."

"It mean—it mean we must—we can't—that—that—"

"Stacey, it mean that no matter what happen, you cannot cry. People with superpowers don't need to cry. No matter how many times you drop off the thing, even if you hit your head, you just have to get right back up and fly again."

I button my lips and wipe my face. Delano relaxes when he sees that I am not crying anymore. He gently pats my hair and fixes my twisted dress. Then he straightens the foot-wipe. "All right, Stacey, you ready to fly?"

I wipe my face and shout back, "Ready! Yes, me ready!"

Before long, the lines on the wooden floor are sailing by. The world is spinning again and I am immersed in the sound of our squealing delight.

In Everything Give Thanks

Grandma says that next to praising God, learning your book is the most important thing in the world. If you believe in the Lord and get a good education, all of God's blessings will come easy to you. I want to ask about Job, whom God used to make a bet with the Devil and caused him to lose everything, but Delano already told me that parables don't really happen anymore. In modern times people have to work and go to school and make their own way in life.

Every evening after school we sit on the back steps and do homework while Grandma cooks dinner in the backyard. Her hands are quick as she pushes the wood and balances the shiny pot on top of three large stones. This evening she is making brown-stewed chicken. As she adds salt and pepper I read my new vocabulary words to her. If I stumble on a word, she makes me read it again. Delano works quietly beside me.

"Grandma, how come Delano don't have to read out him homework to you?"

"Delano is almost six years old. Him big enough to know when him own homework is right! You is not even four yet—now read, before I really have to answer you!"

Delano makes a funny face and dashes out into the yard to chase stray chickens and stone ripe mangoes off the tree. I work on copying the new words Miss Sis has written in my notebook. I love smelling the chicken cooking while I work. Grandma puts the tiny pieces of crispy, salty, garlicky chicken that flake off onto a plate. One by one, she gives them to me as I read. One word seems impossible to sound out. S-A-L-V-A-T-I-O-N. I struggle to make sense of the letters, but nothing comes to me.

Grandma stands over me, one hand on my shoulder, the other patiently positioned on her hip.

"Nuh mind, man. You know the answer! Just try sound it out again!"

I spell it aloud. "S-A-L-V-A-T-I-O-N. Salvat . . . salava . . . Grandma, me just can't get this one right, you can sound it out for me, please?"

She looks first at me, then at the page. "No, you have to do it yourself. That is the way fi learn! Now try again!"

"Savat . . . Grandma, me just don't know it. Just please do this one for me, nuh! Please!"

Grandma nods and looks at the page again. She points at the word and rubs the page. Then she mumbles something I cannot hear. Her breasts go up and down. She touches the page again. Then she closes the book. "Stacey, is time for you to go bathe now. Ask Miss Sis tomorrow. Is fi her job to tell you what the word is. Just ask her when you reach school in the morning."

I look up at her, confused. She smiles and rubs my head. "Stacey, go bathe before night come catch you dirty. And make sure you wash you coco-bread good."

As I lather my legs I wonder why Grandma always tells me to wash my coco-bread good. I know what I should do when I bathe. I am annoyed that she wouldn't just tell me the word. She saw that I was having trouble sounding it out by myself. Her refusal to help seemed spiteful. Then I remember the helpless look she had on her face and suddenly realize that she can't read a lick. I feel like everything bad is happening to me. First my mother runs off and leaves me. And now my grandmother is a big dunce. By the time I am done bathing I am very angry. I don't want Grandma to be my grandmother. I wish I belonged to Miss Sis. Then I would have someone to help me with my stupid homework.

When Grandma calls me to come for my tea, I turn away and mumble, "I don't really want nutten from you!"

"Stacey, is what you say? You really forgetting yourself inside here?"

"I don't have to listen to you. You can't hear and you can't even read."

In one motion she grabs my braid and throws me flat on my back. The smell of the floor polish makes me want to sneeze, but I am too afraid. She drags me up by my braid and brings her mouth right down to my eyes. Every wart on her face is magnified.

Her breath hisses out of her lungs. "Listen to me, Staceyann whatever-you-middle-name-is Chin, listen, and listen good! If you smelling yourself I advise you to hold your skirt tail down. If you ever talk to me like dat again, I will break every bone God use to hold you upright!"

She releases me. "Now get out of your yard clothes and go put on your pajamas."

The dull ache of the coco has already begun. My grandmother must be an obeah woman. Deaf or not, she knows exactly when you say something rude. That must mean something. I don't want to be angry with Grandma anymore. I make myself think of all the good things she knows: how to soothe the terrifying sweats brought on by a duppy; how to wash out dirty white clothes so they are really, really white; how to quickly clean any size house; how to pray and make it sound like a pretty song. But all of that seems like nothing next to reading like Miss Sis.

The next morning, I ask, "Grandma, how come you can't read? Them never have any school when you was small?"

"Ah, me child . . ." Grandma wipes the sweat from her glistening forehead. "Go and get the comb and make me comb your hair while me talking." I want to hear the story, so I get the comb without murmuring.

Grandma undoes each braid and runs the comb through it. When she is done she gathers all the hair and runs the comb through the entire mass. The sharp teeth of the comb rake across my scalp. I try hard not to cry. But soon I am shrinking into the floor and wiping the cascading tears.

Grandma sucks her teeth. "Stacey, is cry you really crying? Me think you did want to hear the story. You don't want me fi tell you?"

I wipe my face and nod.

"All right, then, stop the crying and make me tell you."

She lifts the comb and rakes it across my scalp. I burst into a fresh round of tears. Grandma drops the comb and raises her right hand to God. "Jesus, if you not busy, come take a look at this sorrowful child!"

She adjusts my head for leverage. "Stacey, I don't know why you is so 'fraid of this nice head of hair. Is not soft like Delano own, but it not tough like them little naygar children own either."

She parts the hair in two equal sections, and oils the part. "Your hair is just like butter, soft and nice." Pull. Drag. Plait. Part again. Wail.

"Only Jesus know why you bawling like that! You just want to look like you don't have a good-God soul who own you! You want to go just go 'bout the place with a fowl nest 'pon yuh head? You don't have no mother, but I want people fi know that you have somebody who taking care of you."

I try to picture my mother combing my hair, but I don't know what she looks like. We have no pictures of her. Grandma smears the sticky grease from her hands onto my face. I smell onions and scallions on her fingers as she wipes the snot from my nose.

"All right, all right, Stacey, don't bother cry no more. Make me tell you the story that will show you how much you have to give the Lord God thanks for. Let me tell you how, from the very first day, the God up in heaven was looking after you."

"Grandma, me know the story of how me born already. Me want to know why you don't know how to read."

She sighs and pulls me into the folds of her floral skirt. The fabric reeks of wood smoke, fried chicken, and washing soap. "Stacey, me gal, if I ever tell you 'bout my life—Lawd Jesus, if—" She pulls her handkerchief from her bosom and wipes her eyes. I look up into her eyes brimming with tears. I stop breathing.

"I wasn't even eight years old when me mother, Mama Lou, stop me from going to school. She was a midwife—but she was sickly—so she did need me fi work. She couldn't read either, so she never think that book-learning so important. Me never want to leave school, but me have to do what she say."

I can't think of Grandma as a little girl. And it is stranger still to see her crying. She wipes her eyes and continues. "She send me to Kingston to work with a woman name Mrs. Levy. In all me life I don't think I work as hard as I work for that woman. Eight years old and me was peeling green bananas, soaking salt-fish, cutting up the onion and scallion to cook food. And you have to believe me when me tell you that I don't stop working from then. It was one domestic job after the other."

"But Miss Sis say that them have schools for big people. Why you never go when you was bigger?"

She smiles and touches my face. "Well, things not always so easy, you know. By the time me was fifteen me start to have the children. Me had to work fi feed them."

I don't know what to say to that.

"But because me couldn't read me couldn't get no permanent job. One woman tell me she can't hire me fi cook fi her family because she don't want me mistake bleach fi water and poison the whole of them. Is only God make me find this job at the police station. Them don't pay nothing big, but me don't have to worry-worry meself 'bout finding work every week."

The tears stream down her face. "Me really did want better fi them children, but you grandfather was a worthless man. Him could read and write, so you would think him would make sure them children get some schooling. But that man was a dirty sinner, and a gambler—a careless rum drinker who never come home! Every time me ask him fi stop gambling, him cuss me. If me answer him, him beat me. That is why me don't have much hearing in me ears. Your grandfather beat out all me hearing out of me ears. And that is why me give me life to God. When nobody can help you, you only have to turn to God. Every day me ask God fi make you grandfather help me. But that man was a worthless man. Because of that, you Uncle David still can't read a lick. But you Uncle Harold was different. When Harold was a likkle boy, all the policemen them say him could be a doctor. Him is a big policeman down in Bethel Town now. Your mother was bright too, but because me couldn't afford the clothes she want to wear she stop going to school. But all of that is done and gone. And God know why him make everything happen. We just have to put our trust in him. He know what is best for us wretched sinners."

I am not so sure that I want to put my trust in such a God. "Grandma, what if God wasn't paying attention to you and that is why all those things happen to you? What if God is not listening when you pray?"

"Stacey, kibba you mouth and let me tell you something. And this is probably the most important thing me have to tell you. Trust God, Stacey, trust God and learn you book. Ask God to make you learn it good, good enough so that no man could use you as a beating stick."

"So where is we grandfather now? Him old like you? Him living in Lottery still?"

"Lawd ha mercy, Stacey, it getting late. Is time for you to go to school. Don't worry yourself, man—me will tell you the rest another time. Get up from there and come put on your school clothes."

In My Father's House

The Saturday after Delano turns six, Grandma walks us both over to Miss Cherry's house. She tells me that Miss Cherry is going to keep me for the day while she takes Delano to see his father. My chest tightens as I watch the two of them walking away. I try to get down from Miss Cherry's arms, but she holds me until they both disappear. She carries me inside wailing against her bosom. Marse Jeb lies in the bed moaning. He is covered from neck to toes with white sheets and he smells like cold medicine and fever grass. There is a basin of water with bits of fever-grass floating in it. I use my toe to move the fever-grass blades around.

"Stacey, take out you foot out dat dirty water! Grandma go kill me if she come back here and you catch any cold from dat sick-water. Now you sit down dere and don't touch nothing else."

Miss Cherry does not have a veranda, so I have to stay inside. I wonder when Delano and Grandma are coming back. She gives me a plate with curry chicken and white rice. It does not taste like Grandma's. I push the bowl away. "It don't taste good, Miss Cherry. Me don't want it."

"Aah! Is the salt? Marse Jeb is so sick him cannot eat salt. Lemme put some on it fi you." It still doesn't taste like Grandma's.

Marse Jeb pushes his face into the wall and moans quietly. "Miss Cherry, I think Marse Jeb sick again."

"No, man, him all right! Him just groan like that sometimes. Him all right."

She sits and scoops me onto her lap. "Is not so him did stay all the time, you know. Him used to be a big strapping man who could cut down any bush! Stacey, you shoulda see him with him machete. Him used to sell cane in Montego Bay. Every Saturday him come down with a whole load of blue ribbon cane. Blue ribbon is the softest and the sweetest cane in the world. Him used to bring cane and jelly coconut fi me every week." She sighs. "Well, me chile, God works in mysterious ways, his wonders to perform! Come drink some more water. Children with your color need them water!"

The cup smells like cod liver oil but I hold my breath and finish the water. She tells me to sleep a little while she tidies up the place. Then Delano's excited voice drags me from sleep and for a moment I don't understand why I am in this strange bed with Marse Jeb shaking and moaning beside me.

"Wake up, Stacey! Wake up, nuh! You don't want to hear 'bout Montego Bay? Them have cars everywhere," he screams. "And big buildings and stores with all kinds of things on sale. My father have a big supermarket! Me get fi pack me bag meself. And me have strawberry syrup, fi make red lemonade! And Grandma pick up a whole heap of condensed milk and sugar."

I rub my eyes and sit up.

"Stacey, you listening to me? You shoulda see the place! Them have a drawer to put the money into. And when you press a button the drawer fly wide open! And me father have so much biscuit and bread and crackers and cheese—everything you want is right there in the supermarket. And when we leave there we go up to the big clock and we see Uncle Harold. Him is Grandma big son and him is a policeman. Him have a real gun and a real police car with a big red light on the top of it."

I am so jealous I want to hit him. But I want to hear more, so I ask, "Him make you drive inside the car?"

"Stacey, is a police car! Only criminal must ride in there with the police! Me look like criminal to you? Then we go inside a big clothes store and buy more things fi me."

At home Grandma opens the big bag and puts the things away. There is khaki cloth to make Delano new school clothes. He also got new shoes. Socks and briefs and pencils and pens tumble out of his new schoolbag. Grandma bought a dress for me, but I want a new schoolbag and pencils and socks. I ask Delano if he picked up any school things for me. If my father were the one with the supermarket I would have picked up things for him.

"Grandma, why you never buy no new shoes for me?"

"Stacey, you don't need no shoes. You have your little white slippers."

"But, Grandma, Delano get new shoes and him have shoes already!"

"Stacey, I never buy that for him. Is him father give that to him. And this new dress go look so nice with your little white slippers."

It is one week before my fourth birthday. Delano and I are sprawled out under the ackee tree watching the black ants march from one rotten ackee pod to the next. Now and then I squash one to inhale the rancid liquid that oozes out of its big round bottom. It is Christmastime, so the bright yellow fruits with the shiny black heads are in full season. There are so many open ackee pods on the branches that if I half close my eyes I can see a big green Christmas tree with red bulbs hanging all over it. I wish I could eat ackees every day. I can hardly contain my excitement when I watch Grandma boiling, draining, and frying them up with onions and something salty. Salted codfish or salt-pork or salt-mackerel—it doesn't matter which. My mouth is still watering from the soft, sweet fruit we had with red herring and boiled green bananas this morning. Christmastime is the best time for food in Jamaica. The only thing missing is presents.

"Delano, I wish we could get Christmas presents like the children in Miss Sis storybook. You think the missionaries will send any presents from America this year?"

Delano kicks the ground and sucks his teeth. "Even if them send things, I don't want none! Last year, the little water gun them give me was so crack up it couldn't hold no water!"

Grandma is inside ironing clothes for church tomorrow. I feel bad for wanting presents because Pastor Panton has been preaching against those among us who can't wait for Christmas because their families send barrels of clothes and shoes and tin goods from England, America, and Canada at Christmastime. Such sinners, he declares, are called Christmasmongers. I don't want to be a Christmasmonger, but I wish my mother would send us a barrel with Christmas presents wrapped up in pretty paper. I say a quick prayer to Jesus, asking him to help me to get a present this Christmas.

Delano hears me and says, "If we mother never abandon us, Jesus could never have so much power over we."

"What you mean by that, Delano?"

"Well, Jesus is only important to people who don't have any money. Real rich people don't even have to go to church."

"Your father don't go to church?"

"Me don't know. But me know him don't have to beg-beg God for nothing. And when me go to live with him me won't have to go to church either."

I kill another ant and watch the others run for cover. "So when you going to live with him?"

"When you get bigger. If me leave you, you won't have no big brother to tell you what to do. Me have to stay because you so little. But when me go live with him, you will see that when you rich, things is better for you."

"Delano, you think things would be better for us if we was Jews?"

"What kinda stupid question is that?"

"Well, everything in the Bible is about the Jews them, because them is God's chosen people. Bad things only happen to them when them stop listening to God. But God still send Jesus to come and save them. Even when them give God's only Son to the Romans to kill him."

"No, Stacey, the Romans only kill Jesus because it was God's plan. God did know how everything was going to turn out already because him is God."

"Well, is a good thing me is not God, Delano, because if I was God, and I know who kill my son, I woulda burn up every one of them!"

"God know everything, yes, but him is a good God. That is how we get the chance fi have salvation. And even if them was going against God, him wouldn't just burn them up. Him too good fi that."

"So if God so good, why him burn up the people in Sodom and Gomorrah? Them wasn't even committing blasphemy."

"Stacey, the people in Sodom and Gomorrah was doing something worse than blasphemy. That is why God have to destroy the city."

"Worse than blasphemy? Is what them was doing so?"

"Is something really bad—something that have to do with a man who is funny. If you are a funny man, that is even worse than blasphemy!"

"Worse than blasphemy? What you mean by funny? Like when somebody tell a nasty joke?"

Delano turns away.

"Delano, tell me what you mean by funny. What them was doing in Sodom and Gommorrah that was funny?"

"Stacey, me done talk 'bout that now! You always want talk 'bout things what nobody else want talk 'bout. Come on, it getting late. Make we go inside."

Sunday morning comes and there are no presents from the missionaries in America. I take my seat in the front pew beside Delano. Pastor Panton climbs the pulpit and begins his sermon.

"Brothers and sisters, long before the miraculous birth of Christ Jesus, he saw his own future—yes, he saw himself hanging there from that wretched tree! Dead! Eyes closed, mouth shut—dead! But he had no fear of it because he knew that he had to do this to save us!"

A few members shout back, "Hallelujah! Praise his name!"

"Sinners! Imagine the Son of God—who had to pass through the sinful loins of a woman—nailed to that cross! Imagine that steel sword piercing his heart. Christmas is not about presents! Christmas is not about barrels from foreign lands! Christmas is about sacrifice! Christmas is about abstaining! Abstaining from all you love—abstaining so you have the clarity to consider the greatest love of all! The Good Book tells us, 'Greater love hath no man than this, that a man lay down his life for his friends.' If you are a friend of Jesus, lift your voice and sing!"

What a friend we have in Jesus
All our sins and grief to bear
What a privilege to carry
Everything to God in prayer

People from the congregation are screaming and jumping. Miss Cherry has already fallen to the floor. Her arms and legs are flailing. I see her big white panties as she lifts her dress. The other women gather around her and throw a white cloth over her legs.

"Merciful Jesus, we thank you!"

"Hallelujah!"

"Praise him!"

"Brothers and sisters, if we do not recognize the birth of the Son of God as a part of the death of the Son of God, we are on a one-way train straight into the bowels of a raging fire. Let us use this holiday to confess our carnal sins and have the blood of Jesus wash the stains from our human hearts. If we fail to confess, brothers and sisters, we are all going to hell! Sing with me, brothers and sisters. Sing if you have confessed!"

Pastor Panton leads us into the next hymn and everyone starts jumping and screaming again. I dance and sing along with the brightly robed choir. I don't want to go to hell for being a Christmasmonger. I want to be one with the bloody Christ nailed to the cruel cross. The sunlight is streaming through the stained-glass window. In the blue and red light rays I see Christ rising from the dead. I close my eyes and let the melody carry me away.

I raise my hands to the heavens and beg God to forgive me for being a Christmasmonger. I don't care about presents. All I want is to be washed in the blood so I can be saved from the flames of hell. I will never again think of Christmas without thinking of the bloody body of God's only son, hanging from that cruel cross. I wipe the tears from my face and sing the words of the hymn as loudly as I can.

> *I am dying O Lord*
> *Have you heard my cry . . .*

Delano covers his mouth with his hand. His body is shaking. He is snickering so loud I can no longer feel the Spirit. "Delano, is what wrong with you?"

"Nothing wrong with me, is you is the idiot!" He is laughing so hard he has to lean against the pew to keep from falling.

"Delano Mark Anthony Chin, what you mean by that?"

"Is not so the song go." He hiccups. "You singing the words wrong. Hic! Is not *I am dying O Lord*. Hic! Is *I am Thine O Lord, I have heard Thy cry . . .*"

The other people in our pew are looking at us.

"How you alone can be so fool-fool? Hic! You must—hic! You must have a twin to share that burden?"

I point my finger in his face. "Delano, me don't have no twin, only one brother. If me a fool, then you is also a foo—"

The red hardcover of his hymnal connects with the side of my head. The children behind us are laughing, the old ladies are shaking their heads—everybody is looking at me. Without thinking, I smack him in the face with the word of the Lord, King James version, twice, before he jumps me.

Miss Lerlene, the Sunday school teacher, pulls us out of the service. She narrows her eyes at me and asks Delano what happened.

He tells her, "Miss Lerlene, I never do anything to her! She was sing-ing God's song wrong and I correct her and she hit me!"

"Miss Lerlene, that is not true! Is him take him stinking hymnal and hit me in me head first! I only hit him in him stupid face because him hit me first!"

Miss Lerlene grabs me by the shoulder and shakes me. "Stacey, this is not the place to use those words. And you should speak when you are spoken to. I did not ask you. So just keep that filthy mouth shut, young lady. Now continue on, Delano."

She listens to Delano. Then she turns to me. "Stacey, you are a real problem in God's kingdom. You must learn to curb that mouth of yours. No matter what happened between you and your brother, a young lady does not hit anybody—and certainly not in the middle of the service! In every house someone has to be in charge. Your brother is older and he is the boy. It is ordained in the scripture that a woman must yield to the will of the men in her family. Now, just answer me yes or no, were you making a mockery of the service?"

"No, Miss Lerlene."

"Were you singing the song wrong?"

I don't say anything. And Miss Lerlene lights into me. "Well, Little Miss Mouth Almighty, you will be punished on three counts: one for fighting in the house of God, two for mocking the Lord God Almighty, and three for rising up against those ordained by God! Go straight into the vestry and read Proverbs fifteen, verse one: *A soft word turneth away wrath, but grievous words stir up anger.* When you are finished, write down ten traits of a good Christian woman—please to include obedience and the ability to properly take instructions from a man."

After the sermon, I have to explain to the whole Sunday school class why I must obey my brother. "The Bible says that I must obey my brother because God put man in dominion over all the other beasts of the earth. And because the one time Adam listened to Eve, he fell into sin and was cast out of Paradise by God."

Delano sits in the back row grinning. I wish he was close enough for me to hit him with my stupid Bible again.

Fret Not

Stacey, Grandma say we have to leave this house and move in with Uncle Harold and him wife." Delano drops this bomb as he throws a green mango up into the air and catches it. "Uncle Harold coming to get we tomorrow."

I have a hundred questions I want to ask him. How does he know? Why do we have to leave so quickly? And when are we coming back? Delano is so excited that the questions all die in my throat. He goes on and on about the car that Uncle Harold will drive when he comes to get us. I wish it were our mother coming to get us. That night I quietly watch Grandma pack all our things in a large plastic bag. I want to take the things out and put them all back, but I know that she will only get upset with me and end up packing everything anyway. I ask if we can take our little folding tray, but Grandma says the car can only hold our clothes, not furniture.

The next day a policeman arrives in a big brown motorcar. With a stern face he beckons for us to come closer. I look away, but Delano goes to him.

"Good morning, there, young man. Where is your grandmother?"

"She inside, sah."

"Well, go and fetch her, then."

His voice is too loud and it sounds like it is coming from a cave. We run to the veranda and Delano disappears inside. I watch the policeman through the spaces in the railing. He doesn't move. He just waits there, leaning on the car with one leg crossed over the other. His big black police stick hangs from his belt. Grandma comes out and he tips his hat at her. She latches the front door, wipes her eyes, and fixes her tie-head. She checks the door again, folds the yellow foot-wipe, and walks down to the car. We pad quietly behind her. I worry that Uncle Harold can see my heart hammering at my ribs.

I reach up and take Grandma's hand. "Grandma, please, make us go back inside the house."

"Don't worry, man, nothing more not left inside there. Hurry up come. And oonu say good day to oonu Uncle Harold?"

We stop in front of the man leaning on the car.

"Good day, Uncle Harold."

The smell of him tickles my nose. I press the side of my face into Grandma's dress and try hard not to sneeze. He nods at me, pats Delano on the head, and takes the two bags from Grandma. One has all our clothes and Grandma's Bible; the other one is full of ackee, breadfruit, bananas, and sugarcane that Grandma got for Uncle Harold and his family.

I have never been inside a car. The seats are warm and slippery and the air from the windows moves the hair on my head. Uncle Harold rolls down his window. Then he turns the key, and the car makes a big growling noise. He takes off his hat, hands it to Grandma in the passenger seat, and turns on the radio. Uncle Harold must be rich. We don't even have a radio inside the house.

"Children, please be careful that you do not touch any of the window or door controls back there. It could be very dangerous. Someone could get killed if you do not do as I say."

"Yes, Uncle Harold."

We pass the police station and the church and Marse Jeb's house. I don't want to leave like this. I want to just run up the road and tell Marse George and Miss Sylvie and Miss Cherry that we won't be there next Saturday morning. The road gets wider and wider as we drive farther and farther away. Colorful houses and yam hills whiz by. Children with water buckets on their heads stick their tongues out at us. Goats with long beards amble across the street. Uncle Harold blows the horn to make them move faster. We pass old Indian women, with braids so long they have to sit on them, selling shrimps, peanuts, sweetsops, apples, roasted yams, and fried chicken.

The car is moving so fast, I feel like I have to throw up. I carefully pull the neck of my yellow and blue dress forward and quietly puke into my chest where nobody can see it.

For a long time, we pass only trees and grass and cows standing in large green pastures. I want to go to the toilet but I am afraid to talk over the radio. I press my legs together very hard and pray that we get there soon. Grandma does not ask Uncle Harold for anything. When we finally arrive in Bethel Town, we see a dark-skinned woman with short hair, holding a little baby and standing on the veranda steps.

Uncle Harold puts his arm around the woman and says, "Children, this is your Aunt June. She is my wife. You will be under her jurisdiction and my soundest advice to you is to try your very best not to transgress her house rules."

Aunt June hushes the crying baby. He is very small and his head looks like someone squeezed the sides very hard. His face looks like he is going to the toilet, and he smells funny. The more Aunt June hushes him, the more he cries.

Aunt June hands the baby to Grandma. "Howdy do, Aunt Bernice. I am so glad to see you. I beg you go clean him up for me, please."

Grandma whisks the baby off. I hear her singing and making sucking noises to make the little baby laugh.

Aunt June turns to us and looks us over. "Good afternoon, children." Her voice is very strong and deep. "You will need to take off your shoes before you step inside the living room. And don't leave them scattered all over the veranda floor."

Delano unbuckles my sandals. Their veranda floor is cold and made of red concrete tiles with little white dots on them. The railing is made of concrete too.

Aunt June sits. "Now, children, please tell me, who is who?"

I hop from one leg to the other and look at Delano, who is busy untying his own shoes.

"What is the matter, little girl? None of you have names?"

I stop bouncing and begin the introductions. "Yes, ma'am—me mean, Aunt June. Fi me name is Stacey, and me brother name is—"

Aunt June stands up and smacks her hands together. "No, no, no, no, no! Not a bit of that language in here. In here we speak in proper English. My name is Stacey, and my brother's name is . . . Now say it all again."

I am glad to see Grandma coming back, jiggling the baby, who is giggling with delight. "Look 'pon me baby, look 'pon me baby, look 'pon me baby, now!"

Aunt June takes him from Grandma. "And who is this, smelling so good? Is this Mummy's baby smelling so very good?"

"You don't need me to do anything now, ma'am?"

"No, Aunt Bernice, you should go unpack your bags now. You and the children are going to be sharing that back room with Samantha and Shane."

I hold my coco-bread and jump quickly from one bare foot to the next. "Aunt June, Aunt June, me can go to the toilet, please?"

"Aunt June, may I go to the bathroom, please? Say after me, 'Aunt June, may I go to the bathroom, please?'"

I jump and repeat, "Aunt June, may I go to the bathroom, please?"

"Yes, you may. And let go of yourself. It's not good manners to be doing that in front of other people. Go right through the living room and then the dining room. The bathroom is the blue door on your right. And do not wet the floor on your way there!"

"Thanks, Aunt June."

"Thank you, Aunt June. Thank you, Aunt June—don't tell me I will have to teach you children everything!"

I move very slowly, keeping my thighs pressed firmly together as I walk. Inside, there are two brown doors, both slightly ajar. I can see two beds through one of the openings. Through the other, plates piled on a table. There is a fridge and a dining table and a cabinet with pretty glasses and plates and cups in it. A very old man is asleep in a big chair. He groans as I pass. But he does not wake up. I step over his outstretched feet.

The rugs in the bathroom match the toilet cover. And there is a flushing toilet. I lift the lid to look into the white bowl of clear water. I sit slowly. I don't want to make a mess. I want to go badly, but it takes a really long time for anything to happen. When I am done, I push the little silver lever and everything goes rushing down the hole.

Out on the veranda, I whisper to Delano, "Them have a gas stove and a TV, and a place in the bathroom to put your toothbrush, and plenty, plenty storybooks." He motions for me to be quiet.

"Okay, you two, these are your Uncle Harold's children. This is Garnett, who is thirteen, and Ann, who is fifteen, and Shane, who is almost seven, and Samantha, who is nearly five. And you already saw the baby, whose name is Andrew."

Our cousins look nothing like us. And Ann does not look like the other children. Everybody is darker than her. And she has short hair, like a boy. Aunt June takes the baby inside. Samantha and Shane are the exact same age as Delano and I. Shane smiles at Delano. Delano smiles back. Samantha has short, thick plaits and a round face that would be very pretty if she wasn't making faces.

"Is what happen to your face?" I ask.

"Is what happen to your skin?" she taunts. "Why it so red and ugly? And what is that mark on your chest? You smell stink, like vomit!"

"If you smell vomit is fi your own self you smell it 'pon!" I shoot back. "And why fi you skin so stink and dirty and black?"

"Mummy! Mummy! See Stacey out here calling me stink and dirty and black!" Aunt June is in the room in seconds.

"What? What did you say to her?" Her voice is even deeper now. "We certainly do not use those words in this house! And I hope you do not think you are better than anybody else in here. Your color means nothing in this house, you hear me? Nothing! Now get out of my face before you get a beating your first night here!"

"But, Aunt June, is she did say how me red first. Me never say nutten to her at all."

"Child, what is that coming out of your mouth? Speak properly! Did I not tell you that that kind of language is not permitted in this house? Lord help me with these new crosses I have been given to bear!" She throws up her hands and leaves.

Grandma arrives with a wet rag. She takes off my yellow dress and wipes me down from neck to waist.

Delano is already playing cowboys and Indians with Shane and Samantha. I follow a brown mange-covered dog to the backyard. There are pigs wallowing in a pool of mud in a barbed-wire pen. A black and white goat chewing an old leather shoe is tied to a tall tree with big red leaves. I sit under a tree and watch the chickens scratch seeds from the dust around me. I am grateful for the quiet of the animals. They stare, but it does not feel like they can see me.

At eight o'clock Aunt June says we have to go to sleep. Delano and I are to sleep with Grandma in a big old iron bed. It is much bigger than the bed in Lottery, but here the white sheets smell like bleach. Grandma is not there when we say our prayers. Delano takes the corner. He makes me lie down in the middle of the bed so that there will be room for Grandma when she comes. Samantha and Shane climb onto the other bed. I wait until they fall asleep before I jab Delano's side.

"Delano, Delano, you sleeping?" He does not respond. "Delano! Delano!" I poke him again. "Delano, I really don't like this new house!"

I pull his hair and he elbows me. "Stacey, just shut up and go to sleep, man!"

The fowls squawk in their coop. A door closes. A radio is turned on. I miss the crickets at our old house. I imagine Miss Cherry standing by the road and calling out for us. No one will be there to answer. I cover my head and try my best not to cry. I wonder how our mother will ever be able to find us here. I don't want their electricity or the inside toilet or the stupid TV. I want go back to our little room in Lottery where I am not afraid to open my mouth and talk.

Pa Larry is Aunt June's father. He is so old that he goes to the bathroom in his pants like Andrew. But he smells much worse. When he eats dinner, the whole table is covered with his food. Between Andrew and Pa Larry, Grandma is always wiping somebody's mouth or somebody's bottom. There is no time to talk to her about anything because we also have a lot to do. We start school the following week.

Aunt June makes us try on the uniforms that Samantha and Shane have outgrown. They slip easily over our skinny frames. Aunt June says that fabric is very expensive, but she is going to buy enough cloth to make at least one new set for each of us. Uncle Harold asks her why we have to get new ones if the old ones fit us.

"Harold." Aunt June's voice is impatient. "They cannot go out on their first day in old uniforms. You want everybody to talk about them? They are already getting some old uniforms, and schoolbags and shoes, and this is the first day. They should have something that is not hand-me-down."

"All right, Mrs. Jennings, you are in charge." I think it is stupid that he calls her Mrs. Jennings.

"And just to let you know, Harold, this is not costing you one penny.

I paid for the cloth and I am making them. If my children was with other people, I would pray them would send them through the door looking decent on the first September morning."

She sits at a sewing machine with the word SINGER written in big letters on the side and warns us to take good care of our things because she does not have money to buy new ones. She tells us she does not expect any financial help from anybody. "Not your Uncle Harold, not your grandmother, not your good-for-nothing mother who leave and don't even send one penny to buy an egg to feed you!"

As she cuts and sews we have to try the uniforms to make sure they fit. In between stitches, she bakes and makes sweets and jams. Women pass by and purchase bottles and pans of baked and broiled sweets. They also buy eggs by the dozen. I wonder why she is so worried about money.

One day as I slip out of my half-finished uniform, I ask, "Aunt June, you make a lot of money from the things you sell, and your husband is a rich policeman with a big car. Why you always looking for more money? The Bible say, *The love of money is the root of all evil.*"

The pins prick me as she drags the cloth over my head.

"Christ Almighty! You fresh, eh? What your Uncle Harold does with his money is neither your business nor mine—but the money I make in this house go toward taking care of everybody. You think is easy to feed eight people on a teacher's salary? And now there is you and your brother and your grandmother. It is a blessing indeed that I have the animals so I can sell two eggs and kill a pig or a goat. Only God knows how else we would manage!" She tucks a pleat in the cloth and puts it back over my head.

"Stand up straight! What you don't know is older than you! Sometimes your eyes fail you—sometimes what you see is not what is there. Your uncle could be a rich man, yes. But I cannot question the ways of God! The good God in heaven will never give you more than you can bear. Now take off the thing and let me finish these uniforms so you children have something to wear come Monday morning."

We pack our schoolbags on Sunday. Garnett goes to Cornwall College in Montego Bay. That school is a long bus ride away, so he has to wake up and leave while it is still dark. Ann takes the bus too, but she just goes to Chester Castle All Age, which is not far.

Monday morning Aunt June reminds us that we have to be dressed before Uncle Harold comes home from his night shift at the police station. He takes Aunt June and the rest of us to the Bethel Town All Age School in his car. I pull at the crisp, newly starched uniform that rubs against my neck and waist. The creases jab at me. I ask Aunt June if I can wear one of my dresses instead of the dull tunic.

"What an ungrateful wretch! After all I do to make sure the both of you look like somebody's children!" She is standing at her full height above me. She raises her hand to hit me—

Grandma walks in. "Stacey, is what you say to you Aunt June?"

"Me never say anything, Grandma. Me only ask her—"

Aunt June takes a step toward me. "Who are you referring to as *her*?"

I run to Grandma. She grabs me by the shoulder. "June, is what she do? Tell me so me can deal with her."

Aunt June sucks her teeth and leaves the room in disgust. Grandma pulls me aside and whispers in my ear, "Stacey, why you cannot keep your tongue to yourself? Your mouth set on spring? God Almighty, mind you make June put us out of here!"

I am not sure what I have done, but Grandma sends me to finish getting dressed for school. When we are dressed, we sit at the dining table. Grandma has made fried eggs. Everyone has a whole egg with bread and butter, and hot chocolate. I am too excited to eat, but Aunt June says that food is too expensive to waste, so I should please stop forming the fool and eat. I drink most of the chocolate and eat half of the sandwich. Grandma takes the other half of the sandwich and hides it with the dirty dish towel. She tells me to keep my mouth shut.

At school there is a sea of a thousand million students milling about under the trees. A loud bell rings and everyone scatters. Delano is in grade three with Shane. Samantha and I are not supposed to be in grade one yet, but since Aunt June is the vice principal, she can put us in any class she wants. She is also the grade one teacher. In class, I am supposed to call Aunt June "Mrs. Jennings."

During roll call Aunt June calls out the names of the children in the class. Each student has to say, "Present, Mrs. Jennings!" I forget and say, "Present, Aunt June!"

"Stacey, you must learn to follow the rules. Here, I am your teacher, not your aunt. In this room, I am Mrs. Jennings. Now don't make me have to pull down that belt for you to remember."

My face gets hot. "Yes, Aunt Ju—I mean, Mrs. Jennings."

During the story hour we read *Goldilocks*. Aunt June writes words from the story on the blackboard. She calls on different children to say different words. When she calls on me I take my time and sound out the word like Miss Sis taught me.

"Por-por-rig—"

"Stacey, we do not have all day! Look at the word and tell me what it is!"

"Por-pro-porid—I know what it is, Aunt June, is parridge! Parridge!"

"What in the world is 'parridge'? There is no *a* in *porridge*, the word is *porridge*, with an *o*! Say after me, porridge. If you wish to learn to speak properly, you will have to try much harder than that, Stacey! Now sit down before you embarrass yourself any more!"

During recess I sit on a bench and watch the girls playing bat and ball. I listen to them shouting to each other and wonder if I really sound that different from them. I ask if I can play. Everybody laughs when I speak. Wendy, the very tall girl with gold earrings, dances around me.

"Look at the reddi-bug! How you skin so red, girl? You red like mongoose. I 'fraid to leave my white fowl with you, mongoose-girl. Miss Chin from Lottery is a big fat tiefing mongoose that steal chicken from the chicken coop at night!"

Her other friends, Cheryl and Ava, join in. Wendy pulls my hair and pushes me. They all laugh and push me. I want to answer, but I'm afraid they will make fun of how I speak. Every time I say something, Samantha whispers to Wendy. Wendy whispers to Cheryl and Cheryl whispers to Ava. Then they all giggle and roll their eyes.

I ask Samantha why she can't talk to me at school like she talks to me at home. "You know, Samantha, I am just like the other girls. Except me is your cousin. How you can like somebody like Wendy better than your own cousin?"

"Well, is not like I really like her better than you. But she speaks much better than you. And her mother sends things for her."

"What you mean, her mother send things for her? She don't live with her mother?"

"No, her mother live in Kingston."

"So who is the woman who carry her to school in the mornings?"

"That is her father's wife. Her mother is married to a rich man in

Kingston. And every week she sends a big package with all kinds of nice things in it for her. And sometimes she gives me some of the things. She is my best friend, so if she doesn't like you, I cannot like you either."

October comes and Aunt June announces that Wendy's father has died of a heart attack. After one week Aunt June tells the class that Wendy will not be coming back to Bethel Town All Age School. Wendy has gone to Kingston to live with her mother. Aunt June makes us write a composition about Wendy. We have to write down all the nice things we remember about her. We have to pretend she is still here so we could say those nice things to her.

I don't want to write anything nice about Wendy. I am glad she is gone. I wish I could leave and go back to Lottery. The girls hate me, and I don't hate them. I don't know how to make any of them like me. All day long they tease me.

Ava corners me at recess. "Stacey, Samantha says that your mother run away and leave you. Is that true?"

I choose my words carefully. I know she is just waiting for me to say something so she can run to tell the other girls. I want to say something that will make her want to be friends with me.

"No, she never run away. She get a big job in Canada. And now she is just saving up money to bring me and me brother over there too."

"So when you leaving, then, Miss Big Shot?" She does not believe me.

"For your information, Miss Ava Gail Rogers, I am leaving in one week. I wasn't going to say anything to any of you because I don't want any of you to ask me to send any American things for you when I get there!"

Her attitude changes immediately. "Look, Stacey, I never really do anything to you, so you can't be vex with me. Anyway, your mother buy the ticket already?"

"Yes, so you better tell everybody that them should tell me all the nice things they think about me now, because after me gone it will be too late."

During lunch Ava tells me that she loves my hair. Cheryl says that I have very nice skin. When I respond to their compliments I speak English like the American children on TV.

The girls all give me presents at lunch: greater-cake, drops, and gizarda—every kind of homemade coconut candy. I collect colored pencils, crayons, coloring books, lollipops—everything that is offered. That afternoon, Samantha tries to tell Cheryl and Ava that I am lying, but I tell them she is just jealous that her mother is from Bethel Town and that means that she is never going to go anywhere. All the girls want to sit next to me. I have the best day at school.

I am so happy when we get home that I don't even think about it when Aunt June tells me to change into my house clothes and come straight to her on the veranda. I slip out of my uniform and skip along to her. But then my heart sinks in my chest when she stands up and asks me why I have been telling lies to the other children at school. Her lips are tightly pursed as she waits for my answer. I want to tell her that it was a good lie. I want to say that the girls didn't laugh at me this afternoon because of that little lie. But I can see from the set of her jaw that she isn't interested in any of that. I hang my head and tell her that I don't know. She calls Grandma and tells her that I am a disgrace. She sends me for Uncle Harold's police belt. The strip of plastic is cool and hard against my palm. Without the detachable buckle, both ends of the belt are flat and smooth. My hand shakes when she takes the belt from me. Before she begins, she grabs my arm and tells me that what she is about to do is only for my own good. I am so frightened I feel like I am going to wet my panties. I am not quite sure what she is going to do with the belt. She pulls me to her and says that only the Word of God can save me from the pitfalls of a lying tongue. Then she raises the belt and warns me not to make a sound.

Whack!

"Lying lips are an abomination unto the Lord."

Whack!

"Train up the child in the way he should grow."

Whack!

"And when he is old he will not depart from it."

Whack!

"Spare the rod and spoil the child!"

Whack!

"It is not what goes into the mouth that defiles you, but what comes out of it!"

Whack! Whack! Whack!

I cannot contain myself. "Lord Jesus Christ Almighty, Aunt June! I beg you please stop now."

"Stop taking the Lord's name in vain!"

Whack!

"Oh, God! Oh, God! Oh, God! Aunt June, please, please, please . . ."

"I said to shut up that mouth of yours and stop bawling like an old hooligan!"

Whack!

"Please! No, no, Aunt June, no! Please!"

"If you want me to stop"—whack!—"stop that everlasting cow bawling!" Whack!

The belt descends again and again and again. I swallow the screams until the only sound is the slapping of the leather lashing hard against my bare brown legs. Words I did not know I knew are bouncing off the walls of my head. *You are a dirty ole naygar bitch, Aunt June. I wish I never come to live in your damn, blasted, bumboclaat house! I wish you would just drop down dead in the road and have black johncrow birds come and pick out your stinking dirty shitty batty-hole. I hope you go straight to hell and the Devil beat you in your raashole ten times worse that you beating me now.*

I hate Aunt June. I hate her so much that I ask God to give her a heart attack like Wendy's father. I force myself to ignore the stinging belt and I think again of the gifts I got from my schoolmates. I tell myself I don't give a damn about licks, and Christ, and abomination. I can tell all the stories that I want. Aunt June does not know everything. My mother *could* be sending for me. I think hard about plane tickets and gold earrings and all the pretty things my mother is buying for my room. I wish I could send a message to her so she could come and save me.

As for Me and My House, We Will Serve the Lord

I sit on the back steps tearing at my braid and kicking the stones out into the yard. It is October, so the air is neither too hot nor too cool. Aunt June has taken Samantha and Shane to visit her sister in Darliston. She told Grandma that she wanted to take all of us, but since I can't seem to control my tongue Delano and I should stay home. Delano is a little annoyed to be left behind, but I am glad we did not go. The house feels peaceful and quiet without them. Plus I don't have to watch what I say when Aunt June is not around.

"Grandma, if Aunt June send me to live with somebody else, you going to come with me?" I chew the end of the braid and wait patiently for Grandma to answer.

"Lord Jesus, Stacey! Why you worry-worry yourself so? Nobody not sending you go nowhere. Oonu belong to me. Nobody but God can take oonu away from me. And take that hair out you mouth. You want it to go down in your stomach and kill you?"

"But what if Aunt June send me and Delano away? You would stay with her to look after Andrew, or you would come with us?"

"Lord, man! Settle yourself. You fret like you is a old person. Trust that God will take care of you, man."

Grandma sighs. "You know, Stacey, if you did have Jesus in your heart you would have some peace of mind." I groan and kick the dirt again. I wish Grandma would find something else to say when I ask her a question. I force myself to listen as she continues. "Stacey, me is almost seventy year old now. God is always watching over me. You know why? Because every Sunday morning, rain or shine, me put on me Sunday clothes and go to church to give God thanks for the breath of life."

"Yes, Grandma. But it would be nice to see God sometimes—to make it easier to believe in him. If I could see him, I would have all the faith in the world."

"Never you mind, me baby. One day God will show you the way. Is not you is the first one to doubt him. And you won't be the last. You can read your Bible now. Everything is in there for you to learn."

"Yes, Grandma."

While Grandma hangs clothes on the line, I confess to Delano that I believe in the Nancy Drew mystery books more than I believe the stories in the Bible. He immediately makes the sign of the cross and backs away from me. "Staceyann Chin, God must have a special place in heaven for people like you! Don't come near me! I don't want your lightning to strike me!"

"Delano, I like the stories in the Bible too. But not everything in there can be true. You think a whale can swallow a man and him don't dead? You think the Devil can turn into a snake? You think real bread can fall from the sky?"

"La la la la la la la! Don't talk to me—you is just a Jezebel that go lead me into temptation! La la la!" He puts his fingers in his ears and closes his eyes.

I pull at his hands and shout in his ear, "Look at the people in the whole Bible, Delano, nobody in there look like me or you or Grandma. Everything looks like a storybook. And there is no Black people, or Chinaman, and there is not even one verse about Jamaica—nothing that we have is in the Bible. If the Bible did have everything about everywhere, show me the verse about Jamaica."

He punches me in the face and walks away. I wipe my stinging nose and scream at his retreating back, "And why nobody having fun in the Bible? Why everything have to wait till we get to heaven? I don't believe there is any milk and honey in heaven. If there was milk and honey in the sky, why is rain just plain water?"

Delano turns around and makes his way back to me. He stops and points his finger at my reddening nose. "You are one very presumptuous sinner! That is why Aunt June don't want to carry us anywhere. And if you say one more word to me I going to beat you up and kill you!"

I gather all my courage. "And why would Christ come back after they beat him up, stab him in his side with a big old sword, and hammer him to a cross? He would be a damn fool if he did. Jesus is never coming back to earth. If I was Jesus, I would never come back at all. Them church people would wait till eternity for nothing!"

Delano raises his fist again and again and again. I do not even flinch as his punches fall on my temple, my chest, my neck. He takes one look at my face and pushes past me. I scream, "No milk, no honey, no Jamaica! No milk, no honey, no Jamaica. You hear me, Delano? There is no milk, and no honey, and no Jamaica!" He does not look back.

Delano tells Grandma that I am going to hell because I do not believe that Jesus is coming back. Grandma calls me inside and pulls me to her chest. She says that I am her little Doubting Thomas. She says she will never quarrel with me over God. She says that she has faith enough for the two of us.

"Stacey, I know that one day God is going to come to you and show you the holes in his hands. Just like Thomas, he will make you put your finger in his wounded side. Then you will believe. The only thing me can tell you is that you need God so you don't end up like the life I did have before Jesus save me."

Again, she cautions against the pitfalls of wallowing in sin with a demon-infested, tobacco-smoking, spirit-drinking Black man. "When is that time, find yourself a man who know God," she warns. "One who could help you get closer to your Heavenly Father."

She points to her ear and wags her finger at me. "Take it from me, poor old Bernice, a man who only want to bring you down on you back is a man who will want to bring you down in life. You take to that book-learning. That is good. That is the way to get out of this place where man want to use woman as workhorse. Read everything. The more knowledge you have, the less a man can use you for poppy-show. If I coulda read, your good-fi-nutten grandfather coulda never use me as him beating stick."

While we are away at school, Grandma sweeps the floor, watches the baby, sees about Pa Larry, and prepares the evening meal. After dinner we do homework while Grandma washes the dirty dishes piled onto the wooden table just outside the kitchen door.

Long after Shane and Samantha are done, Aunt June makes Delano and me sit at the table doing extra work. "You children are behind in your classes. This is the only way you can catch up."

"Aunt June, I am not far from catching up, right?"

"No, Stacey, you are doing well, but remember that pride goeth before the fall."

When she goes to change Andrew, I whisper to Delano, "Delano, today I get a gold star."

He barely looks up from his multiplication tables. "That is good, man, Stacey, keep it up."

"I get one yesterday too in Reading."

Delano's brow is wrinkled in concentration. "Uh-huh."

"Delano, you listening to me? Delano!"

"Stacey, wait until I get this one, nuh."

I wait until he looks up at me. "Delano, how come Grandma don't look at our books anymore?"

"Stacey, you are the biggest complainer in the world. You don't see that Grandma busy? You want her to stop doing the work them bring her here to do and look at your stupid homework?"

"Delano, I don't want her to stop working. I just want her to look at the gold star I get for Story Writing and Comprehension." My eyes are filled with tears and my hands are shaking as I doodle.

"Staccy, nuh bother with the crying, man." He picks up the book and hands it to me. "Just take it and go and show her your gold star. Nobody not stopping you. Just take the book and go show her. Go on." His voice is strangely gentle.

Book in hand, I make my way to the back door.

"Grandma!" I open my book and touch her arm. "Grandma, look. I get a gold star today."

She looks down at the page and smoothes my hair. "That is good, man. Is a good ting you have your Aunt June to show you how to do good at the book-learning."

I want to tell her how hard it is to get a gold star in Story Writing and Comprehension, but she looks so confused I close the book and pick up the dishwashing cloth. Grandma only lets me help with the dinner knives and the forks. I cannot touch the sharp knives because Grandma does not want me to cut off my fingers and become a nine-finger Jack. I am also supposed to steer clear of the ceramic cups and plates. I tell Grandma that I am big enough now to wash a plate, crockery or no crockery. "No, no! Leave the things them that can break alone! Me don't have no money to buy back Aunt June expensive cup and plate. Dry the eating knife and fork them. Me will do the rest."

After homework and evening chores we watch the evening news. I like stories about people I do not know. The best news reporters are Dennis Hall and Fae Ellington. I don't like Dennis Hall so much. He looks so old and white. Like he is a duppy. But Fae Ellington looks like a nice lady. She is very pretty. I wonder if my life would be good if Fae Ellington were my mother. I wish I could see her real skin color to see if she is the same as me. But everybody is the same shade of gray on the grainy image of the black-and-white TV.

As Fae introduces the weatherman, Aunt June bellows, "Staceyann! Staceyann Marshree Chin! Come in here right now!"

I follow her voice to the dining room. She holds aloft an eating knife. "What is this, young lady?" I hate to be called that.

"Is a knife, Aunt June, a *dinner knife*."

"You take me for a fool? I know it is a dinner knife. Who washed it?"

"I washed it, Aunt June. What happen to it?" I am annoyed that I am missing the news.

"Jesus Savior, pilot me! Give me strength to deal with the audacity of this child! What you mean, what happened to it? And who you think you are talking to in that tone of voice? You think I am your friend and company?"

Her voice is rising and I am getting a little frightened. "Sorry, Aunt June, you asked me a question and I was just answering you. I never said anything 'bout no friend and company—"

She grabs my wrist and brings the knife to my face. My bladder contracts, but I take a deep breath and press both legs together before I let the air out again.

"Stop sighing at me, child! Stop sighing and look at this knife! This looks clean to you? Look at the food marks on it! You think we live like pigs here? If you wash a knife, it should look like you washed it!" She squeezes my hand so tightly I try to twist my arm away.

"Aunt June, let me go! You are squeezing up me hand!"

"Let you go? Let you go? You think you are a big woman here? You are a child. I can hold you for as long as I damn well please! You do not tell me what to do in my own house!"

Again I try to pull away from her, but she tightens her grip and forces my arm out to expose the inside of my elbow. She then wipes the serrated edge back and forth across the soft skin there and slaps my arm with the handle, over and over. I look her square in the face. I do not make a sound.

Finally, she lets me go and throws the knife at me. "Little girl, you have the Devil himself inside of you! Put this back in the kitchen and find yourself in the bed!"

I turn toward the kitchen, and my heart drops from my chest to my stomach when I see Grandma standing by the door, wiping away tears. I stare at her, but she cannot look back at me. I make my way around her body, carefully lay the knife on the table with the clean dishes, and walk around her again. In the bathroom, I sob quietly against the sink, wishing I had an address to write a letter to my mother. I know that if she had seen what Aunt June was doing to me she wouldn't have just stood there and let it happen.

Later, when Grandma comes to bed, she tries to rub my head. I push her hands away and turn over. The next morning, she is extra gentle combing the tangles out of my hair. I don't want to be angry, but the kinder she is to me, the angrier I get. I stop washing dishes with her. She never asks me to help again.

Be of Good Courage

December arrives and the days shorten and cool. Christmas day, which will be my eighth birthday, is only twelve days away. Samantha says that this Christmas is going to be very special because Aunt June is going to buy a big Christmas tree. And Uncle Harold has hinted to Samantha that he may buy her a special present. She tells me that there may be a present for everybody. Delano and Shane want water guns. Samantha wants a talking dolly. I hope and hope and hope and hope that I will get my own set of Nancy Drew mysteries. Every day all the girls at school sing "The Twelve Days of Christmas" at recess.

> *On the first day of Christmas,*
> *my true love sent to me*
> *a partridge in a pear tree . . .*

Samantha marks off the days on a calendar. Some days she lets me make the *X*. I am very careful not to make it too big or too small. Samantha stands behind me and supervises. Delano and Shane say it is a stupid idea, but every morning before we leave for school they stand by the wall and watch us cross out the day.

> *On the fourth day of Christmas,*
> *my true love sent to me*
> *four calling birds . . .*

> *On the seventh day of Christmas . . .*
> *On the eighth day of Christmas . . .*

By the time we get to the tenth day, the excitement has mounted to twenty girls marching around the schoolyard in a line. Each girl holds the waist of the person ahead and sways to the rapid rhythm of our chant. Every girl is sure that she will get what she wants on Christmas morning. It feels good to be a part of such a big loud group. And everybody is extra nice to me because Christmas day is also my special day. All the girls say that having a birthday on Christmas is like having two birthdays together.

At home the house is busy with the smell of baking. The tables are covered in flour and sugar and butter. Big bowls are atop every surface. Samantha and I park ourselves in the dining room, hoping to taste anything that Aunt June will let us. The sweet fruit preserves are drained and measured and added to the cake mix. Raisins and prunes and dates are from the store and are very expensive, so we only can taste the ones that fall on the floor. Those fruits come all the way from Montego Bay. Aunt June says they really come from a place in America called California.

All year, Aunt June has been collecting the skin of grapefruits. Diced and sugared and soaked in wine and rum, they make up the mass of the bittersweet fruits that will be in the Christmas cakes. We can eat as many of those as we want. As the mixes are made and poured into baking tins, we lick the empty bowls clean. Then we march through the house screaming the words of our anthem at the top of our lungs.

Finally it is December twenty-fifth. It is so exciting to wake up and suddenly be eight years old. The first carolers come by bright and early. "Silent Night" filters into the back room from the front yard and I turn over and pull the sheets up to my neck and snuggle in while I listen. Delano groans and covers his head. Grandma is up already. I can smell the sweet hot chocolate she is making. Hot cups will be handed out to everyone when the singing of the carols is done. The Christmas cake is cut up into thin slices and passed around on a silver tray.

When the carolers are gone, Aunt June tells us to hurry up and get dressed for Christmas service. I bound out of bed and pull the covers off Delano. He kicks me harder than is necessary, but not even the sore spot on my thigh can spoil my good mood. The ride to the church is quiet. Everybody else is sleepy. But I am silent. I don't want to get in trouble on my birthday. The service is quick. By seven we are back at home eating ackee and salt-fish and roasted breadfruit. When the plates are piled into the kitchen, Grandma heads out back to wash them.

We are all excited when Aunt June tells us to come with her into the living room. There is a huge pile of packages on the couch. I am so excited my ears are buzzing. Aunt June announces that she has at least one present for everyone. One by one she calls our names and hands us each a wrapped bundle. Then she calls Samantha and Shane and Garnett and hands them more presents.

When she is done, Samantha has three boxes and a brown paper package. Shane has two boxes and a bag of things wrapped in different kinds of paper. Garnett has three things on his lap too. Delano, Ann, and I each have one thing wrapped in brown paper, tied up with a red bow. Aunt June smiles at me when I dutifully unwrap a pair of blue canvas sneakers from the Bata shoe store. Delano opens his to find a water gun. Ann unceremoniously unwraps a new church dress. Shane has a new Hardy Boys mystery, a pair of church shoes, a water gun, socks, a belt, and some red pencils. Garnett has a new T-square and a school bag complete with school supplies. But Samantha is the queen of the day. A brand-new dolly with a change of clothes, three new panties, a pair of shoes, one new Bobbsey Twins and two Nancy Drew mysteries lay scattered around her. I have to work very hard to keep from screaming out loud and stomping all over their shiny new things.

Everybody is saying thank you to Aunt June. My eyes fill with tears as I look again at the gifts that Shane and Samantha have opened. I should be happy for these sneakers. Nobody has ever given me a present before. I should be grateful, but I think I deserve more.

Aunt June turns to me and clears her throat. I put the shoes back in the brown wrapping paper and look up at her. "Aunt June, thanks for the shoes, but is Christmas, *and* it is my birthday *too*. Everybody else get one present on them birthday. And now they get Christmas presents too. I think I should get two things today!"

Aunt June does not miss a beat. "Well, Stacey, you do have two things there, two things that make a pair. One foot is for your birthday, and the other is for Christmas."

I say thank you again and put the sneakers inside the bedroom. I find Grandma praying under the ackee tree. When she asks me what's wrong with me, I bury my face in her lap and weep. I am tired of being afraid of Aunt June and having to live in her house. I am tired of Samantha always having everything she wants. I don't want to live with them anymore. I want to go back to Lottery. Grandma strokes my head, but it does not make it any better. I don't really want Grandma. I want my own mother. I don't understand why she left us. I cry loud and hard. I smell curry on her hands as she brushes away my tears.

Grandma tries her best to comfort me. "No, no, Stacey. No mind, man. No mind, whatever it is, God can fix it—"

"No, Grandma! I don't want God! I want my mother! And I want my own father! How come is only me one don't have no father? Even Delano have a father! Where I come from? Me drop from sky?"

"You have God in heaven as you father. The Bible say him eye is on the sparrow, so I know him watching over you too. Come, man. Stop the crying."

"Grandma, I know my mother run away, but what about my father here on earth? Him run away too? Is what happen to me why everybody run away from me?"

"Stacey, stop that, man. Dry you face. All right, all right. Let me tell you something, nuh!"

"Grandma, I don't want to hear 'bout no Heavenly Father. Everybody have that. I want to know who my real father is. Delano have one. Shane and Samantha have one. What wrong with me?"

"All right! All right! Dry you face!" Grandma finally relents. "As there is a God in heaven, stop with the everlasting crying! You would drive the living Jesus to sin himself! I going tell you, but you have to quiet yourself and listen."

She strokes my braids and pats my back until I am quiet. Then she leans over and whispers, "Junior Chin. You mother did tell me that your father name is Junior Chin. Him live in Montego Bay."

Surprised, I look up from her lap. I wipe my face as she continues.

"Him used to come to pick up you mother at the house when Delano was a little, little baby. Miss Cherry say him have a furniture store on Barnett Street, right in front of the Montego Bay Police Station. Him is a married man. With other children. You turn eight year old today. And is Christmas day. And you know already that this is the Lord Jesus Christ birthday?"

I nod. "Yes, ma'am, I know that."

"Well, mark this day, and mark it well." She slowly shakes her head and pats my shoulder. "Today, Christmas day, nineteen hundred and eighty—I know that both you mother and you father will live to regret that them leave you by the wayside."

She pauses, sits me upright, and looks into my eyes. "Them may not want you now, but if you make sure you work hard, that you make something of yourself—one day the two of them will come to your door to beg you for a drink of water! The Bible tell you, *The stone that the builder refuse will become the head cornerstone*! Matthew twenty-one, verse forty-two. Is right there in the Good Book! You only have to read it!"

She pulls me to her bosom. "Believe you me, they will beg you to recognize them as father and mother. Just trust in God and he will see you through."

"Yes, Grandma." Something strange sits in my throat, and Grandma's voice is low and hard, as if she is angry.

She gets up and straightens her dress. "I don't tell you these things fi make you feel bitter in your heart. Is just that you getting big now and is full time you know how things really go."

I lie on the bed thinking, *My father's name is Junior Chin. He lives in Montego Bay. Just like Delano's father. Except he does not send groceries from his shop for me. He does not want me.*

Not yet.

Dominion Over Every Living Thing

The summer holidays arrive and the long days stretch out endless before us. During the week Aunt June keeps us under close supervision. But on Saturdays she and Uncle Harold leave to buy the week's groceries. And on the first Saturday of the month Grandma puts on her rainbow tie-head and boards the navy blue van to Montego Bay. She makes the long trip alone to collect food from Delano's Chinaman father. Grandma is gone by the time I wake up. I open my eyes surprised to find her movements missing from the house. For a moment, I worry that she will never come back.

As soon as we finish the chores, Ann and Garnett cut across the green flatland of the front yard and disappear. Beyond the front yard is The Road, which is essentially a dirt track with a sliver of asphalt that runs down its center. We are not allowed out on The Road without permission.

Every day at home without the adults is an adventure. Delano has the best ideas, so he decides what we should do. We all follow him as he slowly circles the house. He uses a stick to poke the hard dusty ground. Then he leads us back to the front. He plops down on the front steps and sighs.

"So what we going to do, then?" Samantha looks to Delano.

Shane looks to the hills behind the house. "We could go tease the madman."

"No, man." Samantha shakes her head for emphasis. "I am not going back up there! Remember what happen last time? Me not going back there at all."

"Ruff! Ruff!" Delano laughs and charges at Samantha. "The man is so mad, him think him is a dog!"

"Delano, that is not funny! We had to run off the track and into the bushes to get away from him!" Samantha sucks her teeth and pushes Delano away from her.

"We should go again, eh, Delano? That was a good joke, eh?" Shane and Delano are laughing so hard they start coughing.

Flat on the ground and exhausted from coughing and laughing, Shane turns to Delano. "So what we going to do, then?"

"We could chase rats!" Samantha throws a rock into the dry gully.

Delano reminds us that the red rats living there are no fun to chase in the summertime. The heat makes the furry creatures lazy, so we end up killing too many. Last summer the stink of their rotting bodies stayed in the air for weeks. And plus, it is no fun to run through a hot cane field in the middle of July.

"All right, Delano, since you knock down everybody's idea, you tell us what to do!"

Delano sucks his teeth and walks away from her. We follow him. Even the animals seem bored. Under the noonday sun, the pigs are fast asleep in their mud-caked pens; the dried slush cracks on their pink skin. They don't even grunt when Delano slaps a whole tin of Nestlé condensed milk in the trough. The goats ignore Shane when he tosses young mangoes at them. The cows only glance in our general direction when we tug at their thick nylon ropes.

Samantha and I follow them, moving sluggishly around the house. The dogs dig holes in the hard ground. They only move from one tree to the other to dig a new hole.

The cats do not get up, even when the dogs move. Only the scrawny chickens squawk when Samantha and I creep up on them and scream, "Supercalifragilisticexpialidocious!"

The boys usually ignore the chickens. They consider themselves above chasing animals that girls chase. Today, however, boredom drives them to join us.

"Today, we are going to do more than chase them," Delano informs us. "We are going to corner them and catch them!"

"Then what?" Samantha asks.

"Shut your big fat clappers and just do what I tell you to do!" Delano snaps.

He takes the left side of the house—that side has no fence. Shane covers the back. Samantha and I are to chase the six chickens from the front yard to the left side. Delano will be right there to catch them.

There are three regular chickens, speckled brown and white, that look like the chickens in our library books. Two of the chickens, senseh fowls, have feathers that make them look surprised. They are bad tempered; they peck first and decide if it is wise later. We all bear scars.

The pride of the pack is the peel-neck fowl. Bald from the shoulders (or at least where a chicken's shoulders are expected to be) to the beak and tiny, it squawks loudly and moves quickly. If any of us were lucky enough to hold it for a second, its cries brought the nearest adult to its rescue, or it found its way out of our grasp so fast, we could hardly boast that we had caught it.

When everyone is in place, Samantha and I rush toward the chickens.

"Chase wide so they will run to the left side of the house," Delano shouts.

He dashes across the yard and meets Shane. The chickens commence a choir of squawking and turn back toward us. The senseh fowls are in the lead. Samantha and I look at each other, then at the oncoming fowls, and take off.

Delano screams, "Shane, circle the house and stop them before they get 'way!"

By the time Shane gets to the other side, every fowl but the peel-neck fowl has escaped.

"That's why I don't like to do anything with a bunch of fraidy-fraidy girls! Look how the both of you make the chicken them get 'way!" Delano is furious.

"All right, Shane, pay attention and don't make Samantha and Stacey help you."

They both close in on the last chicken. In a cloud of dirt and squawking, the animal flies straight up into the air. The copper swirl of dust and feathers is everywhere. I am worried it will be naked when they finally catch it. On its way down, two pairs of hands seize it. It cries out, but the boys do not let go.

Samantha and I are jumping up and down. "Get him! Get him, Delano! Hold on to him!"

The excitement makes my head spin. I am running around the boys as they struggle to grab the fowl. When Delano finally grabs it, I squeal and cover my eyes with my dusty hands.

"Stacey, stop the cow bawling so I can think of something to do with it!" Delano orders.

He holds the chicken by its spindly yellow legs. It is silent now. Its head is hung low, almost to the ground, and its eyes are blinking. It looks like it is waiting to see what will come next. We follow Delano to the back of the house. He sits on the back steps swinging the chicken by its legs. The three of us sit on the ground around him. Delano stands. The sudden movement makes the chicken cry out. We laugh. He swings the chicken back and forth. The squawking eggs him on, making him swing the chicken even harder. The cries drown our laughter as he swings harder still. He now has to stand with one arm out to keep his balance while he is swinging the chicken around in full circles above his head. He keeps swinging until his arm is tired and the squawking has stopped. The chicken is not moving anymore.

"What happen to it?" I ask.

"Nothing. It's trying to trick us, so we will let it go. Swing it some more," Shane says.

"I'm going to tell," Samantha blurts out.

"Nothing is wrong with it," Delano says. "See how the chest is still moving? It's still alive. I'm going to make it scream again."

He slowly moves his arm around. This time there is only a weak cry.

"I'm going to put him down now. Make sure him don't run away."

He gently puts the chicken down. We form a circle around it. The heaving brown body lies there for a tense moment before it struggles to its feet.

"Hold him! Don't let him run away, Delano!" Shane is shouting.

Delano grabs it again.

"See, it not dead, just lazy. I bet it still strong enough to carry all of us on it back," Shane pronounces.

"Okay, let's ride him, then," Samantha suggests.

"I don't think we should," I caution.

"Why not? Shane just said it could carry us!"

Delano says nothing.

"Is 'fraid you 'fraid?" Samantha taunts.

"Yes, is 'fraid you 'fraid?" Shane adds.

The worst thing to do to Delano is call him a coward.

"I not 'fraid of nothing! Make we ride him."

We sit on top of each other. Shane, the biggest, sits first. Then Delano sits on him. There is a thin cry from the chicken when Samantha settles on her brother's lap. By the time I sit, there isn't a sound coming from below.

"Make him move, Shane," Delano urges.

"I'm trying."

"Hit him, like a horse," Samantha volunteers.

"Yuck! I think it's having diarrhea, and it's all over my pants." Shane leaps to his feet.

The rest of us tumble to the ground.

I land on something wet and brown and warm. We scramble to our feet and look at the chicken, which is flat and oozing a dark fluid from its tail. It looks pitiful; its bruised, bald, head twisted to one side.

One eye stares wide open. The other is closed in one-half of a blink, leaking some kind of watery stuff. It's crying, I think, the poor little thing is crying.

"I think it dead." Delano's voice is small in the big backyard.

We all stand there uncertain of what the long pink neck—curved and elegant even in death—means. If I look at one eye, it is alive but tearful. If I look at the other, it is dead.

"I'm telling on all of you!" Samantha breaks the silence.

"If you tell on us, you have to tell on yourself!" Shane counters.

"But I didn't do anything." Samantha is crying.

"Yes, you did!" insists Shane. "You was the one who said to ride it. And you helped to ride it. Maybe it was your big fat batty that make the fowl dead!"

Samantha looks at Delano and me. We both look steadily at the dusty ground. She stands there for only a second before she turns her back and stomps toward the house.

"What we going to do with him?" Shane asks, the next adventure glimmering in his eyes.

"I don't care. You do what you want with it," Delano mutters before he turns and walks away.

I follow my brother to the ackee tree at the farthest end of the back-yard. I think of the chicken blinking when it is alive. Not blinking when it is dead. I can't get the image out of my head.

"Delano, you saw the chicken eye? It look like it was crying, don't? It did definitely look sad, don't?"

"Stacey, right now me nuh care 'bout how the chicken did look. Right now me just thinking 'bout what will happen if Aunt June find out that we kill her chicken. If she and Uncle Harold find out that we was in it, they will think that we ungrateful to them for making us live here. They might make Grandma take us to live somewhere else. Grandma don't have nowhere else to live."

"We could go back to Lottery. The house not big like this one, but is our own. We could go back and go to school at Miss Sis." I miss our old teacher. I miss the head rubs and the smell of thyme. The thought of going back makes me happy.

"How you so stupid?" His anger surprises me. "It was never our house in the first place. We did only rent it from somebody. We can't go back there now. Somebody else live there now."

I know that Grandma tells Delano things she does not tell me, but I am the one who was born in that house. My navel string is buried in that yard. I know I am only in Bethel Town because of Andrew. As soon as he gets bigger we are going to move back to our own house in Lottery. My mother had bought the bed I had been sleeping on in that house.

"What you mean by that? Who live there now?"

"Boy, you really don't know anything, eh?" He takes a deep breath. "Okay, I don't know who live there now, but I know is not our house. Grandma move us here because she retire from the police station job. She never have no money to pay rent. So we had to come."

"But, Delano, how you sure is not our house? Grandma could be renting it to them now, you know!" He doesn't respond. "I don't care what you say. It is our house, with the little blue and white folding tray and the little green veranda. It is our house in Lottery!"

I kick the dirt and wipe the tears from my face.

"Shut up, nuh, Stacey. Just shut up! You think because you say something it just go so all of a sudden? You must learn fi take things as them is. Is so it go. We have to behave or else they will put us out. Is just so it go." He is crying too. Delano almost never cries. Not even when he is getting a beating with Uncle Harold's police belt.

"But Shane and Samantha help kill the chicken too. They not going to put them out," I argue.

"Jesus! Me have to tell you everything? People can't put out them own children. But we don't belong to them, only to Grandma, and not even for real. She is only our grandmother. She only have us because nobody never want us when we mother run gone lef us. Them can put us out, but them cannot put out them own children."

"But, Delano, you can go live with your father."

"Yes, but where you and Grandma going to live? You don't even have no father. And even if somebody take in Grandma, nobody will take you in. Nobody but Grandma want you."

That hurts, but because he is crying so hard, I don't say anything. "Don't worry, Delano, nobody going to find out. None of us going say anything." I am not so sure about Samantha, but I cross my fingers and say a prayer.

Delano looks at me like I am the biggest idiot in the world. He turns away and covers his face with his hands and sobs. I watch Shane lift the limp carcass high above his head and toss it into the gully. The feathered missile looks like it is flying as it hurtles toward its final home. Shane's bright blue Gator sneakers kick dust over the wet spot on the ground.

I hate him. And Samantha. I hate their new sneakers and their new schoolbags bought for them right from the store.

One Sunday morning in July, Aunt June muses aloud that she hasn't seen the peel-neck fowl in a few days. Uncle Harold wrinkles his brows and says, "Mrs. Jennings, I have been telling you for months now that we need to set some poison. A rat or mongoose must have taken that fowl right from the coop."

"Harold, I am tired of telling you that if I set poison for the mongoose the fowls will eat it too. The children just have to make sure that each fowl is accounted for before they close the coop at night."

Uncle Harold turns to us at the table and says, "I hope you are taking note of what you just heard. We cannot afford to lose livestock to these rodents. Just make sure every latch is closed before each of you go to bed at night."

"Yes, Daddy."

"Yes, Uncle Harold."

The second week of July a letter arrives from Auntie Ella. She wants Grandma to take us to Kingston for the summer. I am excited to meet my mother's sister. Auntie Ella is Grandma's youngest child. And Grandma says Auntie Ella was very close to Mummy before she left for Canada.

Aunt June doesn't look pleased about Kingston. She bangs the pots around and says we have to make sure to take both our math workbooks and our next-year reading books with us. "I will not be held responsible for your regression when you both come back from a month in Kingston with nothing between your ears but God's free air!"

The evening before we leave, Grandma packs our bags. Aunt June tells her that she can use a tin of corned beef to make sandwiches to take for the long train ride. Delano picks limes and we fill a big bag with the best ones for Auntie Ella. I pick fresh mint and fever grass. Grandma uses the bruised limes to make a bottle of lemonade. When Aunt June leaves for prayer meeting she takes the other children with her. Grandma feeds Pa Larry and puts him to bed. Then she fries some chicken and roasts two breadfruits. When it is just me and Delano and Grandma, I pretend that this is our house and that we can do whatever we want in it. I wonder what it will be like at Auntie Ella's.

The following morning we get up at four. We do not wake anybody to say good-bye, except Uncle Harold, who takes us to the train station. We catch the first train out of Montpelier station. I didn't believe that Aunt June would really let us go and as the train pulls away I do a little dance. Delano laughs at me. I am so happy to leave Galloway District, even if it is only for five weeks out of the long hot summer. I am not going to Canada, or America, or England, but Kingston is almost like a foreign country. Kingston is where everybody on TV lives. I ask Delano if he thinks Auntie Ella will take me to meet Fae Ellington so I can tell her how much I love when she reads the news. Delano wants to have a shoot-out, with real guns like they have in the cowboy movies.

Grandma cannot eat anything for the whole day on the train. She is afraid she will throw up and mess up the train seats and her dress and everything. Delano says I shouldn't eat anything either because I might throw up too, but Grandma says I cannot stay hungry all day. She puts some newspaper inside my dress and tells me it will make my stomach feel better. Then she lets me eat a little and I throw up into a plastic bag with more newspaper in it. Aunt June would be vexed with Grandma if she knew that I was eating on the train. But Grandma says, "What rat don't tell puss, don't harm dog."

I take small bites of my corned-beef sandwich and look out the window at the trees passing by. The conductor laughs loudly and makes jokes with us.

"How are we doing there, big man?" He pounds his palms on my brother's back, but he smiles and tips his hat at me.

"And how is my little lady?"

I say, "Fine, thank you, sir."

The candy man comes by and asks if we want cotton candy. We say yes, but Grandma has no money. He gives us one tiny piece each and keeps moving, all the while shouting, "Candy man! Sweet, sweet candy! Anybody for the candy man?" I hear him long after he has disappeared. We finally get off the train at the Six Miles stop. There are so many people getting off the train I almost forget to wave good-bye to the conductor. Grandma steps down onto the platform and tells Delano to hold on to me while she puts the bag of clothes on her head. Then she reaches for my hand.

More people than I have ever seen pass by while we wait for the bus that will take us uptown. A pregnant lady and three little children holding on to her skirt wait with us. A man with one arm and a scar that runs from his left eye to the right side of his mouth nods at Grandma. Two old men with white beards approach us and smile at Grandma. They smell like the rum that Aunt June uses to soak Christmas fruits. Both of them are grinning and shaking their hips at Grandma. She pulls us closer to her and looks the other way. They laugh louder and tip their hats before they stumble away.

The bus is teeming with all sorts of people carrying bags and boxes. There is no room to sit. I squeeze Grandma's hand and press my body against her. The air is hot and heavy with sweat. Bob Marley is wailing that he shot the sheriff, but he didn't shoot the deputy. A girl not much older than Delano has a large cardboard box with holes punched in it. She pulls herself away when Delano places his ear close to the box. He leans over to me and whispers that he heard chickens peeping inside. An old man smelling like cow dung balances a bundle of sugarcane and some yellow yams atop his head. I wonder why there are so many people on one small bus.

In no time we are in Half Way Tree. The big bus grinds to a halt and people almost knock us over getting off. We make our way outside and stand on the sidewalk. Grandma tells us to look out for Auntie Ella. The crowd thins and we are left on the sidewalk with a woman with a giant leg. One leg is almost three times the size of the other. I search for Auntie Ella. I worry that we will miss her and be forced to sleep on the road with the old lady with the enormous leg.

"Grandma, I don't know who to look for. What Auntie Ella look like?"

"Lawd, Stacey. She look like anybody. She have two foot and two eye just like everybody else. Just wait yourself and she will come and find us."

Auntie Ella appears in a black-and-yellow taxi. She is tall and pretty and light skinned. She covers her mouth with her two hands and laughs out loud when she sees us. Then she is kissing and hugging us and saying how big and beautiful we are. The taxi stops at a place called Kentucky Fried Chicken for dinner. There is a picture of a white man called the Colonel who cooks it. I order a wing and Delano orders a breast. Grandma says she will take whatever Auntie Ella orders. I am amazed that you can order whatever part you want to eat. I wonder what they do with the parts that nobody eats. I imagine a graveyard of chicken backs and feet and bottoms, forever searching for their missing, matching parts.

The taxi stops in front of a very, very big house, on a street called Sandhurst Terrace. The grass is cut low and there are red and purple flowers in bloom in the garden. The tall concrete walls are painted white and the louver windows are glass. There is a big veranda enclosed with metal grilles. Plants hang from the grilles and the walls. When we get out of the car, I see that the house is even bigger than I thought. The structure is built on a piece of land that slopes. From the front of the building, it looks like a very wide single-story house, but when you peek around the sides you can see that there are two floors.

"Jesus peace Almighty, Auntie Ella! This is where you live?"

"Staceyann, please don't take the Lord's name in vain like that! But yes, this is where I live. But come, hurry up and get the things out of the gentleman's taxi so he can go."

Auntie Ella pays the driver and we make our way inside. Auntie Ella opens the one on the left. I ask to use the bathroom.

"Down the hallway. It is the first door on the left and remember to knock before you open!"

Every part of the house is tiled. And everything inside the bathroom is blue: the toilet, the sink, the bathtub, and the shower curtain. The whole place smells like perfume. I slide my hands over everything and thank God for Auntie Ella and Kingston.

When I come out of the bathroom there is a girl the color of sand sitting in the living room watching a small TV with everybody in the picture in real color. She smiles at me and moves over on the couch. I sit beside her, mesmerized, as I watch the national storyteller, Miss Lou, in a red-and-white plaid bandanna conducting a game of ring-around-the-rosy on the children's show *Ring Ding*. The children are wearing dresses and shirts of every color. Every time Miss Lou laughs the children laugh too. I lean in toward the screen to get a better look at the people in color. Their teeth don't look as white as they look in black and white. I can't wait to see what complexion Fae Ellington is. The girl is looking at me like I am doing something strange. I lean back on the couch and look out the window because I don't want her to think that I am an ignorant country bumpkin who has never seen a color TV before. When Miss Lou waves good-bye, the girl gets up and turns off the TV. We sit there for a moment before I speak.

"So Auntie Ella is your mother?"

"Yes."

"So that means I am your cousin."

"Yes."

"All right. So what is your name?"

"Annmarie."

"My name is Stacey."

"I know."

"How you know that? My brother came inside here already?"

"No."

"Well, his name is Delano. You saw where him went?"

"He's inside." She points to Auntie Ella's room.

"All right."

I don't know what else to say. She kicks her heels against the couch. We sit there in silence until Auntie Ella comes to call us for dinner. At the table, Auntie Ella says that since there are only two bedrooms, Annmarie has to share her room with me and Delano and Grandma. She tells us that she and Annmarie are glad to have us in their home. She says that the place is small but we are welcome. She only asks that in her house we respect the Lord.

The rules are simple. We can watch TV from sign-on to sign-off every day except Saturday. Saturday nights we have to be in bed by nine p.m. On Sunday we have to wake up early and well rested. Auntie Ella says that that is the only way we can be ready to hear the word of the Lord on Sunday morning.

Delano chews the devil out of a chicken bone. The bubbly orange soft drink tickles my nose when I sip it. I ask Auntie Ella what is in the rest of the house. She tells me that the house does not belong to her. She only rents a small part of it from her friend Mrs. Bremmer, who lives in the rest of the house with her family. Grandma gets up to clear the table, but Auntie Ella makes her sit and eat some more.

Delano, Grandma, and I have one big bed. Annmarie has a small one. Grandma smells my mouth to make sure I brushed my teeth properly and we climb into bed. Auntie Ella stands by the bed and prays with us. Her hand rests gently on my head as she asks God to give me strength to love in the face of adversity.

"Father God, I ask you to keep this blessed light afloat in the heart of this precious little girl. Remind her that she is already spoken for in your blood. Keep her body safe. As she ages, help her to navigate the difficulties that lie ahead with hope and generosity."

Each of us gets our own prayer. When the prayers are done, Annmarie quietly slips under her blue blanket and covers her head. Grandma's chest rises and falls as she breathes next to me. I know Delano is not asleep because he is shaking his leg. I don't know if Annmarie is awake, so I move closer to Delano and whisper in his ear.

"Delano, I wish me and you could live here with Auntie Ella every day."

He pushes the covers up under my chin, leans over, and kisses my cheek.

But the Greatest of These Is Charity

Kingston is very different from Bethel Town. Kingston life has telephones and black-and-yellow taxis and streetlights that come on by themselves at night. When the ice-cream vendor comes, he rings his bicycle bells right outside the gate. Grandma says that if you get a good job, Kingston is a place somebody can have a decent life. I ask her if that is true even when your mother runs away and leaves you. She says anything is possible while you work hard and trust God.

I love Kingston, but I don't understand Annmarie at all. I try to talk to her, but she never says more than a few words. She is four years older than me and quiet as a mouse. Grandma says to leave her alone. "Not everybody mouth set on spring like yours!"

Auntie Ella works as a secretary at a big important company called the Jamaica Flour Mills. Every day she brings home pens and pencils and funny-colored paper on which Delano and I copy Bible verses from her King James version. Sometimes there are baked cookies and sweets, but mostly it is just stationery with J. F. MILLS typed in black at the top.

The first Saturday we spend in Kingston, Auntie Ella takes Delano, Annmarie, and me to Hope Gardens to visit the Hope Zoo. Auntie Ella asks what animals we want to look at first. Delano wants to see the lions. We enter through a big black gate and walk down the path leading to the lions. Behind a high metal fence there are three lions sleeping like there is no tomorrow. Delano tosses a rock through one of the tiny holes in the pattern of the fence. None of them move. We keep tossing rocks until Auntie Ella says it's time to see the snakes. As we leave, a sleepy old lion yawns and I see three decaying teeth inside his big mouth.

The snakes are much better. They wrap themselves around tree branches. They slither and hiss at us through the big glass window. Delano wants to take a snake home. Auntie Ella tells him that she wouldn't be able to sleep if she knew there was a snake anywhere nearby. There are goats and pigs and mongooses and rabbits cowering in the corners of various cages. Delano says that all the animals look sad. I remember the eyes of the dead peel-neck fowl.

"If I was in charge, instead of locking up the animal them inside a cage, I would let them run about in the gardens. The goats can eat the grass and the snakes can climb the trees all them want."

Auntie Ella's voice is gentle. "But, Delano, if the snakes and lions were running about, we couldn't come inside the gardens. It would be dangerous for us if they were free."

"It don't matter if we come inside here. I don't like to see them in the cage."

"Okay, sir. We won't come back to the zoo anymore."

I skip ahead to Annmarie. "Hey, Annmarie! You like coming to the zoo and looking at the animals?"

She looks through me and shrugs.

On the way home we stop at the supermarket. The Hi-Lo Supermarket in Liguanea is so big it needs three or more cashiers to take care of all the customers. The groceries are sealed packages: sugar, flour, milk—even the meat comes in a little white tray. Everything looks bigger and better than the goods in the little shop in Bethel Town. Delano says that Hi-Lo is even bigger than his father's supermarket. I stand in the aisle looking at the rows and rows of things on the shelves. It's not fair that Annmarie gets to live with these shiny packets all year long. She walks quietly behind her mother and I try my best not to hate her. She doesn't even look excited to be here. I cannot imagine a better life. To live in Kingston with a speaky-spokey mother who takes you to the zoo and never shouts at you.

Back at the house we take the groceries downstairs. Delano and I are racing to see who can take the most bags down the stairs. Auntie Ella sees me leaping the steps three at a time and tells me to stop or else. I jump and land on my knees, breaking the bottles of garlic and onion powder. Delano takes one look at the broken glass and darts out the back door.

Aunti Ella comes to the top of the stairs. "Stacey, what was that?"

"Nothing, Auntie Ella."

"How can it be nothing when I distinctly heard something break?"

She comes down a few steps and sees me scraping up the glass and powder.

"Why would you tell me it was nothing? Why did you feel the need to lie to me? Lying is an abomination before God, child. Did you know that? Come up here! Leave the thing there and come up the stairs to me."

I know that lying is an abomination. I did not mean to lie to her. I want to move up the stairs toward her, but I bite my lip and stay where I am.

"Staceyann Chin, did you not hear me speak to you?"

I fold my arms and rest my weight on one leg. I stick my chin out and look up at her.

"My goodness! Is this a spirit of stubbornness I see you exhibiting there? Staceyann, come up these stairs immediately!"

I do not move. Auntie Ella makes her way down the steps. My heart is pounding against my shirt as she stops right in front of me. She puts her hand on my shoulder and tilts my face up toward her.

"I never would have guessed that you were like this. I am ashamed of your behavior. Go upstairs and sit in the living room while I clean up this mess you have made here."

I stomp upstairs and park myself in front of the TV. I can't concentrate. I am so worried about what will happen when Auntie Ella comes back upstairs. I turn the sound down very low so I can hear her coming. That means I have to sit right up in front of the TV to hear anything.

"You shouldn't sit so close to the screen, you'll end up hurting your eyes."

I nearly leap out of my clothes. I didn't hear her come into the room, but Auntie Ella is now sitting on the chair beside me. She does not look upset. Suddenly I want her to be my mother. I want to throw my arms around her and cry.

"Auntie Ella, just leave me alone and stop acting like you are my mother! I don't have no mother. Your sister run gone leave me and me brother! That mean nobody can tell me what to do!"

Grandma walks in and sees me shouting at Auntie Ella. She pulls off her blue house slipper and hits me smack in the mouth. She raises the slipper again and Auntie Ella stops her.

Grandma pushes Auntie Ella away. "No, Ella! No. She have no business talking to you like that! You who treat her so good? No, I not going to allow that kind of behavior in here!"

Grandma sends me outside. "Go on! Go out a door and think about why you so fresh! You must be smelling the young green of you-self in here!"

I sit at the top of the back staircase, crying softly, wishing I were living with my own real mother. I hear Delano's laughter coming from the yard next door. I can cry as hard and loud as I want. My brother is too far away to hear me. Everybody is too far away to hear me. I lay my head onto my arms and weep.

"Don't cry, don't cry, baby, I coming."

Through the blur of tears I look down the flight of stairs. An intently reassuring face looks up at me. The little girl is about four years old and rust colored. She has a big nose, thin lips, and very long, very kinky hair. She has the most beautiful smile I have ever seen. As she wobbles up the steps, her wild brown hair waves from side to side like a giant shapeless animal. She smiles again with coin-deep dimples on either side of her face.

"Don't cry, please. I coming, man. Wipe y' face, wipe y' face. I coming."

She looks so funny scrambling up the steps that I start laughing. Finally she makes it to the top. She plops down beside me and hugs me in triumph. Then she pats my face with her dirty hands until the tears are gone.

Moments later a woman with two sturdy braids comes to get her. She tells me the little girl's name is Racquel. I ask her if she is going to beat Racquel. She laughs and tells me she should. "Racquel is just being nasty and running away from getting her hair wash and comb. But I try me best not to beat them too much. I leave the beating to them parents."

"So you are not her mother?" I ask.

"No," Racquel pipes up, "she is my auntie Myrtle and she is our helper."

Auntie Myrtle tells me she lives and works with the Bremmers in the other half of the house.

"So, Auntie Myrtle, if you work for them and live with them, that means that you at work every day, right?"

"Well, sort of. But me don't have to work on Sunday, except to cook breakfast and dinner. After me cook me can do as me please. But how old you is, anyway? Why you asking all these big-woman questions? You is the police?"

I laugh out loud. "No, Auntie Myrtle, my name is Staceyann Chin. Auntie Ella is my aunt and I am here to spend the summer holidays with her."

"All right, Miss Chin, turn over the prisoner and come with me."

I follow them to the concrete cistern on the back veranda next door and stay until Racquel's mass of tangles has been shampooed, conditioned, and braided.

Auntie Myrtle offers me dinner. Racquel and I sit at the table and she puts three plates on the table and yells upstairs, "Chauntelle! Chauntelle! Turn off the TV and come eat your dinner!"

The Bremmers have two girls. Racquel has a big sister, Chauntelle. She is six years old. She has the strangest eyes. They are a brilliant shade of sea green, like she is a white person on a color TV. But she has short thick black-people hair that sticks up off her head in four even plaits. Their side of the house is much, much bigger than Auntie Ella's. Their living room has more furniture in it than Auntie Ella's. Against one wall there is a white lounge chair. Against the opposite wall are a big velvet couch, a dining table with a glass top, and a big wooden whatnot with crystal and wood-carved animals on the shelves and that houses a stereo system with a record player and a tape deck. The giant color TV sits in the middle shelf of the whatnot.

That evening Mrs. Bremmer tells Auntie Ella that she is lucky to have a niece as bright as I am. "She is such a nice little girl. And so pretty! Her hair is so soft and curly! And you know me, Ella, that is the kind of skin I would absolutely die for!" She turns to me. "Listen, Stacey, I am going to America for a few days. Do you want me to bring something back from Miami for you?"

The way she asks makes me hesitate. It's as if she expects me to say yes. I don't want her to think that I am begging her for anything. I also don't want Racquel to think that she is better than me because I beg her mother to bring me something from America. I don't know what kind of things she would bring, but I want them.

"That would be nice, Mrs. Bremmer. But you don't have to bring anything for me. Only if you want to."

"My goodness, she is so sweet! You have to call me Auntie Pam. I will be your auntie too. Ella, be careful I don't steal her from you."

The next morning Auntie Ella finds Racquel—nose pressed against the window—asking if Stacey can come out and play. All day long I show her how to play church, and police-and-thief, and act out the love songs we hear on the radio. We pick hard green mangoes long before they are ready for eating. We add salt and pepper and vinegar and eat the pieces until we are sick. I direct Racquel and Chauntelle in an impromptu concert for Delano. I teach them how to make otaheiti apple and sugar concoctions.

Auntie Pam brings me back coloring books, red ribbons for my hair, and white lace panties—each with a little pink satin bow on the front. She also brings me a pair of shoes. They were really intended for Chauntelle, but they are too big for her. The shoes fit me so well that Auntie Pam says they are mine. She tells Auntie Ella that she refuses to charge her a penny. She says everything looks so nice that I must wear them to Racquel's birthday party later in the summer.

Sunday in Kingston is the best. Everybody gets dressed up from head to toe. Auntie Ella calls a taxi to drive us all the way to church. I love the congregation in Kingston. Everybody smells like perfume. And the ladies hug and kiss each other when they say hello. The preacher doesn't scream at us about hell and damnation. He just talks about the peace and joy that await us in heaven. And nobody screams or falls to the floor during the service. At the end the old ladies ask if I need to go to the bathroom or if I enjoyed the service today.

On the third Sunday we are in Kingston, I put on my blue dress with the brown sleeves and the pleated gathers at the waist. It used to belong to Samantha, but she got too big for it. The dress does not quite fit me; the neck is very wide, so wide that when I dip my chin I see the waistband of my panties peeking up at me. The brown sleeves are ugly, but the big yellow bow in the back makes me feel like a flower. I check my reflection in the mirror.

I don't want to crush my dress, so I sit gingerly on the big couch watching TV. The popular American televangelist Oral Roberts is on the screen, charging sinners to give more of their salaries to God. Auntie Ella comes into the living room and takes one look at my dress and breaks out in tongues. She calls out to Annmarie to go get the little red polka-dot dress. Annmarie throws it at me so hard the zipper stings my right ear. She watches as I untie the bow at the back of my dress.

The dress would be way too tight for Annmarie, but it fits me perfectly. I don't like the tiny black dots on the dress, but the steamed pleats trace the line straight from the neck all the way down to the flared hem. The almost sheer outline has the look of a revival tent. When I twirl around really fast, the fabric flares up and I look like a ballerina clad in loud, sinful red. Annmarie looks like she wants to hit me. She kicks her right heel against the doorjamb. I silently examine the little Peter Pan collar. I discover a tiny white smudge, no bigger than the nail on my little finger.

Delano stands behind Annmarie, looking at me and picking at his cuticle. He says nothing, but his face is begging me not to do anything stupid. I know Annmarie does not want me to have the dress. I rub my thumb against the tiny stain. No one would ever see that little white mark, but I know it is there. The dress is red and pretty, but Annmarie's face reminds me that it is still a piece of hand-me-down. I am tired of wearing things that other children have grown out of. I unzip the dress and let it fall to my ankles.

Grandma nervously searches my face. I kick the dress and she raises her right hand to heaven. "Lord Jesus Almighty! This child ungrateful, eh?"

Auntie Ella is kinder. "Staceyann Chin, this dress looks as if it was made for you!"

"But it wasn't made for me, Auntie Ella. It was made for Annmarie and you can see that she don't want me to wear it!"

Annmarie crosses her arms over her chest. "You are absolutely right. I don't know why I have to give away that dress. It doesn't even fit her right!"

I kick the dress again. "I didn't want it anyway! You can take back your stupid stain-up dress!"

She stomps over to me and points her finger in my face. "My dress is not stupid! Is my favorite dress, and if you think it is stupid you definitely don't deserve it!"

"Annmarie, please take you finger out of my face before—"

Auntie Ella steps between us. "Annmarie, be quiet! Stacey, it is getting late. You need to get dressed. Pick up this dress and put it on."

I straighten the waistband of my panties and fold my arms over my chest. Delano steps out onto the back veranda. Annmarie stoops and picks up the dress. "Mummy, she obviously does not want the dress. Can I go and put it back in the closet?"

"Annmarie, give the dress to Staceyann."

"Even if she doesn't want it, Mummy?"

Auntie Ella immediately launches into her. "Annmarie, she does want it. But she is ashamed to take it because you do not want to part with it."

I tap my shoes on the patterned tiles and try hard not to cry.

Auntie Ella puts her arm around Annmarie. "Look how much God has given to us, Annmarie. The Bible tells us to cast our bread upon the water and it shall come back to us sevenfold. You have to learn to give cheerfully to those who are less fortunate. The dress is too tight for you. It fits Staceyann so beautifully. It would be a sin not to give it to her."

"But, Mummy—"

"End of discussion, Annmarie Lawson. I never thought I would have a child who could be so self-serving. The poor child has nothing to wear on her back, nothing, and you would begrudge her something that is of no use to you. We are going to have to talk about this attitude, young lady. Now get out of my sight before the Devil gets the better of me this holy Sunday morning."

"Ella, you want her to wear it to church this morning?" Grandma quietly offers the question. She fetches the dress and hands it to me. She did not hear the details of the conversation, but she knows that I no longer want the dress.

"Stacey, remember Proverbs fifteen, verse one? *A soft answer turneth away wrath, but grievous words stir up anger.* Lord, child, you have more joys than sorrows to give thanks for this morning. Now pick up you face from off dat floor and go put on the dress in the bathroom! And make sure you don't stay too long. Everybody have on them clothes already!"

Alone in the bathroom, I wonder if Auntie Ella will send me back to the country if I don't take the dress. I don't want to leave the color TV and the telephone and the shiny blue toilet to go back to Aunt June and her black and white TV. And Racquel said her birthday party is going to have a big cake from a bakery. I had better do as I am told so I can stay and enjoy all the wonderful things in Kingston. And maybe Annmarie will feel better about the dress after church.

I slip the dress over my head again. The fabric scratches my skin as I make my way to the bedroom. I avoid Annmarie's eyes and do my best to concentrate on Auntie Ella and Grandma.

I don't realize that five weeks have gone by until Grandma says we leave for Westmoreland in two days. It feels like we just arrived two days before. I wish I could stay with Auntie Ella forever. I hug Racquel when she gives me a red plastic heart that folds in two with both our names written in it. I put the heart in my Bible so I won't lose it. Auntie Pam gives me a pair of navy blue socks and two shiny blue ribbons to match my school uniforms. She gives Delano two pairs of silky brown school socks.

On the morning we are leaving, Auntie Ella gives us each a stack of notebooks and a box of pencils. She hugs me long and close. I start crying. "Auntie Ella, I don't want to go. Please, can I stay here with you?"

"Oh, Staceyann, Staceyann, Staceyann . . ." I hug her closer and sob harder. "Listen to me, Staceyann, remember that Christ is the captain of your ship and that you are second in command. You are a bright and determined child. With God's help you will go very far. You hear me?"

I nod and stifle a hiccup. "Yes, Auntie Ella."

"Your mother was the same way. She was not easily frightened. You have the same spirit. You just have to make better choices, okay?"

I nod and she hugs me again. "There, now, things are not so bad. How about a little smile?" I want to come back next summer, so I stretch my mouth into a weak smile. She hugs me again and tells me to go with God.

The return trip on the train feels longer than it took coming to Kingston. Delano and I do puzzles and take turns sleeping restlessly on Grandma's lap.

When we get there, Uncle Harold is already at the train station in Montpelier. He nods at Grandma and tells us to get in the car. "Make haste, children. I am severely pressed for time."

At home, nobody asks anything about our trip to Kingston. When I attempt to tell Samantha about Racquel, she says, "Kingston is nowhere. Kingston is still in Jamaica. Mummy's sister, Aunt Inez, lives in Kingston. Now, if you went to America, that would be something to talk about."

In September, Delano and Shane start extra lessons after school to prepare for the national Common Entrance Examination in January. If they pass, they get to go to high school. If they don't pass, they have to stay in school and do the exam again. If they don't pass on the third and final try, then they have to go to a secondary school. If you go to secondary school, you will have no future ahead of you.

Every day the boys do Mental Ability drills. I wish I were doing the Common Entrance. I know I could pass. I look at the problems in Delano's English workbook and I can do some of them without asking anybody to help me. They work at the dinner table until late at night. They have no time for police-and-thief and cricket. Samantha and I are not good at playing by ourselves, so we read at the table while they work. When we are done with all the books on the shelf, we read them again. Aunt June says I am going to ruin my eyes reading all the time with the book right up to my face.

The boys study all through the holidays. Aunt June makes them do some math exercises even on Christmas day. Shane asks why they can't take a day off. Aunt June calls all of us together. "When the government or the man on the street can take your house or your car or even your money, no one can take a good education away from you. What you have inside your head is yours and yours alone. Long after everything else has passed away, your education will serve you."

Delano says he knows that he will pass for Cornwall College in Montego Bay. That way he can see his father every day when he goes to school.

Finally the day of the exams arrives. Delano and Shane wear new khaki shirts. School is closed for the rest of us that day. Samantha and I spend the day reading. I can hardly concentrate on the words. Every time I finish a chapter I check the clock. I cannot wait until Delano and Shane get home. Aunt June says, "Make sure not to bother those boys when they come home. They have had a big day. They just need to rest."

Uncle Harold picks them up. Delano says it was very easy. Shane says he is sure he passed with very high marks. They are both certain they are heading off to high school in September. Aunt June says that she hopes that when the results come out the examiner feels the same way. When we play dolly-house or train-wreck or police-and-thief that is all we talk about: the size of the building of their new school, the bus they will take to get to Montego Bay, the shoes they will have to wear, the books, the tests.

When the results come out, the names of all the students who pass are printed in the *Jamaica Gleaner*. Delano has passed for Cornwall College. I am bursting with excitement and pride when I see my brother's name in the national newspaper. I feel as if I have passed the Common Entrance myself. I underline his name so I can find it again on the long list of children who have earned full scholarships to high school. We look and look and look, but Shane's name is not there. Aunt June does not say a word to Delano. Nobody else makes a fuss about him either.

All day, Aunt June just goes on and on, "Delano was behind in every subject when he came from Lottery! He could not even write his own name that well. And you let him come here and pass that exam before you? Shane Jennings, I am so ashamed of you."

Grandma does not understand what is happening. I do my best to explain. "Grandma, Delano pass the Common Entrance! That mean him brighter than the children who don't pass. Him have to go to high school now!"

"But how him go reach Montego Bay every day? Him one can't travel so far!"

"Yes, Grandma. The teacher say that Delano is very bright. Him can do anything by himself! And Miss Allen son go every day. And him Chinaman father will pay the bus fare and buy uniform fi him. You just have to tell him that Delano is very, very bright."

I am jumping up and down so much that Grandma smiles. "Well, if is education, me will have to go to him father. And you say Miss Allen son go there too? P'raps them can travel together."

"Yes, Grandma. And him have to get a big schoolbag. The books for high school is big, big. And him need a folder, with folder paper, and a geometry set. Him need a whole heap of things!"

I am so happy that Delano is going to high school. If he goes, then when I pass I might get to go too. There is no father to pay for my bus fare, but something could happen. Grandma says you must have faith.

Delano is very quiet. I don't understand why. He should be excited about Cornwall College High. He will wear red and yellow epaulets on each shoulder and carry a T-square and geometry set to classes. Everybody will have to give him time alone to study. You cannot study if people are always asking you to do this and that. And best of all he doesn't have to be in Bethel Town all day.

"Delano, you not happy that you going to school in another big town far away from here?" I grab his arm and shake him. "You not happy you going to high school?" He shrugs me off and walks away. I have to run to keep up with him. "Delano, you must feel good that you did better than Shane! That mean that you brighter than him fi true!"

He stops abruptly, and I bump into him. He grabs my shoulder and whispers, "Stacey, is not a good thing that I pass and Shane don't pass. You see how Aunt June vex with me—" He pushes me roughly. "I don't know why I am saying anything to you. You is such a damn fool some-times! I wish it was me that never pass!"

I don't care if Delano is not happy about passing. Even if Shane failed, I am glad my brother's name appeared in the national newspaper. That way everybody will know that even if your mother runs away and leaves you, you can do well, even better than somebody whose teacher-mother is here with him every single day.

The Prodigal

On the first day of July, Uncle Harold calls Delano and me aside to tell us that his sister, Hazel, has decided she is coming to Bethel Town from Canada. At first I do not understand why he is talking to us about his sister. Then I realize he is talking about our mother. My mother. My own mother is coming back to Jamaica. "Jesus Christ Almighty, Delano! Him talking 'bout Mummy!"

I can't imagine what it will be like to have a mother from Canada come back for you. "Delano, you know what that mean? It mean we going to move from this house! It mean our own mother coming to take us out of Bethel Town! That mean we not going to live with Aunt June and Uncle Harold anymore! Hallelujah! Praise the Lord!"

Delano grabs my hand and drags me to the back of the house. He lowers his face and looks me straight in the eye. "Stacey, listen to me! You are nine years old—and that is big enough to understand how things go. If you not careful you could mash up everything! Now, promise me you not go do anything to spoil things for me! Promise me!"

"Delano, you never hear what Uncle Harold say? You don't have to worry 'bout them anymore. Them can't do anything else to we now! We own mother coming!"

"Stacey, just shut up and promise me you not going to be rude to nobody till she come!"

"Delano, don't tell me to shut up. You is not me mother!"

He squeezes my wrist and twists my arm behind me. "Stacey, if you do anything to make Aunt June or Uncle Harold vex with us, I go beat you up every day till we dead! You hear me? Now promise!"

The burning in my shoulder forces me give in. "All right! All right! Me promise!"

"You better!" He releases my arm and pushes me away from him.

"Delano?"

"What?"

"You think she going to carry us to go to Canada?"

Delano sighs. "Stacey, I do not know. We just have to wait and see. But I know one thing. If you don't behave yourself she not carrying you anywhere."

I don't believe him, but I don't want to argue.

"Delano, you think Uncle Howard tell her that you pass? I think she going to bring a lot of things for you. She might bring your T-square for high school."

"Stacey, just wait, nuh? Suppose she don't have no money?"

"Delano, you must be a big fool. Everybody who live in foreign have money!"

"No, that is just people from America. And is who you calling fool? Don't ask me nutten else, then."

"All right. I am only telling you this one time. If you do not behave yourself, them could send and tell her that we rude and she might not come! So is important that you don't get in no trouble. She will be here in two weeks. Can you behave yourself till then?"

"All right, Delano! Is not just your mother, you know! She is my mother too!"

"All right, then! Since nobody can tell you anything, just lef me alone till after she come!"

That evening I think about my mother as I wash my dirty feet. I pull Delano's old blue T-shirt over my head and wonder if she will bring me new blouses with the tags still on them. She must be very beautiful. People who have been on planes are always good-looking. I wonder if the plane makes them pretty or if you have to be that way before they let you on. I hope they will let me get on the plane to go back with my mother.

The next day seems to pass in slow motion. We try to fill it by doing extra chores. Delano rakes the yard before anybody tells him. He feeds the pigs, moves the goats, and gets the eggs without Shane. I wash my panties as soon as I take them off. I sweep the floors and I make sure to say thank you and please to Aunt June for everything. At the end of the day, we watch TV in the living room while Aunt June sews on the veranda. During the news, she sends me to get her scissors from her bedroom. I immediately dash to fetch them and sprint back before she lays out the cloth for cutting. She smiles and takes the scissors from me. She does not say anything.

I smile and say, "Thanks very much, Aunt June."

"Eh, eh! Is what you thanking me for? What happened to you? You swallowed the book of unnecessary manners?"

"No, ma'am! Sorry 'bout that, Aunt June."

I stand there, hoping for another request. "Beg pardon, Aunt June, you need the pincushion too? Is right there on the bedside table. You want me bring it for you now?"

"No, I do not need any pins. Don't you have anything to do but stand there making an ass of you-self?"

"Sorry 'bout that, Aunt June. What about the bag of threads? You don't need them now? I could bring the black threads, or the yellow ones—any color you want, I can just bring it right now, quick, quick!"

"Child! Move from in front of me and stop being a blasted idiot!"

"Yes, Aunt June. I going round the back right now."

In public I am invisible. No matter what is said, if it was not directed at me, I keep my mouth shut. In Sunday school I only respond to the questions Miss Pearle, the Sunday school teacher, asks me to answer. And I only answer with what is in the Bible.

"Staceyann, according to St. Paul's letter to the Romans, what is the wages of sin?"

"Death, Miss Pearle, St. Paul says the wages of sin is death."

"Good. Now, who else can tell me what is the gift of God?"

I know the answer, but she did not ask me, so I only say the answer in my head. *The gift of God is eternal life in Christ Jesus our Lord.*

Miss Pearle leans to the left and taps her stocking-clad right foot, waiting for a response. A few of the girls scurry for their Bibles. The fine turning of the thin school-issued Bible leaves rustle. I bite my bottom lip and tuck my hands under my armpits when the other students look at me.

Miss Pearle quickly rises to the occasion to preach. "Well, children, all of you are surely moving at top speed on the highway to hell! If you do not know the holy gift of God, you do not deserve his infinite mercy! The generous and everlasting gift of God is eternal and heavenly life in Christ Jesus our Lord and Savior! Life, forevermore—no more death and disease, children, just life everlasting—forever and ever, buried in the bosom of the Messiah! At the right hand of Jesus we will sing and shout the victory!"

I really want to tell her that St. Paul's letter to the Romans did not say all of that, but I hold my tongue.

At home we are gracious to Samantha and Shane. We pity them. They do not have a mother coming from abroad. We only talk about her in private. Delano is certain that our mother is better looking than Aunt June. And because she is not a Christian she should be even prettier than Auntie Ella, who only lives in Kingston.

July the eleventh. Grandma said she is coming on Saturday, July 11. On the morning of the tenth, Uncle Harold calls Delano and me out to the veranda. His English Leather aftershave tickles my nose when he squats to deliver his spiel. I lean away from him as his voice booms out at us. "Children, I want you to be vigilant of how far you have come from the barbarism of your previous life. While my sister is in this house, please restrict your conversations to standard English. You will find that though she is your mother, she is a woman of remarkable class and high culture."

He takes me by the shoulder and pulls me toward him. "Do you comprehend these charges, Staceyann?" I don't understand what he is asking me, but I want him to let me go, so I nod vigorously.

"Don't shake your head at me. You are not a dog. Do you understand what I have asked of you, young lady?

From that close, the bumps in his beard look like marbles under his skin, and his breath smells like rubbing alcohol and eggs.

"Yes, Uncle Harold."

He releases me and stands to his full height. He adjusts his belt and puts his arm around Aunt June. "Well, we have done all we can for you children. The rest is in your hands."

Aunt June steps away and sucks her teeth. "I really don't know anything about class, culture, nor what we have done for anybody, but the rest is certainly in their hands." Uncle Harold carefully examines his shiny black police boots.

Aunt June does not look at him, she just looks at us and says, "Just try not to embarrass me in front of any of the strangers she might bring."

I wonder whom else she might bring. I know people always bring *things* from America. But I had never heard of anybody bringing *people*.

After Samantha and Shane fall asleep, I broach the subject with Delano. "Lano, who you think she could bring?"

"Stacey, you really getting stupid now! She could bring anybody! She could have a husband, or other children, or her friend them from Canada, or people from Montego Bay, or even my father."

I never considered that she might have a husband or other children. "What you mean, she have other children? She don't have no other children! She have us! We is the children she have! Me and you. Okay, maybe she can have a husband. But no children!"

I am silent for a minute. Then I am angry at Delano for suggesting it. "And why she would bring your stupid father? Him don't live in Canada! Him just live in Montego Bay!"

"Shh! Stacey, don't talk so loud!" He puts his hand over my mouth. "Listen, her plane landing in Montego Bay, and my father live in Montego Bay. So him might just pick her up from the airport. And who knows, maybe she will marry my father and then we can live in Montego Bay or all of we can go straight to Canada."

I bite his hand and push him off. "So why you think my father not picking her up? My father live in Montego Bay too! Suppose she want to marry my father!"

He looks at his nails and then smiles before he answers. "Well, nobody really know exactly where your father is. And I think him married already. And him don't want anything to do with you. Otherwise, him would send things for you, like my father send for me. But don't worry, man—if she get married to my father, you can come live with us. But only if you learn to keep your clappers shut sometimes, all right?"

I pull the covers over my head and turn my back to him. The sheets smell of blue soap and the mothballs from the dresser drawer. I like that smell. I hope the sheets in Canada smell like mothballs. Minutes later I hear him breathing deep and even beside me.

I lie awake, thinking about my father. To have me, my father must have committed adultery. Psalm 51:5, *Behold, I was brought forth in iniquity, and in sin my mother conceived me.* I wish I could go ask my father why he did not marry my mother. Just show up at his house one day. Maybe he is not even married. Maybe he is just waiting for my mother to come and marry him and take him to Canada.

On the morning of the eleventh no one has to wake us. We finish making the bed, and Delano asks for a time check. I look at the clock in the living room and report, "Seventeen minutes past seven o'clock."

Delano heads out to the pigpen. Pigs fed, goats moved, and eggs collected, we shovel breakfast down our throats. I scald my tongue on the hot cornmeal porridge, but I don't complain. Samantha and I clear the table, while Shane and Delano rake the front yard. Aunt June orders baths for everyone. Grandma pulls out my red dress with the polka dots. I sit in my white panties while she combs my hair. To make sure the part is straight, she runs the comb from the tip of my nose up over my forehead. She measures the weight of the two puffs and makes minute adjustments to ensure the part is just right. Then she oils the white line of visible scalp with Vaseline. Aunt June has given permission for me to use Samantha's hair clips. Water is sprinkled over the top of my head and the hair is brushed until smooth. The two red bubble clips are used to secure the hair. A perfect braid hangs behind each ear. I like when Grandma makes the two plaits fall down the sides of my head. I feel very grown-up.

Grandma sends me for the dress. "Bring it come to me, I don't want you to fuzz up your hair!"

She carefully slips the dress over my head, zips me up, and smoothes my hair again. I put on my blue socks and tie the laces of my brown school shoes. I feel like a princess when Grandma gives me her handkerchief with the yellow flowers embroidered around the edges. I pass through the living room on my way to the veranda. Aunt June stops sewing when she sees me. She pushes the needle in the pincushion and claps her hands. "My Lord! What a thing when dish towel turn tablecloth! Turn around and let me see you!"

I twirl and she whoops some more.

"You are a puss in boots today, Miss Ma'am! I hope for your sake that woman show up today!"

I trip and just in time catch myself from falling. "She coming, Aunt June! Uncle Harold says so!"

Aunt June picks up her needle and jams it into the cloth. "Well, if your Uncle Harold says so, it must be so, right?" Her face gets serious. "Now go on outside. But stay on the veranda. I know you cannot stay clean if you are in the yard."

I take my position on the red veranda. As soon as my mother comes through the gate, I will see her. Moments later, Delano arrives in his yellow dress shirt and black pants. His hair is wet and greased and parted to the side. He looks like a wet rat. But I tell him he looks very pretty.

"Who you calling pretty? Boys are not pretty! Boys are handsome."

"Okay, Delano, you look very, very handsome."

We sit in the blue and white plastic patio chairs and wait. Samantha and Shane play cricket in the yard. Shane is winning. Soon he is bored and calls out, "Delano, come play with me, nuh? This girl-cricket is foolishness. She can't even bat, much less bowl to me!"

"Delano cannot come out there to play no cricket with you. Him will get dirty before we mother come for us!"

Shane throws the ball at me.

"Who ask you nothing, Miss Mouth Almighty? I was talking to Delano, not you."

"Shane, it don't matter who you was talking to, him cannot play today."

Delano kicks the ball back to Shane. "Staceyann Chin, why you can't just shut up? Him was asking me. And I can play if I want to. But me don't want to play now."

"Delano, sometimes you are such a follow-fashion! Why you would let him inveigle you to go and dirty up your clothes when you know your mother is coming from Canada? You are a disgrace to anybody who look at you!"

"Stacey, nobody is inveigling me to do anything. So just shut up your blasted mouth and stop telling me what to do."

"Stop telling me to shut up! Is my mouth and I can open it when me want! Why you want to go outside and dirty up yourself when you look so pretty today is beyond me!"

"How much time I must tell you? I am not pretty! Stop saying that! Before I thump you in your big fat mouth!"

"Delano, I don't care what you say! Is a compliment me giving you—you look pretty today. Is that a big crime, that you look pretty?"

Shane takes up the call and runs with it.

"Delano, you look so, so very, very pretty! Ooh! Ooh! In your pretty shirt and your pretty pants. Delano is a pretty girl! Delano is a pretty girl!"

Delano's face is getting redder and redder with every taunt. "Stacey, me warning you, take it back!"

"Me not taking nutten back, Delano. And you wouldn't dare hit me today!"

Shane runs back and forth across the yard. "Delano, please don't hit me with your pretty little fist. Not today, when your pretty mother is coming from pretty Canada!"

The chair is yanked out from under me and I look up to see Delano sailing toward me on the floor. He rips out the red clips and pulls at my dress. The ripping sound makes me scream and grab at his shirt. The buttons fly off and hit me in the face.

"Fight! Fight! Mummy, come quick! Delano and Stacey fighting." Shane is jumping up and down with excitement.

When Aunt June arrives, we are a pile of rumples and rips on the red concrete floor. "Now there is nothing to say to the two of you. Imagine, God has seen it fit to send your mother from all the way in Canada. As I speak, she is already on her way. There is nothing to be said of man's ungratefulness in the infinite mercy of God! Now get out of my sight! The both of you get up and go put on yard clothes. You obviously are a set of wild animals. You have no idea how to behave like decent human beings. Get up from that floor at once!"

We collect our bits and pieces and go to the bedroom to change. I put on my purple dress with the oil stain on the front. Delano pulls out an old khaki school shirt and some church pants that Grandma made into shorts because they were too short. I try to brush my hair. It looks so ugly. I wish Grandma could do it for me, but I am afraid Aunt June would see me if I go to look for her.

Delano and I do not say a thing to each other. We go back to the veranda and wait for our mother in silence. The morning passes in painful expectation. The sun on the veranda gets hotter as the day gets later. It would be cooler to sit in the living room. But we are afraid we might miss her.

The white van marked JUTA TOURS in big blue letters on the side pulls up a little after two. The driver, his white teeth grinning from his smooth dark face, wears a white long-sleeved shirt and black pants. He jumps from the driver's seat and quickly opens the passenger door.

A tall woman with lots of curly bronze hair slides out. The long white dress falls softly around her slender frame. She holds the hem of the dress aloft as she turns to close the door. She is darker than I imagined and she looks nothing like Grandma. She straightens her sunglasses and stands there for a minute, looking at the two of us standing on the veranda. Suddenly her right hand clutches her throat.

"Oh, my God! Look at my baby. I would know you anywhere. Delano Mark Anthony, you still have the very same face!" Then she is crying and holding out her arms to him. Delano stands there, rooted to the ground.

"Come here, come to your mother." She beckons to him. He walks over to her and she envelops him. I stand aside, watching the embrace.

"You too," she invites, "you can come too."

My mother smells like talcum powder and coffee beans. Her arms are tight, but I do not feel as if she is holding me. I stand very still while her long red nails make scratching sounds on my back. Her toenails are the same color as her fingernails. She smells like something else, but I cannot think what it might be. Something else, like Christmas fruits soaked in rum and sugar. I don't know if I like that smell, so I stop breathing. She hugs us for a long time. I can't wait for her to let me go. Her belt buckle is pressing into my forehead and my neck hurts from the way she is squeezing my head.

Finally she lets go. I inhale deeply and marvel that I could hold my breath for that long. She whispers something to the driver, who immediately unloads the van. There are bags and bags and bags of things. The driver puts the bags in the living room. He asks for a drink of water. Aunt June sends Samantha to get it. He drinks all the water without taking the glass from his mouth before he nods to Mummy and drives away.

She hurries us inside. "Now, June, can you please tell me, where is my mum?"

It takes me a moment to figure out that she is asking for Grandma.

"She round the back, washing," I say.

"No! No! No! She cannot be doing laundry at a time such as this! Please go and get her, now! Right now. Tell her she has to come and greet me this very minute!"

She sinks into the couch and rubs her forehead. "I cannot believe my mom is doing laundry! I have not seen her in ages, and she is too busy with laundry!"

Quicker than anyone expects, she begins to open bags. Aunt June offers her a drink of sorrel.

"Oh, June, sorrel is so sweet. I'm convinced those things are not good for anybody."

"Hazel, you want the sorrel or not?"

"No, thank you, June. I'm afraid it might give me a headache. Now, where is my beautiful son? I have brought him something very special!" She reaches down into a bag and pulls out a small black box.

"Is this a camera? Does it have real film? And is mine? Thank you, Mummy! Thank you very much!" Delano cannot contain his joy. "You see this, Stacey? You see me new camera?"

"Yes, Delano. Is very, very nice fi true."

"Oh, Staceyann, don't be so jealous. I brought you something wonderful too."

Just then, Grandma walks into the living room.

"Oh, Mother! Mum! Oh, my God, you are a sight for sore eyes!"

She falls upon Grandma. Grandma pats her, the way she pats me when I want something I cannot have. My mother is pressing her face into Grandma's chest. "Mum, it is so good to see you! How are you?"

I can see that Grandma cannot understand her. She is talking too fast and her mouth is too far from Grandma's face. But Grandma nods and pats her again.

"I have lots of dresses for you. And I know you adore hats. Are you still into hats, Mum?"

Grandma is just nodding and nodding and nodding.

She hands Grandma a big bag of clothes and tells her, "These are all for you. I shopped very carefully for you. I wanted you to know how much you really mean to me. Even with all the distance, you mean the world to me, Mum!"

Grandma takes the bag and pats her again. "Hazel, I have some washing to finish up. So me soon come back. And I thank God up in heaven fi sen you come back, so me can see you before me dead!" Grandma is wiping tears from her own eyes.

"Okay, Mum. I know it must be hard for you to be so emotional. And I don't want to mess up my face again, so go. Go and finish your laundry. I understand. Okay, so where are we now? Yes, we are opening the gift for my little princess."

It feels like the sun is shining on just me. I don't know what to do with myself. I shift my weight from leg to leg and watch while she finds the appropriate bag. She reaches into the largest bag and pulls out a doll. It is almost as tall as I am. The large blue eyes stare emptily at me. The smooth pink skin is hard and cold to the touch. The dress it is wearing is too short. And she is wearing red high heels. She looks like Jezebel. "Mummy, you didn't bring me any books?"

"Staceyann Chin, do not be ungrateful! I spent the last two days looking for that doll. And it cost me a pretty penny, I'll tell you! Much more money than I could have paid for any book!"

I do not care how much the doll cost. It is ugly and is dressed like a fallen woman. I want to throw the doll on the floor, but I am afraid to make her angry, so I hug the doll and tell her I love it.

Delano and I get lots of new things: shorts sets, dresses, a pair of bright red pajamas, and hair clips—everything but shoes. She did not know our foot sizes, so she couldn't buy us any shoes. Shane and Samantha get a few things too. But not any clothes.

"I don't think any of these will fit you guys. Both of you are so much bigger than Staceyann and Delano. I bet you both like your hamburgers, don't you? But I have plenty of hair clips and socks. You are both welcome to have some of those."

Mummy hugs us every time she hands us a new gift. "Come here and give your mother a big thank-you hug."

Every time she holds me, she exclaims, "You are as thin as a pin! You could be a runway model! What in God's name do you eat? You can't eat anything and be this slim!"

After she says it a few times, Aunt June gets upset. "Hazel, in the nine years you leave these children with Grandma, you ever send one red cent to buy a piece of bread to feed them? You are damn out of order to come here passing remarks about them being fat or thin!" Aunt June gets up from her chair and stands over Mummy. "Hazel, I will let you know this much. You can fool them children with your antics, but I have the power of God in my eyes. I see straight through everything you trying to run from. You do not give a damn about these two children. Not one cent, eh, Hazel, and you know that Grandma was not working. And you know how Jamaica is for poor people! Is not like you never used to live here!"

Mummy begins to pack up the bags of things.

"Look at me, Hazel! When was the last time you go to bed knowing what your children have eaten for dinner? When?"

"June, you are so melodramatic. I think of them every day! Not a night goes by when I am not worried sick about my babies!" Her voice is screeching and odd.

"Well, if such is the case, and you are worried about them being so thin, take them. Take them and go feed them yourself."

"Don't be silly, June, what would I do with two small children?"

Aunt June and Uncle Harold turn away from her.

"June and Harold, I do care about them! I do! I do! I think of them all the time!"

They do not believe her, but I believe her. I feel sorry for her.

"I understand, Mummy. I think about you all the time, too."

She looks at me and bursts out crying. "Oh, Ma Chérie, I know that you do, and I appreciate it so much."

This time when she hugs me, it feels good. And I am glad that she remembers my middle name. I did not even know the correct pronunciation till she said it. It sounds really pretty on her tongue, like I am somebody special, somebody from somewhere else.

When she stops sobbing and raises her head, her eyes look funny. Like somebody had punched her in both of them at the same time. "Staceyann, is my mascara running?"

I have no idea what she is asking, but I nod.

"Okay, then, let me run to the loo to fix my makeup."

When she comes back, she covers her face with her hands and screams, "Ma Chérie, don't look at me. The light in that bathroom is awful. I must look like a scarecrow. I have no idea how June puts herself together in such a small dark place."

She pats her eyes with tissue paper and sits on the couch. "Now, my darlings, come and sit beside me and tell me what great adventures you two have out here in the country!"

Delano tells her that he gets groceries from his father every month. "Oh, Delano, that takes such a weight off my mind. I am so glad he is taking good care of you."

She looks so pleased that I want to tell her something about me. I settle for telling her about Nancy Drew. "Mummy, I can finish a whole Nancy Drew in just one week."

"Oh, Chérie, I am so glad you like learning about other places! Are you learning another language in school? Can you speak any French? Everyone speaks French in Canada. French Canadians are so sophisticated. Not like Americans, who can only speak one language."

"No, Mummy. But I read the stories in the Bible. They tell you a lot about Egypt and Jerusalem and Bethlehem."

"Staceyann, I hope you two are not getting too caught up in this church business!"

"No, Mummy! Delano have a lot of friends at church, but I don't like church at all. Sometimes I wish I could stay home and read, but Aunt June make us go every Sunday!"

"Staceyann Chin! I am ashamed of you. No one can make you do anything. You are your own person. You have to decide what is right for your own life. And June is not in charge of you, I am. And when I am not here, your grandmother is. Don't forget that!"

"Yes, Mummy."

"Now stay here while I go and say a few things to June. She believes she can do as she wishes with my children. Well, I am here to tell her she can't!"

The rest of the day is quiet. We all sit in the living room. Delano snaps pictures of Shane. I comb the yellow hair of the giant dolly.

At about five o'clock the white van comes back. My mother calls me to her and whispers that she has one more special gift for me. She reaches into her pocket and pulls out a little box with a gold bow on the top. She opens it and empties out the finest gold chain with the tiniest cross pendant into her palm. I turn around while she places it around my neck.

"Now, Ma Chérie, this chain is a symbol of my love. As long as you have it, you will know that you are my daughter, and that I love you."

The fine gold chain makes me feel like I am the most beautiful thing in the world. The little cross rests cold on my collarbone. Mummy climbs gracefully into the passenger seat of the van and yawns. "My darlings, my darlings, this has been a wonderful day! It was so lovely to see both your beautiful faces."

She pulls us to her bosom one last time. And then, in a hot wave of blown kisses and perfume, my mother rides away.

Both of us stand watching the van disappear.

"Delano, I did think she was going to stay with us."

"That is what I was telling you. You can't think anything. People do what them do and you can't do nothing about it."

"You think she going to come back tomorrow?"

"How I must know that? You think me know everything? Just relax yourself and wait till things happen how them supposed to happen! Now come make us go and take up our things off the living room floor before Aunt June get vex 'bout it."

Shane and Samantha are sitting with the few gifts Mummy had given them. There is something odd about having more than them. But it still feels good. I quiet the small worry and finger the cross at my throat and remind myself that I am the luckiest girl in the world.

I wear the gold chain and the brand-new flannel pajamas to bed. The sharp edges of the cross make tiny nicks in my throat. By morning I am hot and sweaty and the red dye from the pajamas has bled into the white sheets on the bed. I go to the kitchen to look for Grandma.

She is not in the kitchen, but Aunt June is there, complaining to Uncle Harold over the porridge. "Whatever she do, Harold, she will have to take the two of them out of here today." Uncle Harold is silent as she continues, "You hear her yesterday? *They are so thin!* Where she was when them was eatin? I don't want them in here another night. Them have a mother now, and I going to send them go to her!"

I tiptoe back to the bedroom. "Delano, Aunt June say we have to leave today! That means we going to live with Mummy now!"

"Stacey, why you can't stop telling lies? You can't just wait to see anything happen before you make it up, eh?"

"All right, Mr. Know-It-All, you will have to just wait and see."

By late morning Grandma has packed all of our things. She packs all the new clothes. Only a few of the clothes we had before Mummy came can fit in the bags. The big doll cannot fit, so Grandma says I will have to carry it in my arms.

"Delano, you know exactly where Miss Miles's house is, right? Is right up the road from your father place. That is where you mother staying. Stacey, me don't know if you remember Miss Miles. Me would go with oonu, but Miss Miles's new house is very small. Me don't want all of we to turn up on the poor woman without no warning. Oonu will have to go on the bus by oonuself."

I ask Grandma why our mother can't come for us. I am worried that we will get lost if we are by ourselves. But she says there is no need to worry because Delano is big enough to know where to walk. "Delano, make sure you hold her hand all the time. And look fi car before oonu cross the road. God not going to make anything happen to oonu. Him take oonu this far, him wouldn't let oonu down now."

We take our bags to the veranda. Aunt June stands by the front door. I can't tell if she is angry or sad. Delano tries to say good-bye, but she turns away and tells us to just go. As we exit the gate she waves her arms and yells, "Make sure oonu don't come back here, no matter what that madwoman tell oonu! Even if she put you back on the bus, do not set foot back on my property!"

None of us say anything. Grandma walks with us to the bus stop. She holds my hand while I struggle along with the doll. When we get to the bus stop she gives Delano money for the fare. Delano sits by the window with his face turned to the side. I slide in beside him and stick the doll between us. Grandma carefully pushes our bags under our seat. She sniffles and takes out her white handkerchief. I am suddenly tired of her. I wish she would just stop with the crying so we can go.

"Delano and Stacey, oonu must put oonu trust in God. And be careful, Montego Bay is like Sodom and Gomorrah. Watch where oonu walk! And make sure oonu tell oonu mother fi send word as soon as she can. Jesus in heaven protect the two of oonu!"

She presses the handkerchief into my hand and wipes her nose with her sleeve. Then she licks her fingers and smoothes my hair. I shrug her off. "All right, all right, Grandma. You have to get off the bus now. The driver waiting on you. Good-bye!"

She removes her tie-head and uses it to blow her nose. She stands outside looking very, very sad. I push my head through the window, "Don't worry 'bout us, Grandma. We going to be all right. Delano know the way and our mother will take care of us when we get there."

As the bus drives away, she waves and waves and waves at us. Delano waves and waves back at her. I can't wait to see Montego Bay.

By the time we get to downtown Montego Bay I am so hungry that nothing in the busy city is of interest; the giant clock, the labeled streets, the hundreds of people milling about are too much. We walk from the bus stop to another taxi stand. The taxi smells like sweat and perfume. I lay the doll across my legs. A young man with a gold tooth and a large older woman with very big breasts sit in the back with us. The woman calls the man Sparky.

"Sparky, go over some more in the seat! Why you must sit down with you legs them wide open, I don't know."

Sparky grunts, closes his legs, and looks out the window. The woman puts on lipstick and smiles at us. Her perfume crawls right up into my nose when she leans in to me and pats my cheek. "My word! What a pretty little girl! And is this you brother? Is where oonu going without oonu mother?"

I sit straight up and tell her, "Miss, we are not *without* our mother! We are going up there to her now. And then we are going to live with her in Canada."

The lady pats my cheek again and nods. "All right, little miss, oonu is very lucky to be going away to foreign." She turns back to Sparky. "Sparky, you hear dat? Them going away to America!"

She turns to us again and asks, "Is that where you father is, America?"

"I never said America! Canada is better because they talk French like France! In America they only speak one language—"

Delano pulls me closer to him. "Stacey, stop bothering the woman. We don't even know if we going anywhere yet!"

"Well, children, this is our stop. Oonu take good care of oonuselves when oonu reach Canada. Open the door, Sparky!"

We drive for another few minutes. At the final stop Delano pays the driver. When the taxi drives away he grabs my arm and shakes me. The doll falls to the ground.

"Stacey, why you have to tell that woman that we going to Canada? You have to stop telling people things that you don't know."

"Delano, just leave me alone and stop telling me what to do. You is not my mother!"

"All right, then. Do what you want, but one day something really bad going to happen because of your big fat mouth!"

I am hot and hungry and annoyed with his pessimism. "Delano, is your mouth big and fat and ugly! Just wait till we reach! I going to tell Mummy on you!"

He grabs the two bags and tells me to pick up the doll and hold on to one of the bags. "And make sure you don't let it go. Grandma say that Montego Bay drivers drive like madmen. Just hold on to the bag and follow me."

We pass a big church called the Mount Salem Open Bible Church.

People are singing and clapping inside. Mount Salem Hill is steep and the sun is very hot. At the top of the hill there are rows and rows of houses surrounded by walls and fences. We pass gardens with bright-colored flowers and neatly cut hedges. The street is wide and empty when we turn the corner.

"Delano, how much farther we have to walk?"

"Stacey, stop complaining. Is right here. Just hurry up and open the gate!"

I reach inside to unlatch the metal gate. He puts one bag on the door-step and knocks on the front door. The door swings open and Mummy steps outside, wearing a shiny red robe held together with a wide black sash loosely tied around her waist. Her red nails reach up to scratch her face. She looks up and down the street and demands, "What the hell are you two doing here?"

She pulls the sash tighter. Her face looks very different today. There are little pimples and black marks all over her face.

"Aunt June tell us to come, Mummy." I don't understand why Dela-no's tone is apologetic.

"'Aunt June tell us to come, Mummy'? Is that the best you can do? Is that all the explanation you have as to why you have both appeared unannounced on my doorstep?"

My mother is waving her arms and screaming. The veins in her neck are little snakes crawling under her skin. When she shouts like that I can see that her teeth look funny. They are not really white and they don't all line up in a straight row. I wonder why her teeth are like that. In America, they have shiny wires that hold your teeth in a straight line. The wires are called braces. The braces I see on TV make it look like the person has diamonds on every tooth. Maybe Canada does not have braces. I watch her mouth moving and moving and moving and wonder what she would look like with diamonds on those crazy teeth.

"After all the things I brought for June and her children, this is how she repays me! That bitch! See if I bring another stitch of clothes for her and her little tar babies next time!" She pulls the black sash again and looks down at the two of us. Then she turns and walks inside.

"What are you children waiting for? Come on in! And leave the door open. I need the fresh air. Delano, please put those bags inside and take her to sit in that corner."

She is talking to us like we have done something bad to her. I feel like I should say I am sorry, but she walks toward the back room and slams the door behind her.

I lay the doll on the couch and asked Delano, "What's wrong with her?"

"Shut your mouth, and don't say anything when she come back," he tells me.

I start crying. Delano pinches my arm and orders me to stop. I cry even louder. He lets go of the flesh on my arm and hugs me. "Stop, nuh, Stacey, man. If she come out and see you crying, she going be more upset. Just quiet, man, stop crying and everything go be all right."

He pulls a lollipop from his pocket and gives it to me. Half an hour later, Mummy comes back into the room and sees me sucking away. She almost jumps over the coffee table to get at me. Her long red nail grazes my cheek and hooks onto the gold chain as she slaps the half-eaten lollipop from my mouth. The chain breaks and the gold cross falls down my chest.

"Now look what you made me do! Find the cross and give it to me. You obviously don't know how to care for anything of value. Find it and give it back to me!"

I reach down into the front of my dress and fish out the tiny cross. She reaches over and grabs it.

"Who told you you could eat candy in this house? Who do you think has money to fix your teeth when they go rotten? There will be no candy in this house. Do you hear me, young lady? And sit up straight. Your spine is curved like an African monkey. No grace in these children. No wonder I never came back for you!"

Provoke Not Your Children

Mummy tells us that this wonderful house belongs to her dear old friend Miss Miles. I ask if it is not the same Miss Miles that is Grandma's friend.

"Please don't interrupt me, Staceyann. It's very rude to interrupt!"

I put my hand over my mouth to keep from blurting out that I did not interrupt her, that she was finished with her sentence before I said anything.

"In these last few years, Miss Miles was really getting too old to live under the harsh conditions of the country life in Lottery, so her husband built her this lovely mansion here in Mount Salem." The house does not look like a mansion to me. The living room is very, very small, but I know better than to say anything. "I wouldn't say it is as big as my house in Montreal, but it is a marvelous little place. Did you children see the gardens? The flowers are to die for! Gardens are so romantic . . .

"When I was a little girl, I used to be buddies with Miss Miles's son, Harvey. He was so in love with me. We didn't do anything that could be called *fresh*, but in the evenings while we did our homework, we held hands—nothing fresh. It was such a lovely time in our lives. I know he still thinks of those lovely evenings. He must! It was just so perfect! Absolutely, perfectly perfect!"

She tells us that Miss Miles is out shopping for the day, but that we have to be ready for her at all times, as this is her house.

She stands by the doorway looking out and picking the tiny pimples on her face. Suddenly she tightens her sash. "Okay, my lovelies, what do you want to have for dinner? Franks? Mac and cheese? Spanish rice?"

Those choices don't sound like dinner to me. I bite my lips and wait

for Delano to respond. He hunches his shoulders and looks at his fingernails. "What's the matter with you children? Aren't you hungry?"

"Yes, Mummy." Delano looks away.

She looks at me and raises her eyebrows. "Well, Staceyann?"

"Yes, Mummy." I want to find the words that will make her happy.
"I want some of the mac and cheese and some of the Spanish rice.
I think Delano wants some too." Delano looks at me with murder in
his eyes.

"Okay, my darlings. Let's get you fed. Delano, we have no cheese, so
you will have to go get cheese from your father's supermarket. It's just
down the road. You can easily walk."

Delano does not move.

"What is the matter, Delano? I expect you to move when I ask you to
do something. Now get up from there and go get dressed."

"But, Mummy, I never go over there by myself. Grandma always go
with me."

"Delano, please do not argue with your mother. Just do as I say. Go
and get some cheese from Charles."

He takes a deep breath and stiffens his back. His hands curl into fists.
"No."

"I beg your pardon?" Her fingers still against the side of her face, she
slowly moves toward the couch.

Delano makes his body smaller in the corner of the couch. "Mummy,
I never go in there by myself. Can't you just come with me?"

"What did you just say to me? Are you out of your mind? Did you just
refuse to do something I told you to do?"

He presses the small of his back against the arm of the couch and
slides his bottom up and over it. She edges toward him. He circles away
from her and darts toward the door. "Mummy, just come with me, please.
I will go, but just don't make me go down there by myself."

"Delano, stop being a big baby and try to be a reasonable person.
Look at me! I can't possibly go with you. I am not even dressed!"

He backs away from her. "I will wait for you to get dressed,
Mummy."

"Delano Mark Anthony, stop that bellyaching and go right now! Right
this minute, I tell you!"

"No!"

She reaches for him and just misses his collar as he slips through the door. The hot tar burns his bare feet and he hops from one foot to the next.

"Stop making fun of me!" Mummy shakes her fist at him from the doorway and grabs her own neck with her hands to show him what she will do to him when he comes inside. Her long nails make her thin hands look like claws.

"I don't care what you do to me, I am not going down to the super-market by myself!"

Mummy screams, "Delano Mark Anthony! Do not force me to come out there! Get inside this instant!"

People hear the screaming and look out.

I stand behind Mummy's red robe and watch her clench and unclench her fist. I am a little afraid for Delano. Part of me wants him to come inside and end this, but I'm also glad to see him standing up to her.

The argument goes back and forth. Mummy ties and reties her black sash. A lady from the house next door urges Delano to go in. He tells her to mind her own business. Another woman shakes her head and says it's a pity when people can't control their own children. My brother holds his ground for almost an hour.

Finally Mummy concedes. "Okay, Delano, you have won this round! You do not have to go to the supermarket. Just come inside and put on some shoes. Your feet must be blistering on that hot asphalt."

Delano cautiously makes his way inside. He closes the door slowly. As the lock clicks into place, she lunges at him. She hits him in the head, on his legs, his face, his arms—all the time cursing, "Do you think you can take me on? You little half-breed, ill-mannered dog! I will knock your insolent lights out, you little stinker!"

When he is no longer moving, she tells him to put on his shoes and go to get the cheese from Charles's supermarket. He is crying so hard I ask if I should go with him. She slaps me. "Speak when you are spoken to!"

I sit on the couch holding my face. She tells me to take good note of the incident and consider it anytime I ever think I can be fresh to her. Delano glances fearfully at her before he slips out the front door. She looks me up and down with disgust before she goes into the back room and slams the door.

Forty-five minutes later Delano comes back with the slab of cheddar.

He sits beside me to take off his shoes. I touch his back and he shrugs my hand away. Mummy opens the bedroom door and smiles at him.

"Goodness! You're back already?"

She walks over to him and plants a loud kiss on his cheek.

"Ooh, Delano! I love you so much! Just you wait and see. I'm going to make you something very special! Canadian macaroni and cheese—with milk in it. Have you ever had that?"

She tells us that milk is good for growing children. Milk and cheese—not too much cheese, though. Cheese is very fattening. By the time Miss Miles comes home we have already eaten the gooey macaronis with the sour sauce of milk and cheese. The keys jingle as she opens the door.

"My Lord! Look who is here! Delano, it is so good to see you!" She leans down and kisses Delano. Then she turns to me and whoops before she throws her arms around me and kisses me.

Arms akimbo, she steps back. "Oh, my goodness! Look at you, Stacey! I have not seen you since the Devil was a boy! You are so tall and beautiful. Both of you are such beautiful children. Welcome, welcome to my house."

Miss Miles slips off her shoes and puts her handbag on the dining table. "Oh, children, I am so sorry I was not here when you came. Had I known you would be coming I would have prepared some sandwiches. And I cannot even spend any time with you now because I am leaving for Canada early tomorrow morning and I have so much packing and running around to do. Where is Miss Bernice?"

I step forward. "She's in Bethel Town, Miss Miles. Is she put me and Delano on the bus this morning."

Miss Miles looks up from her handbag. "The two of you travel all the way from Bethel Town by yourself?"

We nod.

Mummy steps in and touches our shoulders. "Don't nod your heads like cows, children. Mrs. Miles has asked you a question. Open your mouths and answer like civilized people."

"Yes, Miss Miles."

Mummy's nails press into my shoulder. "Mrs. Miles. She is a married woman, so her name is Mrs. Miles."

"Oh, Lord, Hazel, never mind that! Everyone calls me Miss Miles. But I must say I am very proud of both of you for coming so far on the bus by yourselves. Hazel, can I have a moment with you inside, please?"

She hugs us again and they both go into the back room. In a few minutes Miss Miles comes back and tells us we can watch TV until it is time to go to bed. Fae Ellington is reading the news. I wish Fae Ellington were my mother. Mummy comes out of the back room and announces that it is time for us to get ready for bed. It is only seven o' clock, but Delano quickly gets our toothbrushes and pajamas from the bags. Mummy is curled up reading on one bed. Delano and I say our prayers and climb into the other.

"Good night, Mummy!"

"Good night, Mummy!"

She does not respond. I nudge Delano and whisper, "You think she sleeping?"

"Please, children, I cannot concentrate with all that whispering."

Delano covers his head and turns his back to me.

The next morning Mummy wakes us at dawn and tells us to shower. She tells me to put on my red shorts with the matching red-and-white-striped blouse. Delano has to put on his blue jeans and white T-shirt. The shirt is a little small, so she tells him to change into his blue polo shirt. He tells her that he wants to wear his white T-shirt. She slaps him on the mouth and asks him if he thinks he is a big man.

"If you are a big man, you should go and find your own accommodations."

Miss Miles makes fried eggs and bread and butter. We say grace and then eat breakfast in silence. I volunteer to wash the dishes. Mummy tells Delano to go and make the beds. Afterward I watch Miss Miles stuff things into the three big bags that she is taking with her to Canada. When she is done she calls a taxi. She hugs us and then she is gone, leaving us alone with Mummy.

The hum of the taxi is still in the air when Mummy calls us into the back room. She tells us that we must never ever go outside. "Staceyann, for years your father has been trying to steal you from me. I don't want his spies to see where I am keeping you." Her hand grips her throat. "I will not allow that bastard to take you! I will never let him have you! I would rather die first. I love you more than my life!"

"Me too, Mummy, I love you more than my life too."

"Thank you, my darling. Let's go take some photographs of your beautiful faces."

We stand outside in the garden while she snaps away with Delano's new camera. We take turns wearing her sunglasses. She takes my braids out and changes my clothes. She brushes Delano's hair and makes him tilt his head. She tells us we are natural runway models, that we were born to be movie stars.

We are all laughing and making faces when we get back inside. Delano wants to take more pictures, but Mummy presses her temples and says, "Children, please. Leave me alone now. I have the most terrible headache." Then she disappears into the back room.

Miss Miles has a lot of books in her house. I find three Hardy Boys that I have not read. I take all of them down. Delano turns on the TV.

Mummy comes rushing out of the back room. "Good God! What in heaven's name is wrong with you children? Did I not say I have a headache? I have a headache! That means you should be very quiet. Why do you need the TV? Television is a lot of crock! Garbage! Turn off the TV and find something to read! Staceyann, why do you need all those books? Are you reading all of them at the same time? And why aren't you playing with the doll that I brought? Jesus Christ! Jesus Christ! Jesus Christ! What am I going to do with you?"

She paces around us. Suddenly she stops. Her arms extend out like she is Jesus on the cross. Then she screams long and hard like she is being pierced in her side and storms out of the room. Delano turns off the TV and tells me to put the two Hardy Boys back on the shelf. We spend the day quietly reading. Lunchtime passes without food. In the evening Mummy calls Delano and tells him to make bread and butter for dinner. "And don't use a lot of butter. I don't want you children getting big and fat!"

The sun goes down and we put on our sleep clothes and brush our teeth. When we are done she emerges from the room. She tells me to take the garbage out.

"But, Mummy, I'm undressed for going outside. I am already in my sleep clothes."

She grabs me by the shoulders and shakes me. "There is no such use of the word undressed! If you are wearing clothes already, you cannot be *undressed*. Repeat after me: 'I am *not dressed* for going outside.' Say it! 'I am *not dressed* for going outside.' Now go and change into the clothes you had on before and take the garbage out. I am not going to be stuck with two children who can't even speak properly! I have no idea what Harold and June have been teaching you all these years, but things are going to be different now!"

The following evening she tells us that she is going out. "I can't spend my whole life inside babysitting you two."

She pulls out a long plastic bag with a green dress inside. She showers and puts a thick white paste all over her face. She tells me that the paste is a deep-skin moisturizer. Half an hour later she washes it off. She catches me peeking at her through the half-closed bathroom door. Her bony fingers beckon for me to join her. The water is patted away with a special face cloth. Then she mists with a spray bottle of strawberry-scented liquid. The cushion by the dresser is plumped. She carefully pencils on her eyebrows. I stand behind her, watching the delicate process. It is magical how she smoothes away the dark spots and pimples and makes her nose look smaller in just a few minutes.

When her face is perfect, she slips into the green dress and asks me what I think. I tell her she looks like a princess. She kisses me. I inhale the sweet scent of strawberries and face powder. On her way out she makes us promise that we won't watch *Dynasty*. We promise.

As soon as she leaves, we turn the TV to *Dynasty* and talk about how much our mother looks like Alexis Carrington Colby Dexter. We fall asleep in front of the TV. In the middle of the night Delano wakes me and drags me off to bed.

The next morning Mummy is tired. All day we fetch glasses of water for her. She only comes out to use the bathroom. In the evening she gets dressed to go out again. I watch her make the transformation from ordinary face in the daytime to Alexis Colby at night. She is beautiful at night. I tell her she is more beautiful than the winner of the Miss World beauty pageant.

"Beauty queens are for a season, love. This face is forever."

She likes when I watch her *put on her face*. At every step of the process I tell her how pretty she is. I sit on the bed as she works. Each day I inch closer to the dressing table. By the fifth day I am leaning on the polished edge just inches from her face. It feels good to be this close to her. She is smiling and I am smiling. We look happy in the mirror. We even look a little alike, except that she is wearing lipstick. I wonder what I would look like with red lips. I reach for the plastic cylinder.

"What are you doing, touching my things?" She snatches it from me and throws it on the table. "Why are you touching my things? Didn't I bring things from Canada for you? Why are you touching my things?"

She slaps my hand and pushes me against the chest of drawers. Her index nail is pointed at my nose. "Don't you ever touch my things, nothing, you hear me, nothing. What is mine is mine, and what is yours is yours; just keep your stinking little fingers off my things and we will get along just fine."

She slaps me again for good measure.

The next day she leaves after breakfast. Elmer Fudd chases Bugs Bunny across the TV screen for most of the day. Delano is jittery and irritable. He checks the door, getting up every few minutes to look down the street. When I ask him what's wrong, he tells me to shut my clappers and don't ask him any questions. We hear the latch on the gate opening before we see her. As soon as she walks through the door she tells us to pack our things. She sends us to bed before seven. She warns us about talking to each other under the covers. "If I hear any whispering, you guys will be in serious trouble."

For the first time since we left Bethel Town, I miss Grandma. I wonder if she misses us. I wish I had hugged her on the bus. I feel like crying, but I am too afraid of Mummy. Instead, I think about the things I will have in Canada. Mummy says that I will have my own room and a little garden to plant in the summertime. I wish Grandma were coming to Canada with us.

The next morning she takes more pictures of us in the front yard. She combs my hair into a big Afro and tells Delano to get dressed. As she points the camera, she tells Delano that he is going to live with his father today. She makes us stand by the flowers that line the fence while she snaps us in various poses: smiling in sunglasses, without sunglasses, my hair in a ponytail, my hair let out in an Afro—she finishes two rolls of film before she sends Delano to get our bags. The instructions she gives to Delano are clear. Go down to the supermarket. His father is expecting him. He will take him where he is supposed to be. Delano slings the bag over his shoulder and closes the front door softly behind him. I ask Mummy when I will see him again, but she tells me to get my bag and stop asking stupid questions.

When I return with the bag, she grabs me. "And where is that expensive doll I brought you? Were you planning to leave it here? Did you expect me to fetch it and bring it to you?"

The doll keeps slipping from my hands, so Mummy yanks the bag away from me. I wonder if she is taking me to my father. I wish she had sent me with Delano. I stop in the middle of the road and tell her I want to go back to the house. She drags me onto the sidewalk and slaps me. I grab her hand and beg, "Mummy, can you please take me back to Bethel Town? Please, Mummy, I don't want to go anywhere else! I want to go back to Grandma! Please, Mummy, please!"

She takes my hand and pulls me along. "I cannot imagine why you would want to go back there. June does not want you in her house. The people I am taking you to are happy to have you. What an ungrateful little wretch you are! Come on and stop the crying! After all I have done to convince these people to take you."

The taxi drops us off at a place called Paradise Crescent. Across from the crowded square there is a shack painted red, green, and yellow. A tall, skinny rastaman is by the door, swaying to Bob Marley's "Redemption Song." I stare at him while Mummy drags me down a small side street called Blood Lane. The street narrows into a steep and rocky pathway. We are moving so fast that I keep falling down. Every time I fall, Mummy screams at me.

Finally we stop at a high wooden gate. An old yellow house with a red stairway sits on four huge concrete stilts. Its paint is peeling off the walls in large patches. The open cellar is higher than two adults standing atop one another. It is strange to see a clothesline underneath a house. The wide eyes of several children stare at me from behind the half-open doors, like little animals watching. There is a tall man looking at me and scratching his crotch. His rough beard covers a multitude of swollen yellow pimples. He winks at me like we share a secret. Behind him a dark-skinned woman in a blue dress leans over the veranda rail and grins at me. I close my eyes and ask God not to let Mummy leave me here.

A big brown dog covered in sores and frothing from the mouth ambles toward me. Another, skinny one barks. I hold Mummy's hand and quickly step behind her. The dark-skinned woman laughs out loud. "Take you time and come up, me darlin'! Don't look 'pon the dog them. Them not going to do anything to you." Her voice is sturdy, like big bells in a church.

Mummy makes me promise to listen to the woman and do exactly as she says. "Remember, now, Chérie, exactly as Auntie tells you or there will be hell to pay when I come back for you!"

I hold on to her hand and press my body against hers. I don't really believe that I am staying until she asks Miss John to take good care of her baby. "Please do not let her father near her, he wants to take her and she is my only daughter. My heart couldn't bear it if he got her. I will be back in two weeks," she says, "with her passport and her ticket."

She kisses me, then pushes me away. She hugs Miss John. "Thank you so much, Miss John. I will do everything in my power to repay you."

She kisses me once more. "*Au revoir,* Ma Chérie. See you soon." She waves the long red nails and follows the rocky track that leads back to Blood Lane.

I Will Come Again

Miss John, who explains that she is my grandfather's youngest sister, tells me that I can call her Auntie. She asks me if I am hungry. I tell her no. She says that the day is so hot I should at least have a plum or something to cool me down. Auntie has a big smile, bright eyes, and a really big bottom. She clears some cloth from a metal chair with no cushions and tells me to sit down, and sends her son, Glen, to go and find me a sweetsop. "And make sure is a nice big ripe one!"

I shift my bag away from my feet so I can take off my shoes. Auntie tells me to give the bag to her so that she can put it inside her room. She tells me not to worry about it, that it will be safe inside. Then her bottom is swinging back and forth as she ambles into her room. Glen comes back and hands me a big round sweetsop. I break the green fruit with the bumpy skin in two equal halves. Some of the seeds fall on the floor. Glen picks them up and tosses them over the rail. I hear them hit the rocky ground below. His shirt is old and torn down the front. And his nose is running. I offer him one half. He shakes his head no.

I don't know what to say to him. He is dirty and he smells a little bit like fowls. He shows me his marbles and asks me if I want to play. Auntie shouts at him from the bedroom, "Glen, leave her alone! Girl children should not play with marbles."

I tell him we can play with my doll. He tells me, "Only batty boy play with dolly! And me is not a batty boy. None of the boy them in this house is no batty boy."

"What is a batty boy?"

"You don't know what a batty boy is? A batty boy is a boy who act like him is a girl and only want to do nastiness with other boys."

"Okay. So how many boys live in the house?"

"Is four of us, but none of we is no batty boy. Me three brother is bigger than me. Jimmy is sixteen. Andy is eighteen and Shappy is twenty. Him is the biggest one, but him is *mad, mad, mad.*"

"What happen to him? Him was mad when him was a little boy?"

Glen explains that when Shappy was younger he was the most brilliant student. He passed every exam with flying colors. Everybody expected him to do very well for himself. But something happened after he moved away for college. Some people say the studying got to him. Others believe it was witchcraft. In any case, he began talking out loud to himself, he stopped going to class, and then he stopped bathing. Eventually he was expelled and now he lives at home, where he steals money to buy weed. Glen says that these days he is obsessed with the FBI, the CIA, and the other people who work for the American government.

I ask Glen where Shappy sleeps. He tells me not to worry, that he sleeps in the back room. I wonder how far the back room is from the room in which I will sleep. No one has told me if I will sleep by myself or with other people. I have never gone to bed without Delano. I hope Mummy doesn't take too long to come back for me. I do not see one book, so I ask Glen if there are any books inside. Aunt June used to say a house without books is like a church without God.

He goes inside and brings back a book called *Sprat Morrison*. Glen stands patiently by my chair while I read the back cover to see what the book is about. *Inside are the exciting adventures of the Jamaican boy called Sprat.*

"Is that a good one? She have other ones in there. You want me fi bring one more fi you?"

"No, man. This seems like a good one, Glen. Thank you very much for getting it for me."

He scratches his head and smiles. There is a streak of snot under his nose. He wipes it away with his sleeve and clears his throat. Then he frowns and shifts from one foot to the next. I look away. Finally he blurts out, "Anyway, Stacey, me have to go feed the fowl them now. If Shappy come out here, just ignore him. Me soon come back, you hear?"

As soon as Glen leaves, Shappy comes up the steps. He walks right up to me. He puts his nose into my hair and inhales. He tells me I smell nice, like perfume. He puts his hand on my shoulder. Then on my collarbone, and then he rubs. I pull my shoulder away from him and hunch down into the book. He sniffs me again.

"You smell like a real woman, but your body still small. You don't even have no breast yet. You sure you not underdevelop? Maybe you is a spy? Is the CIA send you fi come infiltrate me?"

He stands there by the chair. The dog ambles onto the veranda. He kicks the dog in the ribs. "Get you raas outside, you dirty stinking mongrel!" The animal sniffs the ground as it slinks down the stairs. Shappy sits on the arm of my chair, sniffing my hair. I do not look up from my book. He smells like smoke.

"Shappy, move from there and leave the little girl alone!"

The tall man who winked at me earlier waves a red wash rag at Shappy and chases him away. He smiles and tells me that his name is Andy. He wipes his face with the red rag and tells me not to worry, that everything is okay now. I want to hug him when he lowers his voice and asks if Shappy really scared me. He smiles again, but something about the way he looks my body up and down makes me straighten my back and say no, I wasn't scared. He asks me how old I am.

"Nine, but I am going to be ten next December."

"Ten? You body small fi ten, but me can see that you very mature. You like to read? Reading is a sure sign of maturity. That book is for children who is at least twelve years old."

He stops talking to me when another man comes up the stairs singing. Jimmy is the fourth brother. His smile is friendly, but his teeth are rotten. When Andy explains who I am, he warns me not to forget them when I get to Canada. Jimmy disappears and Andy leans in to tell me I am much prettier than all the girls in the house.

Auntie's youngest daughter, Diana, pokes her head out to look at me. She is thirteen years old, but I am almost as big as her. She has asthma, so she doesn't leave her room very often. Diana's older sister, Grace, a tall, fat girl with a pretty face, opens the living room door and slips dentures into her mouth. She says a brief hello and heads down the steps. The dog crosses her path and she kicks it. It does not make a sound. Grace is so fat that when she walks her feet puff up like sausages in her high heels. Andy says she has a daughter, Elisha, who is six years old. I ask him how many people live here.

He lists them. "Lemme see. There is me, Jimmy, Shappy, Glen, Diana, Mama, Grace, and Elisha. Me biggest sister, Dawn, move out long time now. And now there is you. Pretty likkle Miss Chin with the smoothest skin on her legs."

I place the open book over my thighs and try to read a sentence. His shoes are inches away from my bare toes. I look up when a tiny pair of feet appears. The feet belong to Grace's daughter, Elisha. She smiles with even white teeth. Her hands are soft as she touches my bare leg.

Auntie comes out from her room and shouts at her, "Elisha, leave her alone! You don't see her reading? Andy, go round the back and help Glen see about them fowls fi me."

"Mama, Glen can handle the fowl them. Me was just here talking to me cousin," Andy says.

"Andy, leave the pickney them alone and go find something to do! Elisha, get up off that red floor before you wipe off all the polish on you bottom!"

Andy winks at me again before he goes inside. Elisha tugs at my arm. "Hey, girl! You never hear me ask you what you name?"

I put the book on the chair and turn to her. "My name is Stacey. And yours is Elisha, right?"

She nods and asks if I want to go look at the chickens with her. We go through the living room. I bump into Andy standing behind the door. I quickly brush past him and follow Elisha. There is an old broken book-case with some torn books. The kitchen counter is stacked with dirty dishes and everything is black and covered with grease. Elisha exits the back door and hops down the big concrete stairway that leads out to the backyard. I stand behind her and look into wired sections of the smelly chicken coop. Each section has chickens of a different size. Elisha says the pigeon coop belongs to Jimmy, but she and Glen have to help with looking after them. The backyard is littered with old clothes and shoes.

Elisha points out the outhouse. "This is the pit toilet. Nobody use it unless water gone."

Then she leads me under the house. There are piles of dirty clothes and two concrete sinks. "This is where we wash we clothes."

Underneath the house it is like a garbage dump; old clothes, pans, wires, all sorts of things line the length of the cellar. The dogs are nestled in the old clothes. Elisha throws a rock at them and they walk away.

Everybody treats me like I am an important guest. Grace changes the sheets so I can be in a clean bed with her and Elisha. I am cautious but grateful when Shappy brings me sweetsops and small tart plums from the tree next door. Auntie tells Glen that he should get anything I want from any tree in the yard. Diana offers her pile of books. "I have some good romance novels. They are just right inside the door on the floor. Just push the door and take what you want. But remember to bring them back when you done."

The Mills & Boon love stories are more exciting than Nancy Drew mysteries. The vague description of the lovers *becoming one in the flesh* gives me goose bumps. And when Auntie combs my hair I daydream about having long, silky curls that tumble down my back. The women in the stories never have to sit while somebody pulls tangles from their big puffy hair. Everybody in the house pokes fun at me for reading all the time. I laugh when Jimmy taps my head and says, "But wait! It look like we have a big bright star in the house. You going to read every book in the world before you dead, eh?"

But his younger brother, Andy, fingers my neck and ear and whispers, "I like a young girl who read romantic books. That's how me know that you will make your husband happy." His hands are rough and dirty on my skin.

I wonder if my mother and father had a Mills & Boon romance. In all the stories, sparks fly whenever the lovers see each other, no matter how long ago they met. It would be wonderful if they were still in love with each other. Maybe they would *fall into each other's arms and weep.*

I begin to worry when a week passes and we have not heard anything from Mummy. A girl at church, who works at the guesthouse down on Earl Drive, tells Auntie that a Canadian tourist named Hazel is a guest there. At the end of the third week Auntie says that I should go and look for her. We take the shortcut, so the Earl Drive Guesthouse is only a short walk away. She sends the small and snot-nosed Glen with me. The whole time he walks behind me and does not say one word. His feet don't even make a sound. I wish it were Delano here walking with me. At the guesthouse Glen motions me inside. I ask the receptionist for Hazel Jennings. I look behind me to see Glen's shirttail disappearing into the hills.

"Hazel Jennings? No. We don't have a guest here by that name," she says.

"It's my mother. And she is here from Canada. I am her daughter. I am here to see her."

"Hazel Jennings? The only Hazel we have is a Hazel Wickham. And she is here from Canada too. Stay here and let me call her for you."

The woman makes a phone call and tells me to walk around to the pool. I walk past the big pots of flowers and the long white chairs. There are glasses of red drinks on all the tables. People with white skin lie on the chairs in nothing but their underwear and sunglasses. I turn the corner to see my beautiful mother gliding through the large pool of clear blue water.

I clap my hands and shout, "Mummy! Mummy! It's me, Ma Chérie! I come to look for you."

She looks up from her stroke and jumps out of the swimming pool. My arm is almost pulled off my body as she drags me away.

In her room, she slams the door and turns to me. "Staceyann Ma Chérie Chin, what the devil are you doing here?"

I back away and say, "Miss John sent me."

She pulls me to her and slaps me in the face. "Don't you ever visit me here again! No matter what other people say, I am your mother! You should listen to only me! Only me!"

Tears sting my eyes and blur my vision. I have no idea what to say to her. I stand absolutely still as she rummages through her bag and then disappears into the bathroom. While I wait, I trace the raised impression of her fingers on my cheek. Minutes later, she emerges, smiling. She hugs me and apologizes for overreacting. We walk hand in hand to the guesthouse gate. Her long nails graze my palm as she slips me some money and tells me to wait for a Paradise taxi and go straight home. I don't know which taxi goes to Paradise, but I don't want to upset her again, so I stand by the roadside waiting.

Half an hour goes by before she comes out and asks, "What are you doing? Don't you know that your father is looking for me? Do you want to lead him here to me? Staceyann, he wants to kidnap you! That is why I put you at Miss John's. He would never think to look for you there. I will never let him have you! You are *my* daughter and I will do whatever it takes to keep you safe."

I wonder why I can't stay with her if she loves me so much. She pulls me out of the streetlight and makes me stand behind the wall. We wait quietly there for a while. Then she hails a taxi. She tells the driver to take her baby home. I wave good-bye as the car pulls away from her. She waves at me with her right hand. Her left hand covers her mouth. I smile at her and wave harder. I feel like I am in a movie.

Like a Thief in the Night

I hand the money over to Auntie and I tell her that Mummy says I am never to visit her there again. She slowly folds the money into a tiny square and then sends me to go and bathe.

The drain is blocked, so the tub is caked with greasy, foamy soap scum. I wipe the stained porcelain with toilet paper, trying to ignore the sinking feeling that my mother has left me here for good. I hope Delano is better off where he is. Maybe if I find him his father would let me come to live with them. When Andy starts beating on the bathroom door, I change my mind about bathing. He taps me on my bottom as I slip past him. I kick him and he laughs. I wish I were big enough to push his pimply face into the wall and break all his big yellow teeth.

The weeks pass and there is still no sign of Mummy. The summer holidays end and Elisha, Glen, and Diana start school. The house is lonely without them. While everybody is out for the day, I sit on the steps reading romance novels and trying to avoid Shappy and Andy. Finally, on the last day of September, Auntie calls me out onto the veranda. She lowers her face into her hands and sighs. The she tells me that it looks like my mother is not coming back for me this year. The maid at the guesthouse has told her that Hazel left Jamaica more than a month ago. The guesthouse threw her a big good-bye party. In my heart I already knew, but it makes my chest hurt to hear her say it.

Auntie taps the floor with her foot. "And you definitely cannot stay here without going to school. Your mother woulda never forgive me if she come back here and you cannot tell the letter *A* from bull-foot!"

The next morning we go to enroll me at the Chetwoood Memorial

Primary School. It is the only public Catholic school in Montego Bay. Glen and Elisha are already students there. Auntie stays in the office while I follow the small Chinese nun I have to call Sister Cecile to a big classroom to take the placement test. She makes me read aloud the story of Jesus's birth. This is the closest I have ever been to a Chinese person. I wonder if she knows my father.

"Sister Cecile, you are Chinese, right?"

"Yes, Staceyann, my parents did migrate to Jamaica from China."

"So your last name is Chin like mine?"

"No, it used to be Lee-Young, but when I became a nun I took a name in honor of a saint I admire. And that is why my name is Sister Mary Cecile."

"So you have a lot of Chinese family in Montego Bay?"

"Yes, there are many of us, but my primary family is those who belong to the Franciscan order. But come along, now. We have been here for quite a while. It is time to get you back to your aunt."

Sister Cecile tells Auntie that there is no more room in the grade five classes, so I will have to be with the bigger children in grade six. That means I will have to spend two years with Miss McBean. Auntie tells her that that is quite all right.

On the first day of school Auntie combs my hair and tells me that this is the last time she will do it. She says I will also have to wash my own clothes from now on. Diana, who looks very smart in her white Mount Alvernia High School uniform, is to make sure we get into a taxi. But the first taxi that stops she hops in and rides away. We stand among the large group of people trying to get to work. Every time a taxi stops, everybody runs and pushes forward. Glen slips inside the back seat of a white Lada and rides away. Taxi after taxi pass us by. Finally one stops and the driver calls out to Elisha. She shoulders her bag and runs toward the taxi.

The driver is Elisha's uncle. He lectures us, "When me was a boy, five mile was nutten to me! I used to run it without shoes. Oonu children just lazy."

The other people in the taxi nod. A man in a red tie asks, "So, Hector, the little dark one is you niece, right? Who is the other one?"

"Is Junior Chin daughter. You know the Chinaman who own the furniture store in front the police station on Barnett? She look like her sister, eh? When me see her first, me couldn't believe that them have two different mother! Them is like twins! Dead stamp!" I am surprised to hear that I have a sister. And that she looks like me. I wonder how old she is.

We get off in front of Cornwall College High School for Boys. I offer the driver coins for the fare, but he tells me his good friend drives for my father, so I can keep my money. Through the fence, I see the boys on the track and field team doing jumping jacks. I look to see if Delano is among them.

The boys form a line and start jogging around the field. But Elisha is pulling me. "Stacey, come on! You want us to get in trouble because we late?"

We cross the street and cut through the main gates of Mount Alvernia to get to Chetwood. I sit quietly among the bigger girls scribbling away at their sums and looking at me suspiciously. Miss McBean gives me a gold star for getting all my sums right and reciting a perfect times table on my first day. During lunch the girls corner me against the school building and tease me for speaking "too proper."

"Listen to how she talk speaky-spokey!" they taunt. "Listen to my China Royal voice. I should be on JBC TV! Look at my mongoose skin! Listen to my red mongoose voice!"

"Leave me alone!" I scream. "I don't bother any of you. If I am a red mongoose, then all of you are black like john crows and dunce as bats."

"All of you Black children are like Black john crows and dunce like bats! Not bright and pretty like me! Like me! Look at me! I am soooo white and soooo pretty!"

"Hey, Cheryl, you hear how she say her times tables to Miss McBean in class? *Fives times six makes a total of thirty! A total of thirty! A total of thirty! All white girls are dirty!*"

They form a circle around me, chanting, "Nasty girl! Talk-funny girl, Staceyann Chin! You red like mongoose! You red like sin!"

The bell rings and we make our way back inside. Donna, the girl who sits behind me, pulls my hair and whispers, "Dirty, stinking, smell-bad white girl from country." I ask Miss McBean for permission to go to the bathroom.

I stand in a pool of yellow water on the bathroom floor and wonder if Grandma still wants me. When I get back to the classroom, someone has written in pen, *Chinese people eat dead cat and dog with mange,* on the front of my exercise book. I sit and try not to look at the hateful words.

On the walk home Elisha asks when my mother is coming back for me. I don't want her to think I have been abandoned, so I tell her she is supposed to be coming in a few weeks. Every day somebody in the house asks about Mummy. Eventually I stop lying. "So what if my mother left me here? Everybody knows that now! Find something else to talk about or shut up your stupid mouth!"

Diana does not tease me, but she says I shouldn't be living in the house. "Stacey, I know it is not your fault that your mother leave you, but is not fair that my mother, who have all of we to feed, have to take up the burden of you."

Glen is less understanding. "Mama, why you don't send her to live with her father? Him have whole heap of money and him house just down on Leader Avenue. You should just pack up her and the dirty things she have under the bed and send her on her way. Or better yet, tie her up under the house with the dog."

Andy likes to grab me and sniff my underarms. "White people smell like raw meat, eh! Come make me smell if you white, Stacey! Is that why you mother gone leave you? She couldn't stand the smell! Is what happen to you? You allergic to water?"

"Auntie, Andy is outside teasing me about my mother!"

Auntie's voice is tired as she tells them, "Lawd, oonu leave her alone, nuh! She is not responsible fi anything her mother do! Come, Stacey, come get some tea and nuh mind what them say."

Andy shoves me when he passes me in the kitchen. Glen trips me when I walk by him. Shappy keeps asking me if I am ready to become a woman yet. Everything they do I complain to Auntie. Every five minutes I have to complain.

Finally, one morning Shappy steals my taxi fare and feeds my breakfast to the brown dogs hankering on the steps. I run inside to tell Auntie, who throws up her hands and tells me she has had enough. "Lawd, Stacey! How you so pestering? You must ignore them sometimes! Just give me ears a little break and leave me alone, man! One miss breakfast not going kill you and you children can walk to school."

If we walk to school on the road it takes about an hour. But if we take the shortcut, the journey takes less than half that time. We carefully pick our way down the stony path, down past the other colorful wooden houses. The left at the road takes us to the Earl Drive Guesthouse. I still think of my mother taking graceful strokes and smiling before she saw me standing there. Today we turn right and follow the path down past the Rastafarian family. Elisha calls out to them.

"Morning, Sister Love. Morning, Papa Love! Morning, Princess! Precious! Zion! Livity!"

I wave at the army of small children sitting on the tiny veranda. The track narrows and gets rockier. I use my hand to push the bushes out of my way. Elisha says to make sure I don't touch the pepperbush and put my finger in my eyes. We duck out into a clearing with a big concrete structure. On the veranda the residents of the poorhouse sit and stare at the horizon. The old men and women are drooling and falling out of their chairs. One man is not wearing any clothes. He grabs his crotch and screams at us. A big woman in a pink uniform grabs him by the hand and drags him inside. He screams and begs us to please help him.

"Them killing me in here! Help! Help! Them a murder me! Come, little girls, come save your grandfather."

Elisha tells me to mind my own business and stop watching them. I follow her to the gate and we cross the road and enter Cornwall from the back gate. Their school grounds are much bigger than ours. The big field stretches from one side of the school compound to the next. We walk around the field. There is a group of boys standing by the water fountain. From far away they all look like Delano, with their fair skin and jet-black hair. As we get closer I begin to see small differences between them. One boy has little red spots all over his face. Another has a gap between his teeth. One of them has blue eyes.

Delano has his back to me, so I see him before he sees me. I don't know why I cannot call out to him. One of the boys says something to him and he turns. I wave. He waves back. I continue walking and he turns back to his friends.

"Elisha, that one is my brother."

"Which one?"

"The one with his hair part in the middle."

"So why you don't call to him?"

"Nothing. You don't see that him busy? He is in high school. He has a lot of things on his mind. Him don't have time to idle with primary school children."

We walk through Mount Alvernia. All the girls are lined up for devotion. Everywhere you look is the white of uniforms. They stand straight up and sing the hymns so nicely. I wish I were going to Mount Alvernia.

When I take the Common Entrance I hope I pass for Mount Alvernia.

At Chetwood during lunch Delroy and Donna take my biscuits, my icy-mints, and my drops and distribute everything among their friends. Donna pulls my hair every time Miss McBean turns her back. One day she pulls it so hard, bits of it come out in her hand. The roots sting and I rub the scalp to make sure I am not bleeding. She is much bigger than me, so I cannot fight her. Tears well up in my eyes, but I do not let them fall. I bite my lips and take deep breaths. I am so tired of everybody doing what they want with me. Andy, Auntie, my mother, even Delano can just stop talking to me and I have to just take it. I wish I could turn around and stab Donna in the eyes with my pencil. My face gets hotter and hotter. But I know that I would just get into trouble if I hit her. Miss McBean would think it was my fault. I take more deep breaths until my face cools down. When I am able to speak, I turn around and face her.

"You know something, Donna? Everybody knows you are a slut because you have her period already. And you are only ten!"

Her face freezes and the tufts of hair in her hand fall to the floor.

"You know that when you have your period you can get pregnant? If you know what is good for you, you would stop looking at Delroy Johnson!"

She rushes at me and kicks me in the shin.

"Go on, kick me, Donna. That doesn't change how you smell stink when you have it. You smell so stink that even the girls over Mount Alvernia can smell your dirty red-up, red-up panties. If I was you, I would stay home when it comes! I would stay home and wash myself with bleach! And by the way, everybody in the class can see the bunched-up pad in your pantie when you are skipping in the schoolyard!"

I look at her stricken face and drive the final words home. "Go on, ask anybody. Why you think nobody eat from your dirty period hands on *certain* days of the month?"

She bawls so pitifully that Miss McBean hugs her and begs her to say what is wrong.

I take my first beating from Miss McBean in absolute silence. "You think you are a big person, eh? You don't believe I can make you cry?"

The flesh on her upper arm shakes as she delivers the blows. My skin contracts when the belt connects. I stand before her with dry eyes. After seventeen licks, she gives up.

"You are the dead stamp and seal of the living Devil."

She wraps the leather belt around her hand and tells the other children that anyone caught speaking to me for the rest of the day would get even more licks than she just gave me.

B roomie! Broomie! Who say the Broomie?" I trip over myself dashing to the front gate to see the smiling, bowing Rastafarian everyone calls the Dread. Every week he brings peppers. And when it is pumpkin season he brings the striped green produce in a basket. Auntie says that the Dread would sell his mother if he knew people would pay for her. Everybody talks bad about the Dread, but everybody buys from him because his wares are cheap. His goods are also fresher than the produce from the market. The market women have to travel all the way from the country in the hot sun with their callaloo. But the Dread just picks it from his front yard. If you buy more than one item from the Dread, you get a big discount. And plus, he delivers the goods right to your door. Occasionally, we buy brooms.

Dreadie, the callaloo man, makes music of his wares.

Eillaloo, eiper, and yumpkin.
Eillaloo, who need the eillaloo?
Who have need of the eillaloo, eiper, and yumpkin man?

He lifts the brooms down from his head before he bows and speaks to me. "Hello, little bright-eye princess, where is the imperial queen of this house? I have some royal-quality callaloo for this house of kings and queens and prince and princess."

"Hello. Auntie is inside, but she say she don't want anything today."

"All right, sweet princess, maybe next time the queen will buy from the Dread."

His smile is flawless as he hoists the bundle back on his head, singing.

Eillaloo, eiper, and yumpkin.
Eillaloo, who need the eillaloo?
Who have need of the eillaloo, eiper, and yumpkin man?

I sing along. When Glen hears me, he starts laughing. "Yes, man, Stacey, practice up you song, because that is what you will have to do when you get big. You going to have to married de rastaman and sell broom with him on Saturday and Sunday. Nobody going married to you with your big mouth and your dirty sheet them. You can't even wash you own clothes properly, plus you too stink and ugly fi get married to anybody good."

Andy is quick to join in. "Yes, man, Glen! And the way how she cook is just right fi de rastaman style, no salt, no pork, no taste, no nutten but a bellyache! No man no want no woman who can't cook. Stacey, it make sense you just go drown yuh-self, or find a rastaman husband! There is nothing else left fi a woman like you."

Diana leans over the rail. "Lawd, man. Oonu no get tired of teasing her? And even if nobody want to married her, it is none of oonu business! Oonu is her cousins, so who she married is not oonu concern."

Andy tosses a mango seed at her. "I know she is me cousin, but you never hear the saying that 'cousin and cousin make good soup'? If her big head of hair wasn't so knot-up and dirty, me would take pity on her and married to her right now!"

Auntie opens her bedroom door and sends Diana back inside. "All right, all right! Oonu leave her alone! She will learn fi cook in time and then God will send her a good husband."

I tell them I do not want to marry anybody. Auntie laughs and disappears into her room. Andy says he is sorry for the man who will have to marry me. I tell him if these men in the house are any examples of the men out there in the world, I will kill the man before I marry anybody. He tells me to wait and see what happens to me after I get my period. Then I will start begging for a man to look at me and touch me.

"You must be God to know what will be inside my head! I don't like nobody touching me anywhere! Nobody at all! The things that them worthless men want to do to a girl is nasty! And if anybody ever try that with me I will get a gun and shoot them!"

Andy laughs and says I will change my mind.

The next day while I am in the kitchen getting a glass of water Andy pushes me up against the wall and slides his hands up under my dress. I am so shocked I can't move my mouth to say anything. He presses his crotch into my belly and asks me if I like it. I push him away and call out to Auntie. He lets me go and Auntie rushes in to ask why I am bawling out her name like a loudspeaker. I tell her that Andy wouldn't let me go.

"What you mean, him wouldn't let you go?"

"Auntie, I was just passing him and him squeeze me up on the wall. And then him hold on to me and wouldn't let me go."

"Mama, is brush me brush 'gainst her when me pass. The place small and she walk wide like a duck."

"Stacey, me not going tell you again. Stop calling me for everything. You are not a princess or a baby. You cannot call me-call me, for foolishness. If him brush you by accident, just say sorry and go your way. Mark my words, if you call me again for no stupidness I going to pull out that leather belt and beat you. And what happen to your hair? Why it look like a fowl nest?"

Andy is grinning at me behind Auntie's back. After that I try my best to avoid him. I stick close to Glen or Elisha if he is in the house. And I make sure that Grace locks our bedroom door at night.

Two weeks before Christmas, Grace goes away with Elisha's father. They take Elisha with them. I lock the door and wrap the sheet around my body three times before I go to sleep.

I am dreaming that I am drowning. The water closes over me and I cannot catch my breath. I wake up gasping for air. There is something crawling around in my panties. I open my eyes to find Andy on top of me. One hand is covering my nose. His mouth is over mine. The fingers of the other hand are in my panties, pushing themselves into my coco-bread. His nails are hurting me. He moans something unintelligible against my mouth. At first I don't understand. Then he says it again.

"You like it, eh, Stacey? You like this? Tell me you don't like it."

His voice breaks the spell. I reach for my pencil on the bedside table and drive the point into his hand. He lets go of my nose and I scream.

The whole house is awake in minutes. Glen is laughing at me cowering in the corner. Diana looks in and quietly slips away. Shappy says everybody should stop providing an audience to Jezebel and go back to sleep. No one asks me what happened. No one wants to know what Andy is doing in my bed at two in the morning. Auntie drags me to the veranda and pushes me into a chair. "I don't know what is wrong with you! But it going to stop tonight!"

"Nothing is wrong with me, Auntie! Is your nasty son have something wrong with him!"

"What that you say to me?"

"Auntie, is him come in the room with me. I never invited him into me bed."

"Stacey, lemme tell you something. If you do not say anything to Andy, if you keep away from him and walk him out, things will go better for you. I think him just bother you because you do not have any manners to him."

"Auntie, how me must have manners to him, when him want to come do what him want with me when you not looking? If him come near me again I going to stab him with a knife! I swear to God, Auntie, if him come near me, I going to kill him!"

I do not see Auntie's hand snake out. But I feel the sting of her palm across my face.

"Hear what me telling you, Stacey. You are no bull-buck and duppy-conquerer in this house. And I cannot sit here with you, no matter what him do—I cannot sit here with you and listen to you talk about taking the life of one of my children. After all I do for you?" She stands up to her full height over me. "Just stay clear of Andy and don't provoke him anymore! Now get out of me face and go back to you bed!"

Back in the room I put on an extra pair of panties. The moon, fat and heavy, peeks in through the glass louvers. The yellow light makes a funny pattern on the bed. I carefully wrap the sheet around my body again. Then I lie down across the bottom of the locked door.

The Word Became Flesh

I feel like I have hit gold when I find three dirty picture magazines in the pile of abandoned books under the house. I dust them off to reveal a series of blondes wearing very small brassieres over their very large breasts. I read about women who are excited to discover *the orgasm*.

None of the women have any clothes on—and all of them have their legs wide open. I look at the pictures of them rubbing their coco-breads with shiny red fingernails. It is all very strange and *exciting*. My heart is beating fast and then slow and then fast again. In some of the pictures the women look happy and sad at the same time, as if they were eating an ice-cream cone that is not really their favorite flavor.

Looking at the photographs makes me want to touch myself too. And I want to know if my coco-bread looks the same as those in the magazine. I decide the only way to find out is to have a look. I choose the one place nobody would find me. The pit toilet. Day after day it stands empty until there is a water lock-off. Not much more than a woodshed built over a twenty-foot concrete-covered sewage receptacle, the pit toilet is so small that only a makeshift toilet seat of wood can fit inside. And it smells like milk farts all the time.

I look down into the hole. There are giant roaches crawling up the inner walls of the seat. I look farther down. Bits of things are floating in what looks like a big black swimming pool. I climb up onto the seat and slowly squat. My naked bottom hangs over the gigantic opening of the square toilet. I carefully examine my coco-bread. There are tiny black hairs and some little things that look like tiny mouths keeping a big secret. I push the mouths open. The tongue pokes out at me. I poke the tongue and the lips get wet. I poke the tongue again. And again. And again. The lips get wetter and wetter and wetter. I am bouncing up and down so much my foot slips and I fall into the pit.

My right leg and right arm are both completely in. The left arm is grasping at the side of the seat. The left leg is caught in a strange angle that has just barely kept me from falling all the way in. I can't call anyone to help me. The dirty magazine is sprawled out open on the floor with Deviled Daisy's bottom cheeks separated by the spine of the open pages. Luscious Lily's lips are throwing kisses at me.

The stench from the waste below makes it difficult to breathe, and there are things I cannot see crawling along my foot. My palms sweat and make it almost impossible to get a firm grip on the wood. It takes me nearly an hour to drag myself up from out of the mouth of the pit. When I finally collapse, shaking and picking pieces of roach legs off my hip and thigh, I know I am never going to look at my coco-bread again.

Andy tells me that I am the ugliest girl he has ever seen in his life. He has been teasing me for nine months now, so I know better than to get into an argument with him. I make my way down to the small concrete receptacle known as the fish tank. The square is set deep into the dark red soil of the front yard. Hidden under the alcove created by the kissing tops of the sweetsop, breadfruit, and mango trees, the fish tank protrudes a foot or so out from the ground.

I peer down at my reflection and wonder if I am really that ugly. I wish I could make my hair smooth the way Grandma used to do it. I drop a small stone and watch the untidy image of my head break into a million little pieces. Auntie likes to boast about the days when fish used to swim in the once-clear water, but now only the slimy moss moves through the tank.

Auntie leans over the veranda rail and watches me toss another rock in. "Stacey, you see how oonu children treat that fish tank? God going to sin every one of yuh for how oonu destroy that good, good fish tank."

Glen comes running from behind the house. "Yes, Mama, them really treat the fish tank bad."

"If oonu was a different set of children, there would be goldfish and tadpoles and all kind of fish running about in the tank! You see them children on the TV from Africa? God know them would kill themselves for a little niceness like this fish tank."

I am quick to correct her. "Auntie, the children in Africa need clean water! Not this nasty, dirty stink-hole that don't even have no fish in there!"

"Stacey, come up here, make me box you in your face! You don't have no manners, eh? Which child would not want to have a fish tank? You stay there, the time will come when you will look back and see how much the good Lord has given to you in your young days."

It is still morning, but the day already feels hot and long. Elisha joins me on the metal plant stand and offers two of her four sweetsops. We suck at the sticky fruit and toss the seeds into the dark, thick water below.

Before long, we are bored with the small plunk, plunk, plunk as the seeds and handfuls of sweetsop skins crash into the water. Elisha jumps down from the plant stand and swishes a stick around slowly in the viscous water.

"Stacey, you think this water was ever clean like how Mama say it was?"

"Everybody is always talking 'bout how everything was always better before we born. But I think them just say that to make them feel like them know better things than us."

"Maybe if we clean it we can put fish to live in there."

"I not sure no fish can live in there, but I suppose we can clean it. Is not as if we have anything else to do."

Plunk. I throw a rock in the water and tell Elisha to listen for when it hits the bottom. She says she doesn't hear anything.

"Stacey, how deep you think it is in there?"

"There is too much rubbish on the bottom for me to tell. Maybe when we clean it out and we could see how deep it really is."

Elisha bellows for Glen. "Glen! Glen! Come quick! Stacey say we goin' clean the fish tank."

Glen comes running from the bathroom holding his pants together. Elisha and I roll our eyes at each other. Glen is always in the toilet. No matter what time of the day you call him, he rushes out grasping the waist of his pants. Elisha thinks he has a permanent case of diarrhea. I think he is masturbating. But I do not say anything.

"Glen, Stacey say we going to clean the fish tank!" Elisha is excited by the task at hand.

"Clean which fish tank? You must drop and lick you head this morning! You see how nasty that water is?"

"If you don't want to help us, then go on and finish what you were doing in the bathroom. We don't need you to help us. But remember, whatever we find in there is ours. Money, jewelry—any kind of treasure we find, you will not get any of it! You hear?"

It takes him only a second to switch arguments. "All right. I will help, but only because me is a boy and in these kinds of work, a man can do some things that a woman can't do."

"Oh, shut up your stupid mouth! You are almost two years younger than me, and I am ten times brighter than you in school, and I can beat you up anytime!" I take a threatening step toward him and he steps back. I point my finger at his chest and continue, "Yes, Mr. Glenford Mosiah Garvey, what you can do that I can't do? Nothing! Zero! Nil!"

I raise my finger to point it at his nose and tell him, "If you want to help, you can help, but make sure you keep your clappers shut 'bout what a man can do!"

"All right, Miss Staceyann Marshree Chin, I going fix your business right, right now!" Glen storms inside to tell Auntie that we are outside cleaning the dirty fish tank.

"Is about time oonu do something about that thing. It never stay like that until oonu start use it as rubbish heap. When them older ones was pickney, fish used to live in there. Is oonu mash it up so! So, yes, is oonu must clean it up!"

Glen puffs up his chest like it was his idea. "Yes, Mama! I tell them we should clean it up so it look just like how it did look before we was born!"

Auntie says she does not care who came up with the idea. "Just clean it as best as oonu can. Cleanliness is next to godliness, and I believe that fish tank is a gift from God!"

The first order of business is to fish the debris from the tank. I send Glen to get wire hangers from inside the house. Elisha is dispatched to get the green and yellow buckets to bail water from the tank. The dogs are so excited they don't know whom to follow. One stays with me while the other darts back and forth between Glen and Elisha.

When Glen comes back, he points to the rastaman standing by the front gate. "Stacey, you don't see you husband waiting at the gate for you?"

The rastaman waves and calls out to me. "Hello, little princess! I see you working today. You need anything from the Dread?"

I barely wave back. "No, no, we don't need nutten today, Dreadie!"

Even flattened out, the hangers are not long enough to reach in and hook anything without wetting our shoulders. We decide to bail first. We scoop bucket after bucket of fetid water and pour it into the ground at our feet. The area around the tank soon becomes a sea of red mud. After about an hour we see objects pointing out of the water.

I push the dogs away from the tank and reach for a wire hanger. The first treasures are bountiful and without value: three blackened socks, one foot of Glen's grade-two school shoes, Shappy's missing tie, Grace's old brassiere, Auntie's broken leather belt, Elisha's baby blanket. Then the objects we retrieve become things we have no history for: an old bicycle chain, two cowboy hats, a black doll with no head, a ratchet knife with a rabbit carved into its handle.

Glen is quick to claim the best finds. "All of the boy-things are mine! You and Elisha can take the brassiere and the dolly! The knife and the chain and the hats is mine!" He stuffs the blade into his pocket.

"Glen, if you know what is good for you, you put it back on the ground." I say it so quietly, I am not sure I even spoke out loud.

"Stacey, this house is my mother house. Anything we find here belong to me!" He picks up the chain and turns his back to us.

I leap into the tank and scoop a bucket of the muck from the bottom. I stand ankle-deep in the stink and hold the bucket out to Elisha.

"Elisha, hold this!"

In one swift movement I climb over the concrete wall, take the bucket, and swing it high, emptying every drop of the slop onto Glen's head. I grin as the green slimy dirt runs down his face and into his mouth as he bawls. I push him against the mango tree and dig into his front pocket. His screaming brings Auntie running to the veranda. She appears just as I yank the knife from his pocket. She watches as I pull the chain from his hands, shove him to the ground, and step over him. He is crying loud and hard. His open mouth inhales and spits out bits of rotten leaves and snot all over his chest.

Auntie stares and stares and stares at me. She says nothing for a long, long time.

Finally, she calls Glen inside. "Glen, come in here and stop the cow bawling. Is nothing, just dirty water. Meet me round the back and make me wash it off your face. Never mind, man, dirt is not like sin, a little water will wash this off. Hurry up and come."

I ignore the unfolding fracas and go right back to bailing. I don't know what Auntie is going to do to me. But for the first time since I came to Paradise Crescent, I don't care. When Glen is washed and dressed in clean clothes, Auntie leans over the veranda rail and looks at me. I tell myself that if she beats me I will not cry. No matter how hard she slaps me with the belt, I will just look at her and laugh.

"Boy, little girl, I see today that you have the living Devil inside you. Nothing can be done with you. Just like Pontius Pilate, I wash my hands of you and release you into the hand of Jesus. While you are here, you can eat and sleep and go to school. But know from this day that I do what I can for God's sake, not yours. Anything I do for you is duty, not love. Now you have nobody in this world but yourself and God."

I bail and bail and bail. I do not look up from the task at hand. I don't want Elisha to see the tears rolling down my face. Auntie goes back inside to make lime-leaf tea for Glen. Elisha works silently beside me. When we can fish nothing else with the hanger, we bail again. The water level recedes past our ankles. We see the tops of our feet. The dogs jump in with us, but I lift them out and keep bailing. The water level drops till the buckets cannot scoop any more. I send Elisha to get condensed milk cans to scoop the water. While she is gone, I wipe my face on the sleeve of my dress. I feel like sitting down in the pool of muddy water and crying until the tank is full.

The muck is so thick, it is almost solid. We keep scooping with the cans. Then we hit gold. Silver coins plop out of the cans of slush: copper-colored one-cent pieces, silver five-, ten-, and even some fifty-cent pieces! Elisha is bouncing up and down and singing, "Glory hallelujah, we rich, praise God Almighty, we rich!"

I count eleven dollars and eighty-three cents. I gather every penny and lay it carefully inside the hammock I make with the tail of my dress. My steps are measured as I walk up the stairs. I swing open the veranda gate and step into the house. The door to Auntie's bedroom is open. Auntie has Glen jammed up against her on the bed. He is eating milk crackers and drinking lime-leaf tea.

"Excuse me, Auntie, this is the money we find in the fish tank. You can take all of it."

"Child, take you Devil money out of me face. I am not Judas. You will not buy me with yuh thirty pieces of silver. Take it and buy something to eat, but take care you don't choke on it."

I shift my weight from one leg to the next. I can see Glen's gaze moving back and forth between the money and Auntie's face.

Finally he gets up and stands next to me. "Mama, what if we take the money from her and bless it? Then it would be holy money, not Devil money. I can use it to buy icy-mints to suck on in church tomorrow."

"Glen, me boy, some kinds of money can't come clean with all the prayer in the world. What is for Caesar, give it to Caesar! What belong to the Devil, let him keep it, me son. Now go and eat you crackers and shut up your mouth!"

She tells me to make sure I don't drop any of that muddy water on her clean floor. Then she drops her eyes to the Bible on her lap. As carefully as I had climbed the stairs, I make my way back to the fish tank. I walk right up to the edge of the tank and tip my shirt and watch the coins fall in.

"Stacey, you mad? Is what you doing with we money? Is Mama tell you fi throw them back in?"

The last coin plops into the shallow water below. Green bucket in hand, I tell her to get the yellow one and follow me. Underneath the house, I turn the tap counterclockwise and fill the bucket to the brim with clean water. I take Elisha's bucket and set it under the pipe. When it is full, we make our way back to the tank. I scoop handfuls of mud into the buckets and tip both buckets into the tank. The top layer of mud on the ground soon disappears. We have to dig dry earth to make each bucket muddy. We keep going until the muddy water is almost up to our knees. Then I toss in the hats and the socks and the knife and the bicycle chain—everything is returned to the abyss.

The earth around the tank is full of holes now. The brown dog is curled in the biggest one. I deliver my hardest kick into its side. It looks up at me, surprised, before it scampers off to the cellar.

Elisha stares at me. She is covered from head to toe in mud. "Little girl," I say, "look at yuh-self! How you manage to get so dirty? You should be ashamed of how you look. Go inside and go bathe your stinking dirty skin!"

"Stacey, is what me do why you bawling after me so? You think is me make you throw away all that money?" She sucks her teeth and stomps away. As she slams the bathroom door, I kick the fish tank so hard my toe-nail on my big toe breaks and bleeds. I wash off the blood in the brown water. The rastaman has passed already, but I climb up onto the front gate and slowly swing back and forth, softly singing his song.

Eillaloo, eiper, and yumpkin.
Eillaloo, who need the eillaloo?
Who have need of the eillaloo, eiper, and yumpkin man?

Diana's seventh-grade biology book says it is supposed to be "haemoglobin-red." I peer down at the weird fluid, sitting smack in the center of my pink panties, and wonder if the brown stain, shaped like an egg, is "haemoglobin-red."

The glossary in the back of the book defines haemoglobin as "the iron-containing respiratory pigment in red blood cells of vertebrates, consisting of about 6 percent haeme and 94 percent globin."

I toss the book behind the toilet and examine the egg-shaped culprit again. I know exactly what is happening to me. I am having my first period. Every girl between the ages of ten and thirteen should get it. The book says if you do not get it, you might be a hermaphrodite. That is someone whose vagina has its own penis. The book says the proper name for my coco-bread is *vagina*. I don't know if I like the word *vagina*. *Vagina* sounds like it is the name of a disease that jezebel women get. I study the book, reading and rereading everything about the "Peculiarities of the Period." There are supposed to be "adult urges," and dull pains, commonly known as "cramps," and "a flow of menses that is recognizable as life force by its haemoglobin-red hue."

I want to talk to Auntie, but I am afraid she would box me in my mouth for asking her anything about my vagina. But I know I have to ask her for the sanitary napkins.

I pull up my shorts and walk carefully to the veranda. I revel in the thick wetness squishing beneath me. I stand by the door and watch Auntie turn the pages of her big black Bible.

She licks her finger and turns a page. "Is why you standing there watching me like you is a policeman so? What you want?"

"Nothing, Auntie. Is just that—I mean—something—happened to—I think I just—"

She frowns and looks up from the page.

"Stacey, me don't have all day fi listen to you hem and haw. Say what you saying and stop talking like you is a handicap!"

I take a deep breath and blurt out in one breath, "Auntie, I think I just started menstruating and I don't have any of the sanitary pad things to put on."

She sighs and looks out at the banana trees. When she does not say anything, I follow her gaze to the young fruits hugging themselves into a bunch.

"Auntie? Should I ask Diana for some of hers?"

"How old you be now, Stacey?"

"Ten, Auntie. I going to be eleven the end of this year."

Auntie shakes her head and sighs again.

"Auntie, what I must do about the pads?"

"Well, Stacey, to tell you the truth, those kind of things a young lady must buy for herself. But because it happen upon you sudden, I will buy them this time."

I calculate how many mornings I will have to forgo car fare so I can buy the monthly sanitary napkins. I am already walking to school most mornings, and I still can't buy much more than a box juice and banana chips for lunch.

"Okay, Auntie, thanks very much for buying them this time."

"Never you mind any thanks! The only thanks I looking for is from God. I do not do anything for anybody for any reward here on earth. The Heavenly Father has my great reward. Now go inside the room and pass me my black handbag."

After she gives me the money, I fold the notes and head out to Miss Elaine's shop. As I step over the rocks I try not to think about the uncertain red spreading over my favorite panties. I know the smell of Stayfree maxi-pads. I see Diana walking to the bathroom whenever she gets a visit from her red auntie from Red Hills. Stayfree is cheap, but it smells like dead flowers. I worry that people will smell the pads on me and know what is happening to my vagina. I wonder how the pad will stay inside my panties. The Stayfree pads are different from the ones in the book. The one in the book is the one you have to tie to your waist.

At the shop, Miss Elaine stuffs the pack of pads inside a brown paper bag, and then quietly slides it across the counter.

At home, I hand over Auntie's change and dash into the bathroom. I lock the door behind me and rip open the plastic packaging. The flowery-sweet scent makes me gag. I hold my breath and examine the pink and white strip. There is a picture of a hand tearing off the strip. The picture also shows the pad lying lengthwise along the crotch of the panties. I quickly peel the strip off the adhesive and pull up my panties. I check to make sure everything is secure. I am no longer worried the pad will fall out of my shorts. They put a lot of glue on the pad so it can really stick. The book said there would be some pain, but the sharp pulling beneath me is unbearable. I can hardly move from the pinching of my hairs pasted to the sanitary napkin.

"Two hours," I tell myself. "Only two hours, Stacey. Then you can change it."

I carefully make my way to the back of the house. The pulling is too intense. I have to stop walking. I park myself on the back steps, but every shift of weight is agony. An hour later, I am sure something is wrong. I limp back to the bathroom, taking the bag of napkins with me.

This time, I read the instructions on the bag: "Important: Make sure the adhesive side of the belt-less maxi-pad lays flat against the crotch of the panties." I read the instructions again. Then I take a breath and yank the used pad from my vagina. It hurts so much everything goes black. For a few moments I am unable to make a sound. And when my vision clears I see more black hairs on the pad than on my vagina. I try to fold the pad in two. But the sticky part isn't sticky anymore.

Suddenly the day seems so dirty. I want to wash all of it away. I decide to take a shower. Then Auntie begins knocking violently. "Stacey! Stacey, open this door! Open it! Open it before I break it down."

I step out of the shower and pick up the pad before I unlock the door. I stand there naked, soiled pad in hand. Auntie looks at the brown adhesive side of the beltless maxi-pad and grabs me by the shoulder.

"You think money grow on mango tree? Why you wasting the pad? You never see that you put the thing on wrong?" She is shaking my shoulder so hard that everything seems to be happening in slow motion. I hear her voice from far away. "You waste the thing for nothing! For foolishness! Stacey, you believe you are big woman now, eh?"

Her voice drops and the shaking intensifies. "These sort of things must be done secretly! Nobody don't need to see you making a damn fool of yourself. And why you was in here naked? You was in there looking at yourself? Lord Jesus Christ! Don't make me find out that you in here doing anything to yourself!" Her finger is in my face. "If I catch you in here looking at yourself again, I will show you how water walk go to pumpkin belly! Now wrap up that thing with newspaper and throw it outside. Nobody want to see your dirty nastiness!"

Her voice drops to an almost imperceptible rasp. "And make sure you stop talking to those boys over the fence. You must be mad if you think I going tolerate no babies under this roof."

I am confused. "But, Auntie, I think you could only get a baby if a boy put his penis *into* your vagina." The sentence is all the way out before I realize I should have kept my mouth shut.

"Jesus God in heaven! This pickney have mouth, eh? Who ask you for no long argument?" She pushes me against the sink and raises her right hand to hit me.

I duck and raise the brown pad to defend myself.

Her arm freezes in the air and she jumps away from me. Her expression of utter horror makes me want to laugh out loud, but I am too afraid she would kill me. So I wait until she slams the door behind her before I fall to the ground laughing and crying until I can't move anymore.

The Evidence of Things Not Seen

Because her wealthy father abandoned her mother when she was a baby, the stunning and red-haired Summer Delaney is simply unable to trust Blade, the man she truly loves. When she goes to confront her father, he unfolds the yellowed note he has kept for this very purpose and reveals that it was Summer's mother who ran away from him. Everything becomes clear to her as she weeps in her father's arms. He begs her to forgive him for being absent from all the important years of her life. She forgives him and is finally able to give herself completely to Blade.

I close the Mills & Boon romance novel and decide to call my own father after school tomorrow.

When the last bell rings, I quickly make my way to the telephone booths on Church Street. It is Friday evening, so the phones are busy with people checking to see if relatives abroad will wire them money for the weekend. I wait while a woman on the phone asks her daughter if she will ever come back to Jamaica. I cannot hear the answer, but the woman nods as tears roll down her cheeks. She reminds her daughter to send money for the children's school fee. "And don't forget you say you was going to send me a new hat fi Easter. All right, all right! Me know it expensive. Take care and cover up good from the cold." When she says good-bye, her nose is running and she is wiping her eyes.

I slip into the narrow booth. I search for the number in the big yellow phone book. I trace my finger down the long list of Chins. There are four Junior Chins listed right after Joan Chin. I draw courage from the memory of Summer demanding answers from her estranged father and dial the number with an address on Leader Avenue. I jump when someone answers on the first ring.

"Hello." The voice on the other end of the phone is deep, melodic.

"Hello . . ." My voice cracks.

"Yes, hello? Hello? Hello?" His response is impatient. "Is anyone there?"

"Hell—hello. Is this Mr. . . . ?" I have no idea what to say.

"Hello? Hello? Who is this? To whom do you wish to speak? Hello? Who is this? What number is it that you want?"

I take a deep breath and grip the receiver. My fingers ache. "Is this Mr. . . . is this Junior Chin? I want to speak with Junior Chin."

"Yes, this is Junior Chin. Who is this?"

"This is Staceyann Chin and I want to know if you are my father."

The silence on his end of the phone is made louder by the sound of cars honking as they pass by me on the street. I look at a bright red Honda going by and wonder, if he has a car, will let me ride in it?

"Oh, Staceyann . . ."

My name sounds so sad on his lips, not excited like I had imagined. Maybe he is worried about how much money it would cost to be my father. I know that he has other children. And children are very expensive. I want to tell him that he doesn't have to give me any money. I just want him to go places with me and talk to me about the books I read. I want him to know that being *my* father isn't going to be expensive.

I remember Summer's speech to her father.

"I really don't want your money," I begin. "I can take care of myself. I'm going to be somebody someday, a lawyer or a doctor. Doctors and lawyers make a lot of money. I won't need any of your money. I just want my identity. You know, my roots. I want to know if I got my nose from you and my crooked little fingers. People say I must have got those things from you. My mother's nose is different and she doesn't have any crooked little fingers. And I'm a really nice person, I read a lot of books and I get good grades, and . . . and . . ."

He sighs. "Okay. Can you come by my office on Tuesday? Do you know where it is? It's on Barnett Street—right in front of the police station. You can come right after school."

"Yes, sir! Okay, see you on Tuesday, sir!"

* * *

I run all the way to the furniture store. At the front desk a round-faced, friendly woman with clear nail polish on her fingers is talking on the phone. When she puts the receiver down, I say good evening and ask for Mr. Chin.

She wrinkles her brow and asks, "Which one of the Mr. Chins you looking for?"

"I am looking for the owner of the place, Mr. Junior Chin. He said I should come today."

"You have an appointment? And what is this in regard to?"

The phone rings.

"I am Staceyann, his daughter. And he told me to come."

She doesn't say anything else. She just points me in the direction of his office and picks up the ringing phone.

"He is around the back. Is the last door behind the red rolls of upholstery—just go down there and knock."

I navigate my way around the giant rolls of red cloth. I step over the planks of wood and follow the long hallway. I tap lightly on the door.

"Come in."

I hesitate.

"Come in! Just push the door and come in!"

The office is a small room with piles of furniture paraphernalia all over the chairs, the desk, and the floor; bits of red velvet upholstery, wooden legs for chairs, floral cushions for couches, nails, hammers—I have to clear myself a path to a chair.

"Sit down there, young lady."

I sit down in front of the desk. He looks at me for a long time before he speaks. He is kind of handsome, and darker than most Chinese people. His hair is a little wavy and peppered with gray. I never imagined my father with gray hair. The pictures of my mother are youthful and vibrant. Every hair is in full color. He doesn't look like someone my mother could be with. He is kind of old. Handsome, but old.

"How can I help you, little miss?" I am confused by his question.

"Well, I called because—because . . . well, I mean, you are my father. We should get to know each other."

"What are you reading?"

"I beg your pardon?"

"You say you read a lot. What are you reading now?"

I don't want to tell him about Blade and Summer, so I lie. "I am reading a book called *The Silver Sword*. It's about some children who lost their parents in the war and they are going somewhere to try and find them. The children are Polish. They are from Poland."

"Young lady, we have to talk about some things, here." He is silent for a beat. Then he continues. "Do you know how a woman gets pregnant?"

"Yes, of course," I reply. "First, she has sex with a man, and then he gives her sperm and the baby grows in her for nine months, but only sometimes—I was born at less than seven months. That's how I am with everything. I do everything fast. People say that is why I am bright, because I do things before I am supposed to."

"Well, if your mother and I had had sex, *then* you could be my child. But I never really had sex with your mother. There's no way you could be my child."

"But I'm half-Chinese . . ." I don't understand what he is saying.

"I know, but you didn't get any of that from me." He holds my gaze as he says it.

"But people say I look like your other daughter . . ." I am floored.

"I know. I know. It's obvious that you are of Asian descent, but there are a hundred Chinese gentlemen in Montego Bay. It must have been one of them, because it was not me. I am very sorry. But that is the truth. Believe me, young lady, if I had had sex with your mother I would tell you."

His eyes look like he is telling the truth. I don't want to call him a liar. I do not want him to be a liar. It does not matter that people say I look exactly like his daughter Karen or that I have ankles that turn in like his. He says that I do not belong to him and that is that. I want to scream at him and call him a bastard, a piece of shit, a coward. I look at his face again; he believes every word he is saying. He looks right at me and I see that this is very difficult for him. Suddenly, I want to protect him. I say the most comforting thing I can think of. "Well, I guess that's all you can say, there's really nothing more. My mother said you are my father, you say you are not. She is not here to contradict you. Don't worry about it, sir. There's nothing else you can do."

I pick up my bag and stand.

"You know something, Mr. . . . I really appreciate your telling me. Big people don't tell children things because they think we are too young to understand. But we understand a lot more than most people think. The thing is, I feel like a big person most of the time. Thanks again for your time, sir, good evening."

I leave the building with the staff staring and passing comments on how tall I am, how much I look like my mother. Another Chinese man who looks very much like my father stops me at the door.

"Stop there, man. Stop a little bit." He takes me by the shoulder. "What is your name?"

My eyes fill up. His face seems magnified. "Staceyann. Staceyann Chin."

"Okay, Staceyann. Your father is not here every day. But I am here every day. My name is Desmond. So I am your Uncle Desmond. And you can come and see me anytime you want, you hear me? And if you need something fi school—a book, or a pair of shoes—just come here and I will try and see what I can do, you hear me?"

I am sobbing now. Uncle Desmond is very kind, but I don't want him. I want my father. I want my father to call me back and tell me that he was just joking with me. That he made a mistake and that he is sorry.

"Listen to me, Stacey." Uncle Desmond shakes me gently by the shoulder. "If I am not here, ask the lady inside. She is my wife. She is your Auntie Joan. And she will help you, you hear?"

I nod and head out toward the front of the store.

The workmen, staining a new dresser, nod and tell me I look exactly like my sister. "You are the dead stamp. And you have the same body as your mother. She was slim and neat just like you!"

I have never seen these men before, yet they all seem to know my mother. I walk to the taxi stand, hugging my schoolbag to my chest so that I won't fall to pieces. Auntie is going to be upset because I am late. My uniform needs to be washed for school the next day. I want to kill my father who is not my father. I want to be dead.

Part II

God Helps Those Who Help Themselves

I know that if I want to get out of Paradise I have to find a way to go to high school. If I end up at a secondary school I will be stuck doing needlework and home economics, with no chance of ever getting a college education. But high schools cost money and my mother has not sent one penny since she went away almost two years ago.

Andy says that since I am almost eleven years old, I am old enough to get a man to pay for me to attend Mount Alvernia. I want to ask Delano if his father could help me, but since we never speak when we pass each other on the street, I don't know if that makes any sense. The most he will do is wave. I am so worried about the money, I can't sleep at night. Finally, I ask the school secretary if I can just have a word with Sister Cecile. As soon as the door closes behind me in the office, I burst into tears.

"Come, come, now. There is nothing that cannot be solved with the Blessed Virgin and our Lord and Savior. What is the matter, my child?" Sister Cecile's voice is clear and kind.

"Sister, I want to go to high school, but I don't have any money! My father is rich, but he is never going to come and save me. My mother doesn't remember that she has any children, and the boys who live in my auntie's house are trying to rape me every day! I have to go to high school, Sister Cecile!"

Sister Cecile's yellow wrinkled face is still while she listens. She tells me she can't do much today, but if I pass my Common Entrance the nuns might have a word with my father for me.

After school I go back to the store to visit Uncle Desmond. He smiles when he sees me. "Come in, come in, man. Come meet your two cousins. Lief and April, this is Stacey, Uncle Junior's daughter. April, take her round the back and show her where oonu like to climb up."

Lief, who is eight or so years old, nods at me and then disappears. April is a pretty little girl of about six years old wearing the white uniform of Mount Alvernia Prep School. "Come on, Stacey." She takes me by the hand and drags me past my father's office to the stack of mattresses in the back.

"Okay, just hold on to the plastic covering and pull yourself up to the top. And try not to tear the plastic. People don't like to buy mattresses that are not covered."

After much huffing and groaning, we settle onto the crackling plastic-covered stack of mattresses. April digs into her pocket and pulls out a handful of coolie plums. She hands me half of the small tart fruits and looks me up and down. "So you are my cousin, then?"

"I don't know."

"What you mean, you don't know? Is either you are my cousin or you not. Don't Uncle Junior is your father?" I chew the tangy flesh of the plum so I don't have to answer. I wish I were dressed in a crisp white uniform too.

I turn to my books with a fury. In October I study every evening until there is no light to see. November brings long days at school doing mock math tests and multiple-choice questions and reading comprehension from morning till the dismissal bell rings. As soon as we are done, the tests are graded, and the top results are announced right there in class.

In the first week of tests, Miss McBean calls my name for every exam. I walk to her desk and proudly collect the sheet of paper with the big red *100%* written on the front. Every time my name is called I feel I am marching closer and closer to being at Mount Alvernia High School for Girls. I can't wait to see the back of Chetwood.

The whole class prepares for the Common Entrance Examinations with extra lessons after school. The children who do extra lessons do better on the actual exam. But the lessons are very expensive and Auntie does not have the money to pay every week. I ask Uncle Desmond to help. He gives me enough to pay for the whole term. I tell Auntie that Miss McBean says I can do the extra classes whether I have the money or not.

"You see, Stacey. God makes a way for everything."

I nod and turn back to timing myself on the take-home mock exam.

After my extra lessons, I spend the evenings eating coolie plums with April at the shop. One evening, just before the Christmas holidays, Uncle Desmond pulls me aside and tells me that today my father is working in the back office, so we should leave the mattresses and play near the front of the store, "because I don't want to get into any more hot waters with him, you hear?"

I nod, but I hover near the office, waiting to catch a glimpse of my father. Auntie Joan catches me pecking into the office and sends April and me to get an egg sandwich from the store across the street. When we come back, the office door is open and Uncle Desmond tells us we can play on the stack of mattresses again.

I tell Auntie Joan, "I wish I could just go home with you and April and Lief. I wish Uncle Desmond was my father."

She puts her hand on my back. "Stacey, listen to me. It doesn't matter who loves you or who doesn't want you now. You do well. You keep to those books. You are very bright. I hear you are getting nineties and hundreds on the mock tests. Just keep at it and one day you will show everybody what you are made of! And everybody will want you then! But it is getting so late, and I don't want you out on the street too late. Them boys out there getting crazy."

When Auntie asks why I am so late coming home, I tell her that Miss McBean kept us or that I couldn't get a taxi. She says she hopes all this late traveling helps me to get into my first choice for high school.

You are allowed two choices for high school. The better I do on the exam, the more likely it will be that I will pass for one of the two girls' schools that everyone picks: Mount Alvernia High or Montego Bay High. All the boys want to go to Cornwall College, where Delano is. If I lived on the other side of Paradise, in the neighborhoods where the children climb into shiny cars and go to school at Mount Alvernia Preparatory School, I would definitely pass for my first choice. All the children who go to Alvernia Prep will pass for good schools. Their parents have the money to pay for the extra lessons taught inside the very high schools they want them to attend.

Christmas day passes without any mention of my eleventh birthday.

When we get back to school in January, we have only a few days before we take the Common Entrance. On the morning of the exam, Auntie gives me a new eraser and two no. 2 pencils. Elisha wishes me luck.

Auntie tells her that the exam has nothing to do with luck. "Everybody in Paradise knows that she is very, very bright. She is a bright child. I know she will do well. She study hard and last night me say a special prayer for her."

I am surprised and happy to hear that Auntie thinks I am bright. I tell myself I will try harder to make her even more proud of me.

Inside the classroom, which the invigilator refers to as the *examination room,* all the chairs are lined up in four long rows. We cannot speak to each other. We are to write only when we are told and to stop when we are asked. The soft rustle of paper is eerie in a room usually alive with the sound of arguments and beatings and laughter. I finish the math questions and we are given Mental Ability next. When that is done we get a break for lunch. I eat my banana chips alone and head back in at the sound of the bell. The English test is so easy I finish before everybody in my room.

On my way home, I see Delano on the opposite side of the taxi stand. I wave and he motions for me to come over. My heart is beating so fast I can hear the blood pounding inside my ears. I fiddle with my no. 2 pencil in my pocket and cross the street. Up close he looks the same as he did when we left Westmoreland, except that his hair is much shorter. I stand in front of him, surprised to see that we are the same height. It has been almost two years since we have stood this close. I want to hug him and kiss him and tell him about my terrible life in Paradise, but he casually leans against the wall and asks, "So how was the exam?"

I wish I could touch his hair, but instead I step away and put both hands in my pockets. "It was very easy. I think I passed."

"Okay. Me did know that me pass long before, but me never say anything to anybody. Sometime is good fi just hold your mouth and wait."

Our eyes meet, but he quickly looks away. "All right, Delano, I won't say anything to anybody."

He straightens his epaulet. "Anyway, you know where me live now?"

"No." I want to ask him if his father is good to him, if he has heard from Grandma, but he seems so uncomfortable standing there that I just smile and wait for him to continue.

"Is at the foot of Mount Salem Hill—the blue house with the big veranda. Me reach home 'bout five o'clock every evening." He fixes his epaulet again. Now he looks like he is in a hurry to get away from me. "You can come check me if you have the time. Just let me know when you coming first. All right?"

Inside my pocket I grab a handful of my thigh. I don't know how he expects me to let him know before I come. We do not have a telephone and I don't know his number. I start to ask him for his phone number, but he is already walking away. I know he doesn't really want me to come and see him. I know he is just inviting me to be nice.

"Okay, then, I will come one day," I shout after him.

"All right, you better go on home before it get too late," he shouts back, and adjusts his backpack.

"Delano—" I walk after him.

He stops and sighs before he turns to face me. "Yes?"

"Nothing," I say. "Nothing. Have a good evening."

"Thanks," he tosses back. "All right, then, Stacey, take care."

I climb into the red hatchback Lada taxi and slam the door. I wave. He does not wave back.

June comes and my full name is printed in the *Jamaica Gleaner* alongside the thousands of other children who have passed the Common Entrance Examination. I have been accepted to Mount Alvernia High School. I know I will look beautiful in my white uniform in September. I wish there was a number to call my mother and tell her. I remember how pleased she was when she found out Delano had passed.

Auntie says she has no idea how she will manage with both Diana and me in high school. I ask her if she thinks I will be able to go. She tells me not to worry. She will find the money for me to go. She says she has a little money put away somewhere. She was saving it for a rainy day.

"Auntie, what if I ask my father to help me?"

"No! No! No! Your mother tell me not to allow you to go there! And she must have her reason. She tell me that that man is the living Devil. I am not sending you to beg them nutten!"

"But what we going to do, Auntie? I know you don't have a lot of money to send me to high school. What me must do? Me need book and uniform and shoes and—"

"Wait, Stacey, wait! You are a young girl, yes. And you don't have anybody. But you have a chance to get a good education. Anywhere me must get the money, me will make sure you can go. Me glad you pass. Sometimes me sit down outside on the veranda and wonder what is to become of you. Your mother going to have to answer to God for how she treat you and your brother."

"Me don't care 'bout her, Auntie. She can drop down dead and me wouldn't care! I hope she live to suffer like how she make we suffer."

"Stacey, you cannot talk about your mother like that. The Bible tell you to honor your mother and your father. Sometime you look at a thing and you cannot see inside of it! Your mother was a different person when she was young, you know."

I sit on the floor and look up at her. "What you mean, Auntie? You did know her when she was in Jamaica?"

"Lawd, you wouldn't like to see how she was pretty when she was small! I remember when she used to come to the market to visit me mother."

Auntie stops and shakes her head.

"She used to come round to the stall and say good evening to everybody. She was such a nice little girl. She grow up same way to be a pretty young woman. Even after she have Delano she used to bring him come to see me down here in Montego Bay. Everybody wanted to hold him. He was such a white little boy. When him just born, him eye them was blue, blue, blue."

"She did ever carry me come to look for you, Auntie?"

"No, man. She leave the island a little bit after you born. From she start keep company with you father, she become a change person."

"What happen to her, Auntie? Why she change?"

"Cho, man, you too love old people story. Me only want to tell you not to worry. Me cannot buy the world and all its riches fi you go to school, but me will provide what me can. Now get up off the dirty floor and go inside."

The next morning I go to ask Sister Cecile if she has spoken to my father. She tells me that she thinks Mr. Chin might be willing to sponsor a child for high school. She suggests that I go to my father and talk to him.

"Stacey, the Lord might just be planning something we don't know about."

I can see myself standing in the sea of girls in white uniforms and speaking standard English all day long without being teased for it. The girls at Mount Alvernia do not speak the dialect to each other. All their words are said the way they are written in the dictionary.

The sixth-graders get out earlier than everybody else because they have no end-of-year exams. That means I get home long before Glen and Elisha. Usually if I am home by myself I sit on the steps outside, but today the sun is so hot, I have to take refuge in the living room. I doze off reading. I awaken to Shappy sitting down on the couch beside me holding his erect penis. I swallow my fear and slowly close the book. I force myself to walk casually to the door. Then I dash out into the yard. Without pulling up his pants, he follows me outside and chases me around the yard until he catches me. His fingers are steel cables wrapped around my arms.

He drags me halfway up the stairs, muttering, "You take my money and give it to the FBI. We'll see what the president going to do about this now."

I grab hold of the rails and wrap my legs around the veranda gate. I cannot let him get me inside the house. Unable to budge my body, he begins to kick me. The pain shoots electric through my body. I scream and try to turn my face away from the blows. When I can't hold on to the rails anymore, he lifts me up and tosses me over the rails. I fall into a heap on the rocky ground below. My back is cut and I am bleeding so much the blood frightens me. I wonder if anything is broken, but everywhere hurts, so I can't tell. I struggle to get up.

But before I can stand, he is on top of me. His hands run over my body. Then he begins to kick me again. I can hear when his foot connects with my body, but I can't feel anything anymore. When he is done, he spits on me and says, "You tell that to the Chinese government fi me. Tell them that is what we do to traitors when them infiltrate our ranks. And don't worry, I checked already. There are no broken bones."

I sit under the steps and weep. No one is home and I am afraid to go inside. When Auntie finally gets home it is almost dark. I tell her what has happened and she says, "Stacey, me sorry that him was bothering you. But you don't see that Shappy mad? Half the time him don't even know what him is doing. You just have to make sure you stay out of him way when you come home."

I spend the rest of the school year carefully avoiding being home alone and I am so relieved when Auntie tells me that Auntie Ella wants me to come to Kingston for the summer. She says that she doesn't mind me going because she knows that Auntie Ella is a good Christian woman, plus Grandma lives there now and wants to see me.

I am surprised to hear that Grandma lives in Kingston. I can't imagine Grandma talking on a telephone or walking through the streets of Liguanea.

There is no train from Kingston to Montego Bay anymore, so I have to take the bus to Auntie Ella's. The twenty-eight-seat minibus is filled with fifty people, plus the driver and the conductor. I sit in the window seat behind the gold-toothed driver and count the number of people twice. A small Indian woman with a big black Bible sits next to me. Auntie tells the driver to please drop me all the way uptown. She gives him extra money to take me straight to Auntie Ella's gate. He smiles at me and tells Auntie that he will be sure to take the very best care of me.

"You don't see how she pretty, Mammy? Me not going let anything happen to her."

The conductor puts a big bag of yams between my knees. The bus ride is long and jerky. Every town we pass through, the driver has to stop and let people on and off. By the time we reach Spanish Town, I am so sweaty and tired and thirsty that the driver offers to buy me a Pepsi. The old man selling the Pepsi uses his knife to open the bottle. The cool sweet liquid bubbles in my mouth. The driver reaches back and touches my shoulder. His fingers slide over to caress the exposed flesh at my neck. He asks me if I want something to eat too.

I pull away and say no. I finish my Pepsi and sit very close to the Indian woman with the Bible. I ask her how far she is going. She tells me she gets off at the last stop, which is downtown Kingston. I ask where she goes from there. She tells me she goes to Gordon Town.

"Is that far from Sandhurst Terrace?"

"No, man. I actually have to take a bus that go past Sandhurst to get to Gordon Town."

I tell her that my auntie paid the driver extra to drop me at Sandhurst and that she can ride with me and then take her bus from there.

"My word! Is so the Lord always provide for his children! Thank you, Father. I will do just that! What a nice little girl! Are you saved?"

I sort of nod because I don't know if I am.

"Well, that is good. Just trust in the Lord and he will take care of you."

When we reach Sandhurst Terrace, Grandma is waiting for me on the veranda. She looks smaller than I remember. One side of her collar is bunched under inside the neck of her dress. I am shocked to see her back bent like an old woman's. She reaches up and opens the grille. She pulls at my arm and me tells me to come inside. "Come, come inside! You must want something to eat, eh!"

She struggles with my bag, her feet shuffling as she slowly closes the grille. I am taller than she is, so I reach up to help her. She puts the bags in a corner and takes my face into her hands. They still smell like onions, but now they are soft like a baby. I want to stay smelling her soft hands forever.

But she is busy smoothing my hair and straightening my blouse. "Lawd Jesus, Stacey! You grow so big! Look 'pon you hair. It long, long now, eh? Take off your shoes. Leave them there. No mind, me will take them up when me finish. Leave them there! Come, come! The journey from Montego Bay long. You must be hungry by now."

I am glad to see her, but she doesn't feel like the same Grandma I knew. I follow her into the living room. I want her to stop doing things and just talk to me, tell me a story, tell me anything. I wonder if she has heard anything about Mummy.

She opens the back grille. "Ella still at work. She don't come in till about five thirty or six. And Annmarie gone to summer class. Lawd, you look so much like a big somebody. How you have so much bump on you face? Is teenage bumps?"

I nod. Suddenly I am tired from the long trip.

"Never mind. Is so you mother did have them too. You hearing from her?"

I don't say anything. She unwraps a block of cheese.

"You want a cheese sandwich? With cheese and lettuce and tomato inside? Ella never make the house run out of vegetable. She say me getting old now. Me have to eat plenty fish and vegetable."

I sit on the back steps and force myself to eat my sandwich. Grandma brings me a glass of lemonade with ice. "So how is Montego Bay?"

I want her to tell me I don't have to go back to Paradise. I want to beg her to tell Auntie Ella that I have to stay with her in Kingston. But I know that Grandma can't do anything like that, so I just nod and say everything is fine. She has more warts on her face. And more wrinkles. And her hearing is much worse. I notice that I have to say everything two or three times for her to understand me.

"So how you do with school, Stacey? And what happen to Delano? Him still living with him father in Montego Bay?"

I nod.

"You see him when you go to school?"

"Sometimes."

"Me glad fi dat. At least oonu never separate completely. Him still going to Cornwall?"

"Yes, ma'am."

"Him must be tall like a pawpaw tree now, eh?"

I don't answer. I wish I could go sit on the floor of the bathroom and think. I chew the fleshy red of the tomato and try hard not to cry.

"How is Miss John? She treat you good?" Her eyes beg me to tell her that she does.

She seems to me like a little girl. Tears brim over, but I quickly wipe them away with my sleeve. I put on my happiest face and say, "Yes, Grandma. Everybody treat me like me is them sister."

Her face crumples and her eyes fill up. She raises her hand to God. "Jesus Christ be praise! If you ever know how me pray fi oonu! Thank God oonu nah get no ill treatment. I woulda drop down dead if me know that nobody take disadvantage of oonu. You want more bread?"

I shake my head no. I lift the glass to my lips, but I cannot finish my lemonade. I can't stop the tears rolling down my face. I wish there was a way to tell Grandma about Andy and Shappy and the fish tank, but she is crying and praying and thanking God for keeping me safe in his blessed bosom.

"You see why you have to trust God, Stacey?" I wish I could get people to call me Staceyann. "You see how Him watch over you? I don't even want to tell you the things that could happen to a likkle girl without the protection of the Almighty! Thank you, Father, fi you grace and you mercy on me granddaughter!"

She peels an orange and offers me half. We sit on the steps and suck the sweet juice. Her dentures make a clacking sound as she pushes the fruit against them. I don't understand why she seems so old. It has only been two years since we left her in Westmoreland. I take the orange peel from her hands and straighten the collar of her dress. She laughs when I wipe some pulp from her chin.

The house looks much smaller, but I know it is the same number of rooms. Everything looks like it is a less shiny version of itself. I can now reach up and pick a mango right off the tree. When I bite into it, the juice is sour. Nothing in Kingston is exactly as I remember. Everyone has changed so much. Auntie Myrtle has gray hairs now. She hugs me and says I am going to be as tall as a coconut tree. Mrs. Bremmer is still nice to me, but she keeps saying it is too bad about my acne. Chauntelle is now preoccupied with taking dance classes and they have a new baby brother named Joel, who is already walking. Only Racquel seems the same. As soon as I walk into her living room she jumps on me and knocks me to the floor. She kisses my face and asks if I know that she has started Mona Preparatory School.

When Racquel asks if I want to play concert I tell her that I will watch if she wants to perform, but I don't feel like singing.

Auntie Ella comes home and heads straight for me. "Congratulations! Congratulations! Congratulations, my darling!"

Auntie Myrtle pokes out her head from the living room. "Congratulations for what?"

"Hasn't my niece told you? She has passed her Common Entrance Examination! She begins high school in September."

"Lord have his mercy! Come here make me hug you up! Whooooi! Congratulations, girl! You Auntie Ella have to buy something special for you!"

Grandma comes out to the veranda looking confused. "Is what happen, Myrtle? Is what she do?"

Myrtle pulls Grandma close to her and tells her, "She pass fi go high school. She pass. She going to high school September. September. She start in September!"

Grandma claps her hands and spins me around in a circle. "Praise the Lord! Thank you, Jesus! Hallelujah! Come here, Stacey! Why you never tell me? What a thing! You going to high school. That is nice, man. Me glad to hear you still taking the book-learning! Thank you, Jesus. Me know you was going come to something in life!"

Mrs. Bremmer gives me a red folder with three silver rings along the spine and a package of one hundred lined folder leaves. I snap open the folder and put the new folder pages in it. Even Annmarie is happy for me. She already goes to high school. She tries to tell me what it is like.

She is taller. And Auntie Ella has given her permission to straighten her hair. She is still very quiet, but she is definitely more grown-up. Her nails are long and she spends her time drawing on a big white notepad.

At church, Auntie Ella tells everyone I have passed. The day is filled with good wishes and congratulations. Some of the ladies give me little envelopes with money. And after the sermon, Pastor Lightfoot hugs me and pats me on the head and says he hopes I will be a good soldier for the Lord as I make my way into this new world of higher education. Auntie Ella confesses to him that she has no idea what will happen to me in September, because my mother has abandoned me and I do not have a father. "Pastor, the child needs so much for this stage of her schooling. My salary cannot provide for my own family and her. We need help."

An announcement is quickly made on the microphone. Pastor Lightfoot makes me stand in front of everyone while he says a special prayer for me. Then he tells everyone that I am in need of things for my journey. He starts listing, "Folder paper, schoolbags, shoes, uniforms—the list is endless, brothers and sisters. You know what your own children would need. If you are committed to truly serving God, make a donation. Help to meet a need. I am calling on you, brothers and sisters, dig into your pockets and place it in the collection plate going round."

We get so much money that Auntie Ella buys me almost everything I need for school. Shoes, a white slip, training brassieres, notebooks—she even buys me highlighters and different-colored pens. I have so many things she has to buy me a new bag to put them in. The only things Auntie has to get are my uniforms and one English literature book that Auntie Ella could not get in Kingston. Grandma cries when she sees all the things that Auntie Ella has bought. Racquel is very excited for me. We talk about my new school all the time.

She gives me her favorite pencil case. I don't have anything to give her, but I write her a long letter telling her how much I appreciate her friendship. When she reads the part about being my only true sister, she cries and tells me that she will keep the letter forever. I wish I lived in Kingston so I could see her whenever I want. We promise to write to each other all year. She wants to know everything about my first year at Mount Alvernia. In Kingston, everything is easier. Everybody is happy about my going to high school. In Kingston, I feel free. I wear short dresses with no shorts under them. Grandma says that I should be careful of how I sit in those short clothes, but I know that here in Kingston, nobody is trying to look up my skirt or pounce on me when I am least expecting it. All day I open my legs and laze about on the grass with Racquel. We eat mangoes from the tree until we are sick. In the evenings, I watch TV with Annmarie and Grandma. When the JBC signs off, I crawl in the bed with Grandma. The yellow sheets smell like rain. Before we go to sleep she prays for me and Delano and all her children. Then we turn off the lights and go to sleep.

When August draws to a close, I am both happy and sad to go. Grandma makes me a sandwich for the ride. Finally I am packed and tucked into the Montego Bay minibus. Auntie Ella gives me an envelope with the rest of the church money and tells me to make sure I take good care of it. "Make sure you hand it right to Miss John. And tell her I wish I could do some more."

She places her hand on my head and prays, "God bless this child on her journey back home. Watch over her body and deliver her safe into the bosom of her grandaunt."

She tells the driver to find me a seat between two good Christian women. After I am wedged in between a woman who says she sells yams in the market and another who is going home from visiting her daughter, she asks them to please take care of me. Her lips are warm on my cheek as she hugs me. I can see my face reflected in the window. There are two little marks beneath my left ear where Auntie Ella has kissed me.

The walk through Blood Lane is difficult with the big bags. I almost fall over in my haste. Auntie is sitting in the big chair on the veranda. I take the red steps two at a time and dump the bags on the floor in front of her. "Auntie! Auntie! Auntie Ella bought everything that I need for high school. She sent money for you to take care of the uniforms. I have pencils and books and everything. The only things I don't have yet are my uniforms and one literature book. Look, Auntie, I even have a pair of sneakers for PE!"

"Well, me know the Lord was going to provide for you. Is because you never have any faith why you was so worry-worry."

"Auntie, everybody in the church give money! Even the other children put money towards buying my school things."

"What you saying to me?"

Auntie is breathing hard and her foot is tapping the floor when I finish telling her everything. "Is really Ella go beg the church people to buy them things fi you? And that is what you so happy 'bout? Jesus Savior, pilot me! Go put everything inside. I don't want to look at them!" She is so angry she is frothing at the mouth. "And you—you should be shame of yourself! Next thing you will do is beg from strangers on the street corner! Get out of me face!"

I pick up everything and dash inside, happy that she did not make me throw away my things.

School starts in one week. The following day Auntie sends me to go get the missing book for English literature class. I go to the phone booth to call my father.

"Hello."

"Hello, is this Junior Chin?"

"Yes, it is. How can I be of service?"

"It's Stacey. Staceyann Chin. I passed my exam and I need help to go to high school."

Silence.

"Hello, you heard me? It's Staceyann Chin, the girl who—"

"I know who you are. I heard you."

"I know that you said I am not your daughter, but I am not asking you to tell anybody that. I just need help to buy books and lunch money and things like that. Can you help me or not?"

He sighs.

"You don't have to help me, you know. I won't be upset with you or anything. Is just that I know if I don't go to high school, I won't ever make anything of myself. And—"

"It's okay, young lady. You don't have to say any more. I will help you. Do you know where my house is?"

"It's right next door to Upper Deck Hotel on Leader Avenue."

"Okay, just come here tomorrow and we will sort out the details."

The next morning, when Auntie and Grace leave for work, I am sitting by the fish tank tossing pebbles into the still, black water. I wait to make sure neither of them has forgotten anything before I head to the bathroom. I put on my prettiest dress. The black top is stitched with white threads. There are no sleeves, no collar, and the skirt flares in a flurry of red, white, and blue stripes. It's a little small, but I feel beautiful in it.

I take a taxi and get off at the bottom of Leader Avenue. By the time I reach the top of the hill I have convinced myself that the dress is too short, too tight. My hands are sweating and I want to change my dress. I climb the two flights of stairs and ring the doorbell. A small, dark, pretty woman comes to see who it is. I tell her my name is Staceyann Chin and I have come to see Mr. Junior Chin. She looks me up and down and opens the black grille door.

She gestures to the white lounge chair on the veranda. "I am Mrs. Chin. Everybody calls me Miss P. Come inside and sit down. He will be with you in a second."

I sit on the veranda and wait. The view of the city is beautiful. There is nothing between the eyes and the whole city below. I wish I lived in a house where there was no mango tree and ackee tree and breadfruit tree blocking the view. After a few minutes I begin to wonder if he is not coming out. I get up and look inside. The living room is bigger than any living room I have ever seen. The windows are tall enough for a person to walk through. Twenty minutes later he comes out and tells me to follow him into his office.

"Sit down, young lady."

He says all his sentences in the same tone. His voice is soft but full of authority, like he is used to people listening to him. I sit across from his desk and wait.

"I was just finishing my workout. Forgive the sweaty clothes. I just didn't want to keep you waiting too long," he says.

"It's okay, sir. It's no problem waiting for you."

He sits down and asks if I know what the agreement will be. I tell him no. He says that he is providing a loan for me to go to school.

"You will never have to pay it back. The written contract is just to protect me and my family—in case someone tries to use the fact that I gave you money as proof of paternity."

I don't really understand what is going on. But because I don't want him to get angry with me I say that that is okay with me. I want to die when he tells me to sit with my legs closed. I tug the hem of my dress, but it won't cover my knees. I feel naked and dirty under his gaze.

"That dress is too short for such a big girl like you," he says. "How old are you now, eleven or twelve?"

"I'm eleven," I say. "I won't be twelve until next Christmas."

"You are still too big for that dress. If you sit carelessly I can see your underwear. These are things you should pay attention to as a young lady."

He has no right to be talking to me like that. Especially since he says he is not my father. I want to get up and tell him to go to hell. I want to tell him that what I wear is none of his business, but he is already writing up the agreement, and I know I need the money to go to school. There is a column with the date and another with the amount loaned and yet another for my signature. Every time I come, he will fill in the date and the amount. I will sign in the column next to the date. He hands me the cardboard-covered notebook and asks me to sign my name.

"And make it legible. I want to be able to read it."

"I know what legible means. You don't have to define it!"

I write my name as neatly as I can. He closes the book and puts it in a drawer in his desk. He hands me the money. He does not put it in an envelope.

"There should be enough there to take you through to the first of October. I hope you use it wisely."

I take the money and stand up. My father reaches for my hand. I have just completed my first business transaction.

"Thank you very much for your help."

"No thanks necessary, young lady," he says. "Just work hard in school and make something of yourself. That is all the thanks I will need."

I use the money to go on my first shopping spree. I pick up a dozen wire-ringed notebooks, some sketching paper, an eraser with a drawing of Scooby-Doo on it, and two packs of coloring pencils. When the woman in the store asks me how I am going to pay for all of it, I take out my stack of bills and ask her to pack everything inside the backpack hanging on the hook behind her. I cut my finger pulling the tag off my new schoolbag. So I head to the pharmacy to buy a box of flesh-colored Band-Aids. At Kentucky Fried Chicken, I stuff myself with a hearty meal of crispy chicken, french fries, and Coca-Cola. Even after all that I still have enough money left to divide into three separate stacks to hide. That way if Shappy steals from me he won't take everything.

Put Away Childish Things

On Monday morning I scrub my skin until it is red. I dry myself and slip the white uniform over my head. I wet my hands and carefully smooth my hair into a single ponytail. It takes three attempts before every strand is tucked neatly into the elastic band. I wrap the blue ribbon around the brown band and tie the bow as straight as I can. With my hair pulled back, the pimples don't look so bad. The blue tie at my neck makes me look important. My new shoes glisten in the morning light.

On my way out the door Auntie gives me lunch money for the whole week. She says I am getting big enough to learn how to manage my money. "Make sure you don't spend all of it today. Remember you have the whole week to eat lunch." She also adds that I am getting older and since I am a girl she doesn't want me lingering in the streets after school. I am expected to come right home. If she catches me walking about and going to other people's houses, I will be very sorry after she is done with me. She warns that friends can be wolves in sheep's clothing. It is better to be by myself, she tells me. I nod, but inside I hope I make a hundred million friends on the first day.

My knapsack is pleasantly heavy on my back as I make my way down Blood Lane. At the taxi stand everybody tells me I look nice in my white uniform. Because I am now in high school I have to pay more for my taxi fare, but it does not matter because I have enough in my pocket to pay five taxi fares. All the people without running water in their homes are gathered at the public standing pipe in the square. They whistle and call out to me, "Take me with you, nuh, Stacey! No, stay home with me and me will teach you everything you need fi know!"

I ignore them and flag down a red Lada with one white door. I am in high school, so I can sit in the front. I get off at the Cornwall College gate and take the familiar route in through the gates of Mount Alvernia. Only, today I do not pass through. I join the sea of white uniforms.

I am in grade seven-one. Every grade has classes one through six. Everyone looks happy and a little confused. Our prefect reminds us to keep our hands at our sides while we sing the national anthem. Then we pray. Then the principal, a tiny Chinese nun called Sister Joan Claire Chin Loy, talks to us through a loudspeaker.

I am surprised at how easy it is for me to make friends at Mount Alvernia. The first girl I meet is Sandy. A tiny, light-skinned girl with a black mole on her cheek, she stands behind me in the line at the water cooler, staring at my shoes and smiling. At first I am afraid that she is laughing at me. Then I look at her shoes and see that she is wearing a similar pair.

"You're wearing my shoes!" I say, smiling.

"No, you are wearing my shoes! When did you buy them? Let's see who got them first!"

It turns out that Sandy and I are seated side by side in class. We sit behind Andrea Albermire, a very skinny girl with blond hair and blue eyes and the whitest skin in the world. She was born in America, but since her father owns a hospital in Montego Bay, the whole family lives here from September to June. I can't believe I am sitting right beside someone whose father owns a hospital. She must get anything in the world she wants from her father. She tells us she has just got back from spending the summer in their second home in Florida. When we ask what Miami is like, she tosses her long hair and tells us that she can't wait till she graduates from high school. She really *must* get back to her real life in America.

Then there is Natalia Grawley.

Natalia has the best figure in the class, hands down. She is exactly one week younger than me and is already wearing a B-cup brassiere. Natalia and I have the same complexion, but her face is free of acne. And her long braids fall neatly down her back, while my hair is an unruly tangle barely contained by a rubber band and blue ribbon at the back of my neck. Natalia's hair is straightened every six weeks. So when she takes it out it is nice and bone-straight and shiny. I cannot take my hair out, since it has never been straightened. When I ask Auntie for permission to straighten my hair, she says she doesn't have money to waste on foolishness. Natalia's mother, whom everyone calls Auntie Bamsey, is a professional hairdresser. So she keeps her daughter's hair in very good condition. She offers to do mine for free, but Auntie still says no. She believes that if God wanted me to have straight hair he would have put it on my head at birth.

The Grawleys live in the well-to-do neighborhood of Mango Walk, which is just on the other side of Paradise. I tell everyone I live in Paradise, but I am careful not to say which neighborhood. In the evenings Natalia offers, "Listen, Stacey, Daddy says if you ride with us we can just drop you off on our way home. He told me I just have to find out which part of Paradise you live in."

I never want Natalia to know that I live behind Blood Lane. "No, Natalia! It is quite okay. If my auntie sees me getting a ride from your father, she will get vex and beat me. Just drop me off at the top of your road and I will walk the rest of the way."

"Okay, you know whatever is better for you. Oh, and Daddy says that you can just come by my house after school. We can do homework together and you can have dinner with us!"

I want to go home with Natalia, but I have to figure out what to tell Auntie first. "I don't know if Auntie will let me," I tell her, "but I will ask."

Everything about Mount Alvernia is new. There are no boys in the school. And the girls are nice to each other. Nobody teases me at lunch.

After school I walk downtown with Sandy. Her mother, Miss Buchanan, a stylish well-dressed woman, works at Vic Walton Department Store. I like Sandy's mother. She laughs out loud and says to me, "You look like you is one of my daughter them! You sure them never send you home with the wrong mother? Where is your mother? I want to see her to make sure you are not my long-lost daughter. You look just like Sandy."

I don't say anything. My eyes fill with tears. My face gets hot. Miss Buchanan touches my head and walks away. Sandy is looking at me questioningly. I force a little laugh and point to the tiny lace panties on the display. "What you think those are for, Sandy? You should ask you mother to buy one of them for you!"

Sandy looks at me for a second and then says, "Is for when you have a boyfriend—ooh, ooh, look at the lacy panties Stacey buy for her wedding night!"

"Sandy, I tell you I am never getting married! And if I do, I certainly won't be wearing any floss-pantie up in my bottom!

We laugh and I am grateful that Sandy doesn't say anything about my tears. I wonder if things would be different if Delano were a girl. Then we could do things together like Sandy and her sister Lisa. Maybe Mummy would not have split us up. When we leave the store, she asks what is going on with my mother. "You never talk about her, and you don't talk about the people who you live with. Where is she? She in America?"

"No, Sandy. She is not in America. And I don't talk about her because I don't want you to get jealous. My mother is very pretty, prettier than yours, and she lives in Canada. She sends things for me all the time. I call her at the phone booths at Church Street and she asks me what I want. Then she sends me a barrel for school every year. You see this knapsack and all my notebooks? Is she sent them for me."

"Okay."

Because I don't want Sandy to suspect that my mother is not sending me anything from Canada, I do things to show her that I have lots of extra money. I buy my pens and pencils by the dozen. I boast to her that my brother is very rich. That his father owns a big supermarket from which I can go and get anything that I want.

Soon enough, I begin to tell more elaborate stories about my mother. "My mother thinks the school system in Jamaica is better than the one in Canada, so I have to finish high school and then she is going to file for us to go to Canada. My brother might not want to go, because he is okay with his father. My father wants me to live with him. He is rich too. He has a big house up on Leader Avenue."

"So why don't you live with him, then?"

"Because it would break my mother's heart. He still takes care of me. I collect money from him every month. Maybe one day I will take you with me. I would visit more, but my mother would not be happy about that. She hates him. And he hates her, but I think they are still in love. That's why they are so passionate about each other."

"Okay."

I can see she doesn't believe me. I raise my voice and pretend to get angry. "You don't believe me? Everything I say is true. I have plenty of places to go." I don't know why it feels so urgent, but I know I have to convince her in this moment that what I am saying is true. So I blurt out, "Okay, then. I'm going over to my brother's house today after school. He likes it when I visit him. You can come with me if you like."

Sandy looks at me like I am crazy and declines my invitation. I tell her that that is fine, but to prove to her that I am not lying, I climb into the taxi with her and tell the driver to take me to the foot of Mount Salem Hill. I watch the taxi disappear before I begin to look for the house on foot. The walk is long and dusty. I want to just turn back and go to visit April, but I know my father sometimes stops there on Friday evenings. But I don't think I would have any fun with him there. Plus, when I am with my father I have to remember to act like he is not my father but only a man who is helping me with money for school. And when I am at the store, April is my cousin and Auntie Joan is my aunt and Uncle Desmond still tells people that I am his niece.

Finally, I spot a big blue house with a huge veranda. I hope it is the right house. I walk into the yard and knock on the front door. A woman with a black tie-head answers the door.

"Good afternoon."

"Good afternoon, ma'am. My name is Staceyann Chin. I am Delano's sister. Is this where he lives?"

"Oh! Of course! Come inside, man. Come inside. Me cooking, so me cannot stay long with you. I am Miss Winsome. Richard mother. I work with Mr. Charles."

I sit in the living room. The house is very big, but there is almost no furniture in it. And there are all sorts of things that do not belong in a living room. There is a big bag of cement and pipes and some tiles. Under the window, a big church bench leans upright against the wall. There are no curtains on some of the windows. I watch the cars passing.

"You want to watch TV?"

Miss Winsome's arms are covered in flour.

"No, ma'am."

"Okay, him soon come home. Him don't really stay too long after school."

"Okay."

Delano pushes the door open and sees me sitting on the couch. He motions that he will soon be back before he disappears into his room. I hear water running. When he comes back he is wearing a pair of Levi's jeans that Mummy had brought for him from Canada. I am surprised that he can still fit into clothes that he'd got so many years ago. The things she brought for me are all too short or too tight.

"So how things?" His voice is casual.

"Okay." I work to make mine casual too.

"Them treating you good up at Miss John house?"

"Yeah, man. How things with you?" I don't know why I am lying to him. I really want to tell him everything, but he seems so different from the Delano I knew in Westmoreland. He doesn't look at me when he is talking and he doesn't seem excited to see me.

"Okay. I'm okay."

"Your father treat you good?"

He hesitates. Then he nods. "Yeah, man. Everything good. Perfect."

"Okay. I passed the Common Entrance."

He laughs. "Me can see that. You wearing a Mount Alvernia uniform."

I laugh too. "Yeah! And you not blind. And you must have seen my name in the newspaper, right?" I don't know why, but I laugh again. I am not quite sure what to say to him. He isn't really interested in anything I say. I ask if I can use the bathroom.

"Yeah, man. It's just right through there, on the right-hand side."

The bathroom is as bare as the living room. There are no toothbrushes in sight, no rugs on the floor, no creams or soaps or anything on the side of the sink or bath or on top of the toilet. It looks like a bathroom at school, except there is a bath. When I get back, Delano is sitting on the couch playing with a Rubik's Cube. He hands it to me and tells me to do the yellow face while he times me. I finish in ten minutes.

"That is not bad. You almost as good as me!"

"How long does it take you?"

"Under six minutes. And that is when the colors are really mixed up."

"Okay."

The front door swings open and Delano jumps. A short stocky Chinese man enters. His adjusts his thick glasses as he covers the ground between us.

"Hello! Hello! Everything all right?"

Delano does not answer. I don't know if I should.

"Eh, man! I ask you if everything all right. And who is this, your girl-friend?"

Delano's voice is even, resigned. "Yes, Daddy, everything is fine. And this is me sister, Stacey. She live up at Paradise. She just come to check me."

"Oh, okay. She look like a nice little girl. Everything all right? Is Junior Chin is your father, right? When you reach home, tell him hello for me. You hungry? You want something to eat?" I nod yes.

"Miss Winsome! Miss Winsome!"

The floured hands quietly appear. "Yes, Mr. Charles?"

"This here is Junior Chin daughter. She want something to eat. What you cooking?"

"Corned beef and boiled dumplings."

"Well, make sure she get some when it done."

"All right, Mr. Charles." She leaves as silently as she had come in.

Mr. Charles reaches out and slaps Delano on the back. "How was school today, Delano? You learn a lot of things? School too expensive! Make sure you make use of it!"

Delano nods his head and says nothing. His father then turns to me. "What about you? You do good in school?"

"Yes, Mr. Charles, sir. I just pass my Common Entrance for Mount Alvernia. This is my first year there."

"What? That is good, man. That means you bright. Here is some money. Take it and buy something for school. And remember to tell your father that me say hello."

"Yes, Mr. Charles."

"No, man—I am your Uncle Charlie. All the little schoolchildren call me that. Me is your Uncle Charlie, you hear?"

"Yes, Uncle Charlie."

"Good, good, then. And make sure you get that food."

He goes to his room and slams the door. Delano turns the Rubik's Cube over and over without saying anything. I sit quietly until Miss Winsome calls me to come and get a plate. Delano says he is not ready to eat yet. I cut and bite and chew the food in silence. Uncle Charlie comes out of the bedroom and waves good-bye. I wave back with my mouth full. When there is nothing left on the plate, I take it back to the kitchen.

"Thanks, Miss Winsome."

"Is nothing, man. There is enough food. Richard eat nuff, but Delano don't eat too much."

"Who is Richard?"

"Me tell you that already, man. Richard is me son. Him is Charles youngest. Delano little brother."

"I thought you worked for Uncle Charlie."

"Yes, man, I work for him, but I also have a son for him."

"Okay. So do you live here too?"

"No, dahling. I tell you I only work here."

"Okay." I still don't understand, but I decide not to ask any other questions about that. I lean against the wall and watch her rinse the dishes. Standing there makes me think of Grandma. I wonder if Delano has been to Kingston to see her.

"So how is your mother?"

"I don't know, ma'am."

"How you mean, you don't know? When last you talk to her?"

"Almost three years now."

"Three years! How you mean? She don't call you?"

"No, ma'am. We don't have a phone where I live."

"My goodness! Delano call her sometimes from here. You should make him call her so you can talk to her. Is a good God shame when a little girl have to say she don't talk to her mother in almost three years."

In the living room, Delano turns the Rubik's Cube. He has solved the red face. I want to grab him and shake him, but I sit there beside him and wait until he has solved the green face before I take a deep breath and ask, "Delano, Miss Winsome says that you call Mummy from here. Is true?"

He slowly puts the cube into his pocket. "Yes, I call her. But I call collect. Is not all the time that she accept the call. So don't think me call her every night and talk to her."

"So you do have a phone number for her?"

"Yes, Stacey, but is not for calling her for stupidness!"

"Delano, what you mean by stupidness? You know I have not talked to her from she leave me at Auntie's house. Not one word. And she tell them she was coming back for me in two weeks. And you talk to her? What does she say about me?"

"We don't really talk about you."

I don't say anything, but my eyes fill with tears.

"Stacey, man. Don't bother with that! Is not like you think! She just talk to me about her garden and the weather and her flowers. And as soon as she get on the phone she say that she have to go. Long-distance phone calls are very, very expensive."

Even though I do not want to cry, the tears roll down my cheeks and onto my white uniform. I use my tie to wipe my face. I fold my arms and press my back into the arm of the couch. Delano is turning the Rubik's Cube again.

"All right, Stacey, you want me to call her now?"

I nod yes. He gets up from the couch and goes into his bedroom. He lifts the phone and dials the operator. He tells her he would like to make a collect call to Canada. Then he gives her a number that begins with a 514 area code. He waits. Then he hangs up.

"What happened? Delano, what happened? She's not there?"

"Stacey, me tell you already that is not like how you think. She is there, but she pick up the phone and say that she cannot accept the charges. Sometimes she accept, and sometimes she doesn't."

"Well, give me the number so me can try on me own, then."

"But you don't have no phone up at Paradise."

"No, but me can call collect from the phone booth on Church Street."

"Okay, me going to give you, but make sure you don't tell her that is me give it to you. She tell me not to give her phone number to any and anybody who ask for it."

I am not any and anybody, but I remain silent. I'm afraid if I say anything he will change his mind. He writes the number down on a loose folder leaf. I fold it eight times and put it in my knapsack. It is almost five thirty. I tell him I have to go.

"Okay, then." He tucks both hands into his jeans pockets. "Well, Daddy like you, so you can come anytime."

"You sure? You don't have to ask Uncle Charlie?"

"No, man. As long as you doing good in school, him will give you money. Him love when other children do well."

"Okay. Take care of yourself."

"Don't worry 'bout me, man. Everything cool."

"Okay."

On the way home I read and reread the ten digits over and over again. By the time I get to the bustle of downtown, I have committed the unfamiliar sequence to memory. And I am in Paradise when I realize I can say the number backward and out loud while thinking of something else. Now, no matter what happens to the piece of paper, my mother's phone number will always be in my head.

As a Bear Lying in Wait

The more lies I tell at school, the more I have to do to cover my tracks. I begin to preempt the follow-up questions to my stories and prepare my answers beforehand. I learn to pause as if I am thinking hard about the question and give answers that leave room for reinvention later.

One Friday, I decide that I am riding to Paradise with the Grawleys after school. When the final bell rings, Uncle Hartley is already parked at the gate. I am both nervous and excited as we make our way to the white pickup truck. If Auntie finds out that I am riding with people she does not know, she will kill me. The truck can only fit two adult passengers, but Natalia says three children fit easily. Her father is a tall white man with a full graying beard. He looks very stern in the face, but as soon as he sees me, he smiles.

"You must be Stacey. I hear you hitching a ride on the night train to Georgia. Welcome aboard!"

"Thank you, Mr. Grawley."

"No! No! No! We have no misters on this train. If you ride in my vehicle you are doomed to become family. I am Uncle Hartley to you and all of Natalia's friends. Ask Natalia. Everybody at Mount Alvernia Prep knows me as Uncle Hartley. Now, Toni-Ann, jump in so Miss Chin can squeeze in between the two of you."

As Natalia shuts the door, the strangest sensation washes over me. Packed in between the two girls in their father's truck, I feel like Stacey-ann Grawley. Uncle Hartley makes funny jokes all the way. "You sure you not making the car too heavy, Stacey? I feel like we are a little heavier than usual. You sure you didn't eat a rock for lunch today?"

A police car with the sirens wailing whizzes by. "Stacey, you didn't tell me you were on the run! But don't worry! I won't let them get you. Just duck, and I will floor the gas!"

Natalia and Toni-Ann are beside themselves with laughter. I don't know what to do with my red face. I sober up a little bit when we pass by my father's house. The long stairway doesn't look so long from inside the truck.

When we pass Blood Lane, I try not to look at the women standing in the road in their slips and brassieres. One of them is stark naked and bathing under the public standing pipe right there in the middle of the square. Children in dirty clothes wipe their runny noses on their bare arms. My face is hot and red. Uncle Hartley turns to me. "Which direction do we take to drop you off at your palace, Princess Stacey?"

I do not tell him that his truck could not drive the rocky path to my palace. "Just go up a little more, Uncle Hartley. Go way up, past Blood Lane, and leave me at that big house at the corner. I will get in trouble if my auntie sees me in this truck. I am not supposed to accept rides from people. I will walk the rest of the way, Uncle Hartley. Thanks for the ride home."

"That is very sensible advice from your aunt, man. I should just come and say hello to her. Maybe she would feel better if she saw my handsome countenance. Then it would be okay for you to ride with the girls in the evening, because she would know who we are."

A woman clears her throat and spits in the street.

"No, Uncle Hartley! I—I am just afraid that she will beat me. She doesn't like when people come to the house without me telling her before."

"Okay, Lady Chin, I will leave you to give her some warning. Maybe tomorrow evening, then?"

"Okay, maybe tomorrow."

The next day when he asks, I tell him to drop me by my father's gate. As I jump out of the van, I want to ask Uncle Hartley to wait for me, but I don't. I need Natalia to think I spend the whole evening visiting with my father, so I just open the door and say, "Thanks, Uncle Hartley. See you tomorrow, Natalia."

At the top of the steps I tap on the grille. From the top of the stairway, I can hear April squealing with laughter. I wish I were Uncle Desmond's child. Then I wouldn't be out here waiting on the steps like a stray dog.

Finally, Miss P. appears with an envelope. I wish I could go in and spend time inside the house like his real children. I sign in the right column, thank her, and promise myself that one day I am going to ask to use the bathroom or say I am thirsty—anything just so I can be inside the house. More than a month's worth of lunch money and taxi fare in hand, I walk to the bottom of the hill, where I flag down a taxi that takes me home to Paradise.

Everybody in the seventh grade wants to be Natalia's friend. The girls who have been to her house after school say she has the nicest things: a waterbed, a personal computer, wall-to-wall carpeting to match the peach on her walls. Parents encourage their daughters to cultivate a friendship with Natalia. I like to think my mother would also want me to have a friend like Natalia. But Auntie is so backward she can't even see how it could benefit me to develop a friendship with someone who is pretty and rich and popular.

It is getting harder and harder to refuse when Natalia asks me over to watch a movie or to swim or to do homework. At night I have dreams about living with her family. In the dreams we do everything together. And because I am no longer living in the squalor of Auntie's house, my pimples go away and I develop a beautiful figure too. Natalia and I look like twins and everyone tells us how beautiful we look walking downtown, holding hands, and smiling.

At home, every time I mention my friends at school, Auntie tells me that the only good company is the company of the Lord. I know that she will never give me permission. So one Friday morning, as I am going through the door, I tell Auntie that the debate team is meeting after school and I am thinking of joining. When she asks what time the meeting ends, I say I don't exactly know, but since the school has offered to pay part of the school fees of the students who make the team, I think it is a good idea to go. She grunts and tells me to make sure I am home before the sundown.

I know that Auntie would beat me to death if she found out that I told her such a baldfaced lie. But I am too excited to worry about that. That evening I climb into the truck and announce that my aunt has finally given me permission to go home with them. Uncle Hartley looks at me like he does not believe me. I look him dead in the eyes and ask if it is still okay for me to come along.

He smiles and says, "Hmm, I really don't know if that house can stand to have any more pretty girls in it, you know. Natalia and Toni-Ann blinding everybody as it is."

"Uncle Hartley! Is it okay or not?"

"It is fine, as long as your aunt really knows where you are."

"I asked her before I went to bed last night and then I reminded her this morning. She says she don't mind if I go, as long as I don't stay out too long."

"Okay, ma'am. I really would love to talk to your aunt. But if she is not up to that, then . . ."

Their driveway is longer and much more beautiful than my father's driveway. Trees line the pathway and there are plants everywhere. We enter through the side entrance. There is a separate room for doing laundry. The helper, Marcia, is dressed in a blue uniform. She smiles and waves at us as she stirs a pot. They have a very large living room that has peach carpet all over the floor. There are big comfortable couches and a big TV. Then there is a second living room with very expensive furniture in it. Outside, I can see a big satellite dish and *their very own* swimming pool.

Uncle Hartley says all hands have to be washed before we can have any dinner. Natalia and Toni-Ann have their own bathroom. The shower curtain is clear plastic with little yellow ducks all over it. Their brother, Mark, has his own bathroom too. And Natalia tells me that there is another bathroom in her parents' room, and another in the den.

"Natalia, what is a den?"

"Well, everybody in the family has their own bedroom, and then there is an extra bedroom, which guests sleep in, or a room where we can just relax and chill—that is what we call a den."

"Oh, okay."

Uncle Hartley has a satellite dish, so we can watch American TV. Dinner is served on dinner trays and we watch *Love Connection* while we eat. I wonder if I will ever have a Love Connection. As it is, I don't even have one person who I can say loves me, except maybe Grandma. But she is so far away.

Uncle Hartley rouses the girls and ushers us off to do homework. I marvel that everybody in the house has a bedroom. After homework I watch CNN with Uncle Hartley while the girls shower. I like being at Natalia's house. I like watching the American news in a large clean living room with an easy chair and remote controls for turning up the volume. I wish I could live here forever. I wish I never had to go back home.

"Stacey, what is wrong with you? Why are you crying?"

I don't realize that my eyes are filled with tears. I stuff a piece of pork into my mouth and quickly mutter something about the food being extra spicy. I take my tray to the kitchen. Then I get my things and tell everyone that it is time for me to go home. When Natalia presses me to call Auntie to ask if I can spend the night, my heart expands and contracts at the same time. But I shake my head no and say very loudly and firmly, "Thank you, but we don't have a phone. Plus, I really like to sleep in my own room at night. I really want to just go home now."

I hoist my backpack onto my shoulders and wave good-bye. My legs feel like lead as I make my way down the asphalt path to the gate. I try my best not to look behind me. But I can't help thinking that the long, beautiful driveway is even longer when you are walking.

I hate waking up on the weekend in Paradise Crescent. At night, I can close my eyes and pretend that I am in Montreal. In my dreams I speak fluent French. My mother takes us to restaurants. I have Cheerios for breakfast and we have coats on because it is so cold. In the morning, it is hard to dream with the dirty wooden walls staring back at me.

Aunt June's house in Bethel Town had wooden louvers: brown cedar slats separated by thin white strips of light with manners enough to creep quietly and slowly into the room. Not so in Paradise, where, as soon as the sun comes up, the harsh light of morning is immediately in my eyes.

On Saturdays, Auntie wakes us early. The whole day is filled with cleaning the living room floor, dusting the furniture, and washing all my clothes and my big smelly white sheet. When the washing is done, I pick up garbage and sweep the yard. Then I burn the garbage in the dump behind the house. If it is my turn, I have to cook dinner. By nightfall I am so tired I don't feel like bathing. I only have time to drag the sheet from the line, wrap myself in it, and fall into bed.

But Sunday mornings are the hardest.

Sunday is a day that begs the body to stay asleep. And I am already tired from the day before. The music on the radio is soft and slow. The shops are all closed and people speak in quieter tones. At dawn, the coolest hours of the day, all I want to do is snuggle down under the covers. But no, I have to get up to catch Sunday school. At twelve years old, I know I am too old for things like Sunday school. On Sundays I wake up already annoyed with the day ahead.

"Stacey! Get up, is time for you to go to church. Stacey, is time for you to wake up! Gal, get up out that bed before I throw cold water 'pon you!" It is not even seven o'clock yet, and Auntie is already shouting from the veranda. I lie there, covered from head to toe, pretending I am asleep. Before long she is in the room pulling the sheet off me. She stands there until I sit up. She drops the sheet on the floor. "I don't know who in them right mind would put that thing over themself at night. You really come from that nasty China breed that don't give a damn about soap and water."

I am not in the mood to listen this morning. I pick up the sheet and roll it into a bundle. "Please excuse me, Auntie. I think it is time for me to go to the bathroom now."

"Put that thing down." When I don't drop it immediately, she grabs it and tosses it back on the floor. "I said to leave it there. I want everybody to step over it when them go to bathe. Maybe shame will make you keep your things clean. Only God knows how one little girl can smell so stink!"

I wish she would just shut up and leave me alone. I drop the rolled-up sheet by the bedside.

"And make sure this evening when you come home from church you wash that sheet and every piece of your clothes clean, clean, clean."

"Yes, Auntie."

The toilet is broken again. I peel off my T-shirt and shorts. Auntie is right. My clothes do smell like wet dog. I pee in the tub, because I am too lazy to fill the basin and flush. The water is cold, so I just wash the "necessaries" and quickly drag on clean panties. I wish it were Monday and I was going to school instead of church. I have to figure out a way to go to Natalia's every evening.

Auntie's voice pulls me back to reality. "Stacey, is what you waiting on to leave the house? Is almost eight o'clock already!"

I pull my yellow dress over my head and slip into my white heels. I hate going to Sunday school. I hate heels. And the leather is chipped and peeling from walking the rocky path leading away from the house. Auntie is outside humming one of the Sunday school songs.

I have a great big wonderful God
I have a great big wonderful God
A God that's always victorious, always watching over us
A great big wonderful God

The songs are all so stupid. And the miraculous stories are even worse. Everything about church is beginning to feel very strange. Most of the stories we read in Sunday school are about telling the truth. First we read Bible passages aloud. Then we answer questions about them. The person who gets the most right answers is seen as having a deep understanding of God as truth. The winner also gets to take home a New Testament Bible or a bookmark with a Bible verse printed on it. I usually answer the most questions correctly. But I always want to tell them that the winner of their truth-telling championship is the biggest liar in Montego Bay. And that, often, I lie about what I think the real answers are so I can get the prize that I don't really want. I am really beginning to loathe coming to this church.

And I don't like the way Pastor Gentles keeps looking at me.

It is the first Sunday of the month, so I have to wait for Auntie while she takes Communion. Glen stays inside with her. I am not baptized yet, so I cannot take Communion. I tell her I am going to wait outside and she looks at me like she wants to hit me, but she just grabs Glen's hand and moves closer to the front. I make my way to the wall outside, but the sun is too hot. So I steal into the vestry. I hear the droning voice of the congregation singing. They sound like a thousand bees. Pastor Gentles delivers the benediction and the whole church says, "Amen!"

I know it will take Auntie a while to get out. She has to ask everybody how is the knee and did the pressure go down before she is ready to go home. I lie down on the table and pull my knees up to my chest. My dress falls away from my legs and my bottom. I am enjoying the freedom of my almost nakedness in God's holy vestry so much I do not hear the door open. I look up to see Pastor Gentles watching me from the doorway. He motions for me to be quiet as he closes the door behind him. He slides the lock closed. I force myself to sit up slowly. Inside my head I am humming "Rock of Ages." He walks right up to me and tells me he has been waiting to tell me something for quite a while now. I fiddle with my Bible and hymnal and straighten my dress.

I hold my breath and wait for him to continue.

His palm on my head is very gentle. "Stacey, the Lord has laid it upon my heart to tell you that he sees promise in you. He has blessed you with a pleasing countenance so you can serve him well. Your body is the body of the Lord! You must learn to surrender it to him. That is why you are not baptized yet. You do not know how to surrender. Let me show you how . . ." He puts his hands on my head and slides them down my back. Then he grabs me by the shoulders and pulls me to him. His breath smells like sour milk. The scent turns my stomach. He pushes me back and places his hands on my breasts. "Praise be to God, little sister! You have the most glorious breasts I have ever seen on a girl your size!"

Suddenly something about him seems small and weak. I use all my strength to push him away from me. My heart is pounding, but I am not afraid of him. I pick up the hymnal and point it at him. "Pastor Gentles, if you ever come near me again, I will tell everybody what you just do! And I will even tell them things that you never do! I will say all kind of other things! You should be ashamed of yourself. You are a pastor. You should be different, but instead you just want to do the same things like every other man in the world. You just want to touch people how you want to touch them, and that is not right. I hope you repent before God strike you and send you straight to hell!"

He backs away and straightens his jacket before he unlocks the door and leaves the room.

When I get home that evening, I tell Auntie I don't want to go to church anymore, but she says as long as I live under her roof, I have to do as she says. "*As for me and my house, we will serve the Lord,* Stacey. It is there in the Bible. If you read it more often you would know that the church is the best place for the young and wayward. It is the only place that going to keep you safe from the dark desires of that young flesh." I want to tell her about what happened in the vestry, but I already know she would find some way to make it my fault.

The next morning no one has to wake me for school. As soon as the sun rises I roll out of bed and head to the shower. I can't move fast enough to get to school so I can hear about Natalia's weekend. I wish I could tell her about Pastor Gentles's sour-milk breath, but I wouldn't know how to say something like that. And since nothing actually happened to me in there, there's actually nothing for me to tell.

Let Him Kiss Me . . .

Miss Hall, my history teacher, asks when Columbus discovered the West Indies. My hand shoots up. When no one else volunteers, Miss Hall sighs and points to me. I am confident in my answer. "Miss Hall, Columbus did not discover Jamaica. When he landed here, people were living here already. The only reason they not right here in the class is that the Spaniards killed them."

"Staceyann Chin, I did not ask for an essay, only a date. Whatever your opinions are about what happened, the first order of history is about dates. So do you know when he *landed* here or not?"

"In 1494, miss."

"Thank you very much, ma'am."

"You are welcome, miss."

Miss Hall walks to my desk, puts her hand on my shoulder, and says, "You know, Staceyann, you would be the perfect student if you were not such a performer. It is a good thing you are bright and focused, otherwise you would be a sore on the backside of this school."

Her voice is firm, but her hands are kind on my shoulder. I like Miss Hall. She says what she thinks and lets me know that she is not being mean to me. She uses her ruler to gently tap me on the head before she smiles and gets back to the lesson.

After school I try my best not to go straight home. Sometimes I stop at my father's store to see April. One evening I actually go home with her for dinner. I chew a mouthful of rice and peas and wonder what my father is having for dinner upstairs. My little brother, Ruel, dashes in and out. I want to talk to him, but I don't think he would talk me, so I just sit there and chew while he gets his juice and leaves.

Most evenings I end up at Natalia's. After dinner and homework, Uncle Hartley gives us permission to swim. I don't have a bathing suit, so I have to wear my PE clothes in the pool. I think I look stupid swimming in shorts, but Natalia says not to worry, I look fine. I spend a good part of the evening holding up my shorts because whenever I move too quickly they slip down. And the water makes the white T-shirt transparent and causes it to stick to my chest. I ask Natalia if she thinks I am too naked. But she says I should relax and enjoy being in the water.

Natalia's brother, Mark, jumps in. It feels a little funny to be so close to a boy with my shorts in danger of falling down, but I remind myself that he is not Andy or Shappy. I am having so much fun splashing and ducking underwater that I stop pulling at the shirt sticking to my breasts. Suddenly Mark points to my chest, laughing and shouting, "Stacey, you don't see your breasts making a public announcement?"

I am so shocked I grab my towel and run to the bathroom. I know that Mark did not mean anything by it, but I want to die from embarrassment. I cover my head with the towel and lie on the floor crying. Natalia knocks softly before she pushes the door open. She asks if she can sit on the floor next to me. When I nod, she squats and squeezes into the space between the bath and the toilet with me. My T-shirt is suddenly cold and heavy against my skin. I remember Mark's laughter and bury my face into the towel again, sobbing.

"Cho, man, Stacey, Mark was only making a stupid little joke." Natalia's voice is soft and cajoling.

I wish I could tell her about Shappy and Andy. But Natalia's life is perfect and there is nobody in her house trying to have sex with her. She would never understand anything about my life. I wish she would just shut up and leave me alone. She strokes my hair and tells me that Mark feels bad for embarrassing me.

I am not crying anymore, but I am still very sore. "Well, Natalia, you should tell your brother that he shouldn't make jokes about things that him don't know about."

"I know, I know, Stace, but you know boys. Them just stupid sometimes."

She is sitting so close to me the hairs on her legs brush my thighs. I hug my knees to my chest and rock back and forth on my haunches. "Natalia, I know you don't understand, but I just wish I had a real bathing suit. That way your stupid brother don't have to see my nipples when I am in the pool."

Her hand is warm on my knee. "I know, Stacey, I know."

"Natalia."

"Yeah?"

"You ever feel like you don't like boys very much?"

"Yeah, man. Especially when them being stupid and them thinking that them sooo cool."

"Yeah. Like when them think them being slick by touching you and pretending it was a mistake!"

Natalia bursts out laughing. "Exactly! Exactly!"

"Talia, sometimes I wish I could just forget about boys altogether and just get married to a woman when I get big!"

Natalia is laughing hard and holding her stomach. I don't think it is that funny, but I laugh out loud too. "Can you imagine, Tal? You and me and the priest saying, 'I now pronounce you *woman and wife*!'"

"Stacey, stop! Stop! You going to make me laugh until me dead in here!"

Natalia gets up from the floor and, still laughing, limps away.

Days later I hear her laughing and telling the joke on the phone: "That girl is so weird sometimes. She says the most hilarious things."

I can tell who is on the other line by how loudly she talks. When it is a boy she likes, she whispers. I listen to her lowered voice and I draw hearts in my notebook. I wonder why she lets me come over so much. I close the book when she hangs up.

"Stace, guess who I just talked to! Carl Kingsley!"

"Oh, yeah? What's his claim to fame now?"

She falls back on the bed and stares up at the ceiling. "He says that he likes my eyes. And my hair. And my eyebrows."

"Your eyebrows? That is so stupid! So anyway, what that mean? That him want to love you and marry you and give you two little white children with perfect eyebrows?"

"I'm serious, Stacey. He just asked me to be his girlfriend."

"Sorry, Tal. I was only joking. So how many boys like you now? Seven?"

"I think it's eight or nine now, but"—she clutches her chest and sighs— "it really doesn't matter in light of the way I feel about Carl Kingsley.

You know what I mean, Stacey? I think I want to be his *wife*! You think I should say yes?"

I suck my teeth and roll off the bed. Natalia pokes me with her toe. "What happen to you now, Miss Miserable?"

"Nutten. I guess I don't know nutten about no boys. None of them ever like me because I am ugly."

"Staceyann Chin, you are not ugly! And what happen to you all of a sudden? You never care if no boys like you before!"

"Yes, I do. I want somebody to like me too. But nobody ever will! Because my face is shaped funny and my forehead is big and flat at the same time. And I have pimples—lots and lots of pimples. My teeth stick out of my head like scissors. And my feet are like duck feet and my legs are too skinny. And look at my breasts! They are much too big for my body!"

Natalia gets down on the floor beside me. She is so close I can smell her strawberry-scented body lotion. "Stacey, I have no idea what you are talking about! I mean, you're not like Miss Jamaica or anything, but you are a nice-looking girl. You have a nice body and you are very bright. And you know more big words than anybody I know."

"So you think that I am pretty, then?"

"I don't see a thing wrong with how you look."

A warmth creeps into my belly. Still, it worries me that I am twelve years old and not one boy has told me that he likes me.

I tell Nellie, who is my only friend at church, that I think I should get a boyfriend. Nellie already has a very cute boyfriend, Garry, who loves her very much and has told her that he wants to marry her. I worry that I will die without ever experiencing true love. Nellie says I have nothing to worry about, but I know that it isn't easy to make anyone fall in love with you when you have acne. She suggests we ask Garry's younger brother, Troy, who is not as good-looking, if he wants to be my boyfriend. I am too afraid he will say no. But she goes ahead and asks him if he likes me anyway. When she comes back, she is all giggles and good news. Troy likes me very much and has asked Nellie to ask me if I want to be his girlfriend. She says I have to give her an answer to take back to him by the end of the service.

During the reading of the first psalm I ask myself if I could marry somebody with such skinny legs. I stare hard at him and wonder how I would kiss him with that long nose in the way. Just before the benediction he turns and smiles at me. He's not as handsome as his brother, but he does have a nice smile. I could do worse than Troy for a boyfriend. Plus no one else has expressed any interest in me. I tell Nellie to tell him yes.

From behind the fence at school I watch him playing soccer with the other boys. His skinny frame moves as quick as lightning as he makes a beeline for the goal. And he is one of the fastest boys on the Cornwall College track team. I wonder if he knows Delano. Troy likes to laugh and make jokes all the time. Being with him makes me feel like I am like everyone else. I write little notes to him and I hurry to Sunday school so I can see him before the service begins. I can't talk to him during Wednesday-night prayer meetings, but I still go with Auntie so I can look at him from my pew.

Nellie says I should start coming to young people's meeting on Saturdays. "Our group leader, James, is here on Saturday and he is not very strict, so you can really get to talk to Troy."

Auntie is pleased to see me take an interest in church. "Yes, of course you can go to youth meeting. You can always go to anything, as long as it have to do with the Lord."

The elders do not come to youth meetings, so the young people get there early to sit around and talk. And after the meeting we sit on the wall surrounding the church. Troy sits beside me. I don't know how I know, but the way he is sitting on the wall and not saying anything to me makes me feel like he wants me to keep sitting beside him. We sit there until it is time to go home.

On Monday I inform Sandy that I have a boyfriend.

At first she is shocked and delighted. "What? Him cute? You can't have a boyfriend that is not cute!" Then she is worried. "Well, you better be careful with them boys. I hear them always want you to have sex with them."

I tell her that she doesn't have to worry about that. Troy is a good Christian boy who would never think of asking me such a thing. I do not tell Natalia my news at school. I want to be able to tell her everything in private without any interruption. I wait until we are finished with homework and dinner. When the plates are in the sink, I usher Natalia into her bedroom. "Talia, I think I have a boyfriend."

"Stacey, what you mean, you think? Is either you have one or you don't!"

"Okay, okay. I have a boyfriend."

"Is he cute? Like Carl?"

I don't want to talk about Carl, but I don't know how to say that to Natalia. "No, he's just okay-looking."

"Oh, okay. Did I tell you that Carl called three times yesterday and two times on Saturday?"

I really wish she would just shut up about Carl. I can't see what she sees in him. His grades are bad and he uses words incorrectly.

She places her hand over her heart and sighs. "And then he came over here last night and I kissed him. You kiss your boyfriend yet?"

Something turns in my stomach. "Yes, man! I kiss him all the time!" I decide that I have to kiss Troy. I am disappointed that Natalia does not ask more questions about him.

The next week at youth meeting I tell Nellie to tell Troy that he can kiss me. All during the program I wonder what I am going to do during the kiss. I wish I had asked Natalia to tell me exactly what she did when Carl kissed her. Then I would know what to do. Thinking about Carl and Natalia makes me angry, so I walk over to the wall and sit with my legs very close to Troy's. He smiles nervously and clears his throat. "Well, Stacey, you know that we have been girlfriend and boyfriend for one week now. I think it's time we make something serious of it."

He scoots closer and takes me by the arm. He is a little rough, and I really do not want him to kiss me, but I don't know what to say to stop him. And I feel bad that he doesn't know that I am pretending to be in love with him. His face moves closer and closer to mine until his eyes are so close they look like two big bug-eyes. He puckers his lips and I do the same. Suddenly he opens his mouth and almost swallows my nose. He sucks on my lower face for what feels like a million years. While I wait for him to finish, I think of ways to make the kiss sound more exciting when I tell Natalia about it. His lips make a smacking noise when he finally pulls them off mine.

The whole event is so wet and cold I wonder why everybody makes such a fuss. Troy chews on a blade of grass as he tells me that he is willing to kiss me anytime I want. All I have to do is let him know when. The way he says it lets me know that he has not even considered that I may not want him to. I wish I could just tell him how I really feel about kissing him. I wish I could tell Natalia how I feel about Carl. I wish I could just tell everybody how I feel about everything. I am tired of pretending. But I am too afraid that no one will like me without the parts of me I have worked so hard to make up.

You Shall Have Treasure

The daffodil-printed one-piece bathing suit is a little baggy in the crotch, but my body looks good in it. It is hard to believe the girl in the mirror is me. I wish I had long straight hair so I could let it all out and shake it like the women on TV. I settle for adjusting the yellow straps and tucking in the stray pubic hairs poking out from the sides.

"How me look, Elisha? It make me skin look darker, don't it?"

"Lawd, Stacey, it look sooo nice. Me can't believe is you that look so boasty in a French-cut bath-suit!"

"Elisha, I know it look nice, but it make me skin look any darker too, eh?"

"Not really. You still look white to me. But what you want to look Black for? You don't know that Black people don't really get ahead in life."

"Elisha, stop that old naygar talk! I think all that Black people and white people foolishness is just mouth talk! And Natasha say it is good for you to look like you have a tan. Rich people go to the beach to get a tan."

"You can think anything you want think, Stacey. Me don't know nutten 'bout no tan. But me know what me know. Why you think Auntie don't like you?"

"Because me back-talk her too much. And because me mother not sending no money come from Canada."

"No, I don't think is just that! I think is because she and the rest of we not white like you and your friends and your brother!"

"Elisha, how much time I must tell you? I am not white! I am *half*-Chinese!"

"White, Chinese, Syrian—is the same thing! You not Black like we.

You can get ahead in life. The rest of we just have to stay right here till we dead."

I look away to avoid Elisha's gaze. From the small wood frame the loops glow golden against my naked shoulders. I untie the bows and make them tighter. I can see my nipples pushing at the stretchy fabric.

"Elisha, the bosom part good, eh? Not too loose, not too tight, like them did measure me for it."

The bath-suit is truly the prettiest thing I have ever owned. I carefully retie the strings in long loopy bows on top of my shoulders.

The body is a cool dark blue. Bright yellow daffodils hold hands in a ring around my waist. Matching yellow piping traces the scooped neck-line to become the straps. The legs are cut higher than anything I have ever worn before.

"So, you don't think it make my breast them look funny?"

"No, man, you look just like a model in a magazine. Like you rich and have nuff white people friend. Everybody go think you look good at Porto Seco Beach."

"Yes. Is true. My breast them look smooth and sexy fi true. You think Troy will like it?"

"Yes, man. Him will really like it, especially how the breast part look nice and smooth!"

I usually dislike the feel of the fleshy stones of my bosoms brushing up against my loose T-shirt, but in the vise of the spandex glove, both of them sit upright and immobile. I feel like the bath-suit is holding every part of me together.

But the biggest problem with breasts is men. Men liked to pinch breasts. And it seems like every man in Paradise wants to pinch mine: Andy, Shappy, Pastor Gentles—no matter how I cover them, no matter how I position my body, some man finds a way to pinch a nipple when I walk by. And having breasts this big makes me feel bigger than thirteen years old. But in this bath-suit, in this mirror, the breasts on my chest look sort of normal. Not like breasts that everybody feels they have the right to touch.

I can only see the top half of me in the dresser mirror. To see my lower half I have to climb up on the bed and then stoop down. Cross-eyed and crouching, I can barely see the tops of my thighs, but my stomach is flat and my bottom looks nice and round.

"So when you going to tell Mama that you get a new bath-suit?"

"Elisha, the bath-suit isn't really new. It used to belong to Natalia. She was very sad to part with it too. It was her favorite one. But she say it would be wrong to keep it when it don't even cover her breasts anymore. Personally, I think she shame that I was swimming in her pool in my PE shorts every week. She was very nice about it, though. She says she won't tell anybody that is she who give it to me."

I know Auntie would not like it if she knew I was taking things from other people like I was in the almshouse. I was just going to use it at Natalia's, but the youth group at church is going to Porto Seco Beach next Saturday, and all the young people have real bath-suits—not sports shorts or cut-off pants or dresses tied up around the waist.

I wish I could just hide it and wear it on the trip, but Auntie might hear that I was in a fancy bath-suit and kill me for wearing it without her permission. If I show it to her she might make me throw it away. I can't lose this bath-suit. It is the nicest piece of clothing I own.

"Elisha, can you check to make sure me bottom cover up good?"

"Yes, man, everything look good. All of your bottom is inside it. Just go on and show it to her. It fit you so good, she must bound fi like it!"

"Okay. All right, then." I take a deep breath and step out onto the veranda.

"Auntie, look at me!"

"But Jesus Chr—is what that you have on?"

"Is a bath-suit, Auntie! You don't like it?"

"That color don't fit your complexion. You skin too white fi wear flowers. And why the bottom so tight-up under you crotches?"

"Is so the style go, Auntie! But I can fix it."

I hook my fingers under the elastic and pull hard until the tops of my thighs are covered. The straps bite into my shoulders and my breasts strain against the blue spandex.

"That suit look like the dressmaker run out of cloth before them finish. You too big for it and your breast pushing out like you is a old Jezebel whore! Is where you get it from, poorhouse?"

"No, ma'am, is Natalia give it to me. It cannot fit her anymore."

Auntie's face hardens into an unreadable mask. She pushes her right foot back and forth across the shiny red floor.

Without expression, she asks, "Stacey, is beg you go up to Mango Walk to beg that girl for her clothes?"

"No, ma'am, is she just give it to me. I never ask her anything."

Auntie finishes her cup of fever-grass tea and puts the cup on the rail. "Uh-huh. Go inside and get the belt."

"But, Auntie, I swear to God in heaven that I never ask her—"

"Stacey, stop taking the Lord's name in vain and go get the belt."

"Auntie, you never listen to anything I tell you. Is better if I did tell you a lie! No matter what I tell you, you always think is a lie!"

"Stacey, stop the talking and go and get the belt. Because not even God above can hold me responsible fi anything that happen to you if I have to go get it meself."

I bite my lips and fold my arms across my chest.

"You hear what I just say to you, little girl?"

"Yes, Auntie. Can I go take off this first?"

"No! Is you did want to wear it. Keep it on. Just bring the belt and come."

I enter the darkness of Auntie's room and wait for my eyes to adjust. The sheets on the bed are the same color as the bath-suit. I walk around the barrel of canned food and move Auntie's black handbag out of the way. The coins in the bottom jingle. The belt hangs ominously from a nail by the window. I reach up, unhook it, rub the smooth length with my thumb, and inhale the slightly greasy sheen.

I walk back to the veranda. Auntie takes the leather strap and wraps one end like a bandage around her palm.

Leather and skin meet and my skin tightens around my whole body.

Whack!

"How many times I must tell you?"

Whack!

"Little girls should not beg anybody for anything!"

I tell myself, *I will not cry.* Whack! But the tears come anyway. Whack!

"You is not a leggo beast in a pasture!"

Whack!

"You are not living inside no poorhouse!"

Whack!

"We are not beggars under this roof!"

Whack!

I will not give her the satisfaction of screaming. Whack!

"What is wrong with you, eh, Stacey? Why you so bloody stubborn?"

A rumble begins in my belly.

Whack! Whack! Whack!

"Why when you leave here you must go and beg people things?"

It pushes up from my insides and toward my throat.

"You want me tie you up like that dirty dog under the house?"

Whack! Whack! Whack! Whack! Whack!

"No! Please. No! Jesus Christ! Help me, God! Murder! Help! Father God! Jesus, no!"

I am not aware that the sounds are coming out of me. I only start to make sense of them when I hear them circling above me.

"Stop, Auntie! Stop now! I'm going to give her back the bath-suit! Just stop now. Please, I beg you, stop hitting me now."

Whack! Whack! Whack!

"Now you only have mouth fi bawl out, eh?"

Whack!

"Me tired fi tell you!" Whack! "You is not a big woman!" Whack! "You is a child!"

Whack!

"No! No, Auntie, no! Stop! Please, please, please don't hit me any-more . . ."

I am curled into myself on the floor. There is no other sound in the room but my sobbing. The shiny new bath-suit is covered with red floor polish and dust.

Auntie winds the belt into a tight leather roll and hands it to me.

"Get up from that floor and go put this back where you find it. And go and take off that thing. Girl children not supposed to wear bikini bath-suit."

"Auntie, is not a bikini!"

"What you saying to me?"

"A bikini has two parts. This bath-suit is a one-piece, so is not a bikini."

"That mouth of yours is what go lead you straight into hell. Mark this day as the day I tell you that! Now get out me sight before I change my mind and give you something to talk about! And make sure you put that thing in the garbage!"

"But, Auntie, me don't have another bath-suit and the beach trip is tomorrow."

"I couldn't give a dyam 'bout that. Wear the pants that you get from Diana."

I replace the belt on its hook and brush past Auntie on my way back to our room. When I am well outside of her reach I mutter under my breath, "Well, I just won't go, then."

"What you say? Don't make me come in that room after you! If you know what is good for you, you would keep your stinking mouth shut!"

I peel the spandex off my bruised skin, fold the bath-suit into the tightest ball I can manage, and stuff it back into my clothes bag.

"Stacey, you throw away that thing yet?"

"Yes, ma'am. I throw it in the garbage heap over the fence."

"Good. Now get up and go find something to do."

"Yes, ma'am."

Elisha says, "Stacey, if you wear the bathing suit on at Porto Seco tomorrow, I won't say anything to anybody."

"I know, Elisha. But is not you one will see me. And Auntie might do worse to me if she hear that me wear the thing anyway."

"So what you going to wear, then?"

"I going wear what I always wear when me go to the beach. It don't matter what other people say. If them don't like me because of some stupid bath-suit, then them shouldn't be me friend anyway."

"Stacey, me really sorry you not going get fi wear it tomorrow. It really did look nice 'pon you."

"Elisha, you don't remember how it did make my breast look funny? As a matter of fact, I like the shorts better than that tight-up bath-suit. I probably woulda never wear it, make everybody see me on decent Porto Seco Beach looking like a Jezebel whore!"

I go to close the chicken coops. It is night already and all the fowls are inside their cages. I shut each cage and wonder why the stupid chickens come back to the coops every night.

The Sins of the Father

I am fourteen years old and Auntie still spends every waking hour telling me what to do: when to sit, when to eat, when to read, when to speak. And even when I do as she says, it is never good enough to please her. I am tired of trying to stay out of her way. She is like a scratched record. And because my life at home is such a big secret, I have to pretend that I am not going crazy living under her roof.

For the first project in the ninth grade, our English teacher, Miss Ritgard, gives us the choice between keeping a private journal and summarizing the journal of someone significant in history. I choose to write down my own thoughts. What appeals to me most about the journal is that no one is allowed to read what we write, and we won't be penalized for anything we write, no matter how offensive or controversial. I use a brand-new notebook as my journal.

In my first entry, I write just basic information, my mother's name, my father's name, and what I know about them. In the second, I scribble a two-page rant about Auntie. I write down how much I hate her and how much I hope she will die. Every day I write something. After a few days I begin to write down things I would never say out loud to anyone. I confess how much I hate kissing Troy. As soon as I get home in the evenings I reread the journal from cover to cover and add more.

October 19, 1987
   Dear Diary,
Today I went to visit Delano. He wasn't there, but his father, who I call Uncle Charlie, was home. He gave me money and told me that I was very pretty and

bright and he wouldn't be surprised if I got very far in life. Sometimes I wonder why Uncle Charlie gives me all this money, but I never ask him and he never says anything.
    Yours truly,
      Staceyann

At night I sleep with it under my pillow. During the day I wrap it in my sheet and stuff it under the bed. By the middle of the notebook I am writing how I feel about everything and everybody, but most of the journal is about Natalia.

October 21, 1987
    Dear Diary,
Today Natalia came to school with a new haircut. I wish I had a hairdresser for a mother. Then I could get my hair done every week and look as stunning as Natalia. She is definitely the most beautiful girl at Mount Alvernia High School. And I am very lucky to be able to say she is one of my closest friends. I wish Natalia were a boy.
    I really wish there was a boy I liked that was half as wonderful as Natalia. Then I might consider getting married and having sex and giving him a baby.
    Until next time,
      Staceyann Chin

On Friday, the thirtieth, I come home and the journal is missing. I hope with all my heart that Shappy or Elisha or Glen has taken it. But my stomach sinks when Auntie tells me to change out of my uniform and come to her on the veranda. It takes me forever to unbutton the white tunic and put on my house clothes. She already has the belt in her hand when I get there.

"So you want a baby, eh?"

"No, ma'am."

"Shut up your mouth and stop tell lie! I read what you write with me own two eyes. You can mind baby?"

I hang my head and button my lips.

"Answer me when I talk to you! You know how to mind baby? You know how much money it take to look after a baby? Me think you did have more sense than that! You don't even have the good sense God give the fowl out a door. You can hardly take care of yourself. That sheet you have under the bed stink like the dog under the house. What you going to do with a baby? Answer me! What you was going to do with a baby? Live here?"

My mouth opens of its own accord. "Auntie, I never write that I want a baby! I wrote down what conditions I would have to have before I would *consider* having a baby! That is very different from actually wanting a baby. If you just read the thing closely you would see the difference!"

Auntie gets up from her chair and grabs me by the front of my dress. "As God is my witness, I cannot take any more!"

She raises the belt and the blows begin. I do not utter a sound. I stand completely still until she is finished.

"Now go inside and get that dirty sheet and wash it!"

"Auntie, could you please give me my journal? I need it for English class at school."

"You will have to write another one. That is not fit to give to any teacher!"

"So what you do with it?"

"Get out of me face and don't question me! If I was you, I would start making up a new one so you don't get into trouble at school. And please to bring it to me so me can see what you write."

"That is not a journal if you read it. It supposed to be private. Miss Ritgard says that nobody is supposed to read it."

"Stacey, if you want another beating, just stay right there and keep working you mouth."

I head to the bedroom to get another notebook. I do not have a new one, so I tear the used leaves from my Spanish book and write three new entries. I know the handwriting is sloppy, but I don't care.

October 7, 1987

My name is Staceyann Chin. I am fourteen years old and I live in Paradise Crescent with my grandaunt and her six children. Her granddaughter Elisha lives here too. She is 11 years old.

October 9, 1987

I go to Mount Alvernia High School. I am in grade 9. I have one brother. He lives in Mount Salem. I am five feet two inches tall. I like to read. I go to Albionview Baptist Church. I was born in a small rural district called Lottery.

October 15, 1987

My favorite subject in school is English literature. My second favorite is English language. I also do very well in mathematics and science. In ten years I think I will be grown up with a good job. I am not quite sure what I will be but I know I will be able to take care of myself.

Auntie reads the entries and tosses the book back to me. "That is much better than the foolishness you write before. The writing look like crab toe, but is your business that, not mine."

I do not add any entries before Miss Ritgard collects the journals. She takes one look at the first entry and tells me my handwriting is trash. She tells the whole class that my penmanship is not even worth the grade for effort.

"Staceyann Chin, I wonder if you even try when you write anything down. Your answers are always correct and the grammar is good, but all of that is of no consequence if no one can read it! Come and take it and write the entries again. And this time make sure the words are legible."

"Miss Ritgard, I thought we would get a grade just for doing it. I did it. It doesn't matter how the writing is if you weren't going to read it!"

"Bring the journal to me! Bring it here this instant!"

When I bring it to her she tears out the entries, folds the pages into halves, and throws them in the garbage.

I walk up to her desk and snatch my book from her. "Miss Ritgard, you have no right to throw my things away like that!"

I am so angry I want to hit her. But I don't want to be expelled, so I pick up her folder, rip out five pages, and throw them on top of the pile of papers that used to be my homework. She tells me to sit at the back of the class until the end of the session. Then she walks me to the office and reports the incident to Sister Joan Claire. Sister Joan Claire pokes her head out of her office and invites me in.

"Sit down on that chair, young lady."

I sit and look at the small round face in front of mine. Very quietly, she asks me why I have destroyed Miss Ritgard's property. I tell her everything about the journal, including the fact that I had written it once before. "Miss Ritgard said that no one was supposed to read it. She said that we could write anything we wanted. But my auntie found it, took it, and then beat me because of what I wrote."

I am crying so hard Sister Joan Claire gets up from her chair and brings me some tissue to wipe my face. The tissue is in shreds by the time I am finished.

". . . and my mother run gone leave me, Sister, and my father don't want to have anything to do with me! And my brother goes to school right across the street and I never see him unless I go to look for him—and everything I do is wrong and everybody just want to take advantage of me!"

I am hanging off the side of the chair and weeping.

"Come on, Staceyann! It cannot be all that bad. You are in school and doing very well. It is only a matter of time before you get out of the situation you are in."

She leaves her side of the desk to come and hug me.

"Child! Child! God is not sleeping. He makes a way for all his creatures. You just have to have a plan of action and some faith."

When I am quiet she tells me to go into her private bathroom to wash my face. When I get back she tells me to go back to class.

"But you must pass by the staff-room and apologize to Miss Ritgard. Whatever the problems you may be experiencing, that is not the way to solve them. And when you are finished saying your regrets, please ask her to come and see me when she has a moment."

Miss Ritgard is nicer to me after that. But she writes a bad comment on my report card at the end of that term: *Staceyann is a student with unimaginable potential, but she is rude and has little concept of boundaries. She has miles to go with reference to good manners.*

Auntie reads the comment and is livid. She asks me to explain. I stand there, lips buttoned and arms folded across my chest.

"Stacey, I am talking to you! Please to answer me when I ask you a question! Why the teacher write that you don't have any manners?"

I sigh and shift the position of my feet. I do not care anymore. Everything I say is rude and everything I do is wrong. I stare back at her and wait for her to finish.

Auntie shakes her head and points a finger at me. "You know, Stacey, you really getting too big for your bloomers! I don't know what else to do with you. What you need is a strong man-voice. A man could make you listen! And if you still refuse to behave, well, he would have the strength to cut you ass for you!"

I roll my eyes and sigh again.

"Stop blowing down yourself when I talk to you!"

"Auntie, I am not blowing down myself on you! I am just breathing. Just like every normal person in the world!" I sigh again.

"Stacey, I am warning you. Do not blow down when I talk to you!"

"Auntie, what you want me to do? Stop breathing? You want me to just stop breathing and just dead? Is that what you want?"

I am waving my arms at her and shouting. "Everybody just want me to drop down and dead! If I was born dead it would be better for my mother and my father and everybody in this house and you!"

Her arm snakes out and her palm lands smack across my cheek.

The sting is sudden and surprising. My arm shoots up to prevent the next blow and the back of my arm hits hers. I am as shocked as she is.

"No! No! No! No!" she screams as she drags me forward by the collar and then slams me against the wall. "Is either me go kill you in this house or you go kill me. I will put you out before I let you raise your hand to me!"

"But, Auntie, it was an accident! I never mean—"

She slams me into the wall and grabs me by the throat. "Not another word! Not one single word! Something have to change before I make you cause me to commit murder in me own house. You have the Devil living inside you! I don't know what I have to do, but whatever it is, it will have to do something soon."

After school the next evening she informs me, "Your grandfather is coming over here tonight to have a talk with you. And you can form the fool and don't show him the appropriate respect! He would take off his belt right here and strip you naked and put you in you place!"

As I wait for him to come, I am a little afraid. But I vow to myself that I will kill him first before I let that man hit me. After how he treated Grandma, he has no right to come and say anything to me about my behavior. I put a sharp rock in my pocket and sit on the veranda, caressing the jagged edges.

It is almost dark before my grandfather arrives. The tall skinny figure opens the gate and my jaw nearly drops off my face to see how frail he is. I am sure this is not the man in my grandmother's stories. He carefully closes the gate and coughs a muffled howdy-do. I am disappointed in this slow carcass, bent and shuffling toward me. Then I am angry. I feel cheated. I want somebody I can fight.

His face has the tissue wrinkles of a kindly old gentleman. He takes Elisha's hands into his wrinkled gigantic palms, kisses her on her cheek, and I recall that Grandma once told me he liked to kiss women on the cheek and "accidentally" kiss them on the mouth. He sips the glass of water that Auntie makes me get for him. He nods at Glen and tells him he had better study hard and to take his book-learning seriously. "Otherwise you won't be able to get a wife and children."

I want to ask if when he was a gambling drunk it prevented him from having a woman and children at home.

His lanky frame is neatly clad in cream-colored serge pants. The lines are creased so sharp the legs seem to be standing up on their own. Beneath the whispering cloth I see his pointy knees wobbling as he walks toward me. His careful gait is comic. I press my lips together to keep from laughing.

The scent of him is equally unexpected. I had expected him to smell like liquor and cigarettes. He smells like cheap cologne. His red-and-white-striped shirt might have been the rage once, but the collar is now a mass of threads that stick out when he hangs his head. It is buttoned up to the last button, exposing silver strands at the base of his throat. His head is covered with a dusting of fine hairs that look almost blond in their whiteness.

He sits beside me and looks through the open window for about five minutes before he says anything.

"Stacey, you auntie tell me you getting on bad, man. You getting too big now! You must stop that foolishness! Is time for you to settle down and stop all of that now."

He still does not look at me.

I had played this scene over and over in my head, fantasized about how he would be so sorry when I was done with him that he would go straight to my grandmother, fall down on his knees, and beg her forgiveness. In my fantasy I would be there to ensure that she refused his pleas. But his discolored false teeth look so pitiful smiling at me, I find myself wanting to be kind to him.

"What them tell you that me do?" I volunteer.

His head jerks up so fast, the perfect almost-smile nearly falls out of his mouth when he speaks.

"Well, they tell me you coming home late in the evening and reading all kind of big-people book. Them things dangerous, you know. You not ready for baby and man and all of that!"

I don't remind him that Grandma was not far from my age when she had her first child for him. I wish I could tell him that I am not with any boys in the evening. I wonder what he would say if I told him I only visited my brother and April and Natalia and my almost-father after school. But I say nothing about that. I know Auntie would prefer to think that I am chasing a man than visiting people who allow little girls to wear pants and have helpers and look like me.

So I simply swallow the odd scent of his cologne, clear my tightening throat, and say, "I have never had sex with anybody in my entire life, so there's very little chance of my ever getting pregnant. Don't you know anything about biology?"

His eyes light up. His borrowed teeth break into a smile and I see a sparkle of the man who used to charm the ladies with gifts he bought with my grandmother's hard-earned money.

"What! You don't start them tings yet? You never do nothing with them dutty-foot bwoy from round the district here? Bless me eyes! So you is a virgin! A genuine young Jennings virgin! Well, me grampickney, Ah proud o' you, keep it up, me chile."

With that, he stands up, pats my knee, and walks away with the swinging stride of a man who has accomplished the job he came to do.

I want to shout at him. Scream my denial at the red stripes on his disappearing back. I wanted to call him back and shout in his ear until he is deaf too. *I am a not a Jennings. I will never be a Jennings and have no desire to be a Jennings or a Jennings virgin. I am a Chin and even though my father doesn't want me I am always going to be a Chin! Even if by some miracle I get married I will hold on to my name. And I am glad that it has nothing to do with a man who is only a wife-beating, rum-drinking, cheating Black man.*

I want to tell him all the things that are bouncing around in my head, but his white hair is gone before I can even open my mouth.

With the Kisses of His Mouth

It is summertime and there is nothing for me to do. Natalia and Sandy have both gone away for the holidays. I don't have school, so I can't fool Auntie with an excuse about studying and slip away to visit Delano or April. The only place I can go is church. And the only reason I go is to see Troy, but I am getting a little tired of him. He wants to kiss me all the time and I don't know how to tell him that I don't really like it. I am just waiting for a good excuse to break up with him.

One day we are sitting on the wall and he tells me we have to talk about something.

"What happen?" I asked him.

"Well, we have been girlfriend and boyfriend now for quite a while and I think it time we make our relationship even more serious."

"What you mean by that?"

He sighs and chews on a blade of grass. "Well, most men would leave already under this condition."

"What you mean? What condition? And who you calling a man?"

"You know what I mean, Stacey. Why you always have to make things so difficult?"

"Troy, I would really appreciate it if you would stop talking in parables. Leave that to Jesus. If you have something to say to me, just come right out and say it!"

"All right. I think is time we do something serious—something that will take our relationship to another level of seriousness."

"Troy Christie, are you saying you want me to have sex with you?"

"Is not just me want it, you must be wanting it by this! You think all that kissing is just for nothing?"

"Let me tell you something, Troy. I don't have one living soul who really care about me or what I want out of life. The only person who can really do anything to save me from being worthless is me. Sex equals baby! And baby equals no school. And no school equals worthlessness! And I am not going to have sex with anybody and turn worthless!"

"But you don't have to get pregnant! We can use things like—"

"It doesn't matter what you say! Condoms can break. The pill is not one hundred percent safe—and my bio book says that I am too young to take the pill anyway. If you had any respect for what I want in life, you wouldn't ask me that."

"Stacey—"

"Stacey nutten! I don't even want to talk to you anymore. I don't want to be your girlfriend! Go find somebody who will let you do as you like with her!" I get up from the wall and go inside the church building.

He sends letters and messages through Nellie. But I tell her to stop delivering them. Two weeks later when Nellie tells me he has another girlfriend I tell myself that she will be pregnant with three children by the time she is twenty.

I tell Nellie I am looking for a priest to be my boyfriend. She tells me she has just the right boy.

Randall, Nellie's cousin, is in Montego Bay for the summer. He is a fifteen-year-old tenth-grader at Monroe College for boys. Nellie says he likes me. One afternoon he kisses me on my left ear and runs away.

All summer he sends me sweets and flowers. I never send anything back and if he smiles at me I quickly turn away from him. On his last day in Montego Bay he slips me a letter written on pink paper and smelling like perfume.

> *Dear Staceyann,*
> *I will always love you, forever and ever and ever. You are the one true love of my whole life. Please do not worry that I am after your stuff. I respect you and would never want to touch you down there. I will only hold your hand. I do not even want to do any nasty things with you. I have enclosed my address. Please write and tell me if I can write to you again. I have so much to tell you about my school, Monroe College.*
> *Until we meet again,*
> *All my love,*
> *Randall*

I am a little disturbed that he does not even *want* to do anything nasty with me. I hope he is not one of those batty boys who don't want to have sex with girls. But just in case he is a normal boy, I pen my response on yellow paper. Sandy says that yellow is a neutral color.

> *Dear Randall,*
> *I am not saying that I love you or anything. But thank you for your lovely letter.*
> *Enclosed is my post office address. I hope to hear from you again.*
> *Yours truly,*
> *Staceyann Chin*

Back at school, Sandy tells me she met a boy on her holiday in West-moreland. His name is Robin and he has promised to write to her. If any boys write to us, we have to collect the letters from Mrs. Burnett, Nellie's mother, who is also the postmistress for the Montego Bay Post Office.

Sandy and I race downtown to the post office. We go every day for three weeks. On Friday evening Mrs. Burnett hands me a yellow envelope. "A letter from Monroe College. My, my, somebody must like you a lot! You know how much a stamp cost these days?"

Randall's handwriting is small and neat. And there are little hearts drawn in red in the margin.

> *Dear Staceyann,*
> *The new term has started and I know I am going to die if don't see you soon.*
> *I think about you after curfew every night. This boarding school for boys is*
> *unnatural. Girls give boys a reason to dream of pretty things. After supper and*
> *homework, all I do is think of you till lights out. And then I think of you when*
> *the lights go out.*
> *I promise you my thoughts are pure. I think of you while I am in the chapel.*
> *I don't ever think about you in any sexual way. I do not picture you naked. And*
> *I do not think of orgasms or anything like that. I think of you fully clothed*
> *and smiling.*
> *I am yours in purity and love,*
> *Randall*

I get my dictionary out in order to respond. I want to make sure our interactions are intellectual. I believe if he is stimulated mentally he will forget about the feelings of the flesh. Still, I write my response on pale purple writing paper and draw flowers around the edges of the page.

> *Dear Randall,*
>
> *I am glad you are luxuriating in your supper and your dreams. I hope the term continues in a manner that is beneficial to you and your studies. Things are excellent here. I am busy with both schoolwork and church.*
>
> *I am extending my most heartfelt gratitude for your very illuminating letters. I know the cost of stamps has become quite astronomical. If you can, please pray for my soul when you go to chapel. I will continue to advocate to the Good Lord on behalf of all the boys at Monroe College.*
>
> *Yours truly,*
> *Staceyann*

"Good evening, Mrs. Burnett, any letters for Staceyann Chin today?"

"Stacey, you were here three days ago and you got a letter. You expecting another one again today? Is Randall writing you all these love letters?"

I turn red in the face and say, "No, Mrs. Burnett, they are not love letters. We are just pen pals. Is there anything for me today?"

"No, ma'am, and there is nothing from Westmoreland for Sandra either. Come back next week."

A few weeks later another letter arrives. The envelope reeks of cologne. When I open it there are flower petals inside. And he has drawn little hearts and lips all over the back of each page.

> *Dearest Staceyann,*
>
> *Thank you for writing back to me. Your letter was very moving. But too long has gone by since I have seen you. I miss your hair and your hands and the way you use big words that no one ever understands.*
>
> *I miss your pretty legs. I miss every part of you. Even the parts I have not seen. Yet. I must tell you, Sweet Staceyann, I have slipped and fallen off the wagon of purity. The other night, I was sleeping and dreaming about you. I awoke to feel my hands in my pajamas. I continued to pleasure myself until I fell prey to an Orgasm.*

That Orgasm was so pleasurable and so satisfying that I knew I was meant to give you your first Orgasm. I hope I am not offending you. I know you are a good Christian girl. But if you allow me to take you into the unknown forest, I promise I will definitely marry you as soon as we get old enough to do so.

Please let me know your answer in the next letter.

Your Loving Husband to Be,

Randall Peterkin

I am shocked by the letter. I am also a little excited by its contents, but I know I cannot allow the relationship to go any further. If we keep writing to each other he will think that I am the kind of girl who will have sex with him before I am ready. I immediately tear a page from my notebook and quickly scribble the note on the lined white paper.

Dear Randall Peterkin,

I have no idea to which personage you were addressing in your last letter, but I know it could not have been myself! I am disgusted by your suggestions and your words. I would never marry you if you were the last boy on earth.

I am asking you to cease and desist from writing any letters to me. I hope your life turns out favorable. I say farewell now, because I will never speak to you again.

Your past friend,

Staceyann Chin

P.S. Please try to respect my wishes and refrain from writing to me again. You have already disrespected me so much. You may redeem yourself if you at least try to respect my wishes now.

Randall does not write again. But Nellie tells me that he always asks about me when he calls.

Take Up Your Bed and Walk

When Grace straightens Elisha's hair, I am so jealous I tell Auntie that if she doesn't give me permission to straighten mine she is cruel and unfair. She laughs and turns back to her Bible. The next day I remind her that Natalia's mother will do it for free, that straight hair is easier to manage. The week after that I tell her that straightening it would give me more time for schoolwork. I am sure to get better grades. But no matter how much I beg, the answer is always no. Almost every girl in my class has had her hair straightened, I whine. Her response is quick and without apology. "Them other girls don't live here. And as long as you live under this roof, what I say go. Your hair is fine as it is. You have good hair. Not like them other children. Leave your hair the way God give it to you!"

Frustrated and angry, I complain to Natalia.

"So why don't you just do it?" she asks.

"You mad, Talia? Auntie would kill me!"

"Don't be dramatic, Staceyann! She cannot *kill* you. Think about it. If you went ahead and straightened it, she couldn't do anything. The most she can do is beat you. And then what? Your hair would be straight and that would be that. You can't just reverse the process overnight."

The next day I tell Auntie Bamsey that Auntie finally said I could straighten my hair. As I sit in the swivel chair and watch her separate my hair in four equal parts, in my excitement I try not to think about Auntie and what she will do to me when I get home. Auntie Bamsey applies the sticky cream and leaves it in for about ten minutes. My hair smells like it is being roasted. When she combs through the messy paste, my scalp feels like it is on fire. I am glad when she washes it all out. Little sections of the straight hair are smoothed onto curlers and pinned into place. I sit under the burning-hot dryer for an hour and a half, wondering why anyone would do this every six weeks. But when the curlers come out and the hair is blown into smooth waves, I understand.

I stare into the mirror at the new me. Long straight hair, with just a hint of a curl, hangs past the back of my brassiere. Perfectly formed large loose curls frame my face. If I shake my head, the curls move individually. My hair looks just like Andrea's blond-white hair, except it's black. I look almost exactly like April and Natalia. For the first time in my life I feel beautiful. Now I really look like my father could be Uncle Hartley or Uncle Charlie or Junior Chin.

I step through the front gate with my heart in my mouth. I know I am going to get the biggest beating of my life tonight and I am not certain that I am ready for it. Auntie watches me as I make my way carefully up the stairs. She does not respond when I say good evening. And she does not take her eyes off me either. Elisha also watches me from across the room, but she does not say a word. We are both waiting for what Auntie is going to do. I stay in the room and read until it is time to go to bed. For most of the night I lie awake waiting for her to come and say something, but she doesn't. The next morning when I am leaving for school, she tells me, "Stacey, I see that you are a big woman now. And since two bulls cannot reign in one pen, it is time for you to move out of this house."

"What? What you mean by move out, Auntie? Where I must move to?"

"You should have think about that before you go out there and do what you want. Please to collect your things together and take them out of this house."

"But, Auntie—"

"No but. Just get your things and go. You are a big woman. Go and live by your own rules."

I ask if I can take enough things for the weekend and come back to get the rest later. I just need some time to talk to Uncle Hartley. He will help me figure it out.

She says, "No. If you take anything, take everything today."

I promise to come back for my things later that day. At school I tell

Sister Joan Claire what has transpired. I ask her to call Auntie Ella in Kingston for me, but when Mrs. Bremmer answers, she tells me that Auntie Ella has emigrated to America. And no, she's sorry, but she doesn't know where Grandma is living now. When she asks what's wrong, I hang up. Sister Joan Claire sits with me while I cry. She might be able to find someone to take me in, she assures me. But I am not sure what she means when she says *take me in*. I know I don't want to be a charity case anymore. I don't want to go to someplace where I am a burden to anyone. I am tired of not having a home. I try not to panic as it dawns on me that I have nowhere to live. Natalia is sure that Uncle Hartley will let me stay with them until Sister Joan Claire finds me a place, but I am not so sure. My experience is that people are nice until they have to take me in.

I am quiet as Natalia fills Uncle Hartley in on the ride home. He listens and nods and taps the steering wheel as she tells him that nobody in the world seems to want me, that I have never really done anything to deserve my situation, that I get such good grades in school, and that I won't be any trouble. Uncle Hartley nods and nods and nods. It is only when Natalia says she knows I will repay him for his kindness that he interrupts her. "No, Natalia, no." His tone is serious as he continues, "When you do something kind for someone, it is not something to be repaid. You do it because it is necessary, not because you expect something back. And Stacey, let me tell you something. You are welcome to stay in the house, but no thank-yous are necessary. This is a critical year in your life. It is your second-to-last year in high school. You have final exams next year. So if you are without a place to live and you are my daughter's very good friend, it is my duty to take you home. You hear me?"

I nod because I cannot find any words. Natalia gently pats my arm while I wipe the tears from my eyes and blow my nose into my tie.

Two weeks pass before Sister Joan Claire finds me a room with a woman named Mrs. Lyn. Mrs. Lyn's husband died last year and her only daughter is away at college in Miami. Sister Joan Claire gives me the address and tells me to go there after school on Monday. Mrs. Lyn's house is on the nicer side of Paradise. That side is called Paradise Acres. Uncle Hartley drops me there after school. Paradise Acres is just a short walk from the taxi stand at Blood Lane, but the neighborhood feels like a whole other country. The houses are all concrete. And everybody has metal grilles over the windows and doors.

Mrs. Lyn is a tiny half-Chinese woman who speaks very softly. She opens the door and motions me in. She points to the big plush red couch and I sit down. "Good afternoon, Stacey—or is it Staceyann? Which do you prefer?"

"Ah—I—I like to be called Staceyann."

"Okay, Staceyann, Sister told me about your situation. She told you what the room and board will be?"

I nod and reach into my pocket, but she shakes her head. "No—no, you don't have to give it to me until you come with your things. We just have to go over some basic rules. First thing is first, I will not touch anything that personally belongs to you and you will afford me the same courtesy, right?"

I nod again.

"Second, if you are not coming home you have to call and let me know before ten. And if you forget, please call first thing in the morning. I am an early riser, so it doesn't matter how early you call, okay?"

"Yes, Mrs. Lyn."

"Another thing. All the boarders who have stayed here have called me Aunt Lyn. Mrs. Lyn sounds so formal for people who are sharing a house, you agree?"

"Yes, Mrs.—I mean, Aunt Lyn."

"Don't worry, it will take a while before it becomes habit. Now, you can eat what you like as long as it is not without consideration. The helper cooks every day, but she leaves at three, so you have to share out your own dinner when you get home. It will always be there in the fridge. Eat it if you like. Leave it if you don't. Come with me."

We leave the living room and head to the back of the house.

"This room in here is yours. The bathroom in there is yours alone. The helper will clean it once a week. If you want it cleaned more often, you will have to do that yourself."

I follow her to another room with a concrete sink.

"The washing machine and dryer are in this back room. Sheets and towels go in the laundry basket back here. You will be responsible for your underwear, and that includes your brassieres too. If you make a mess—for example, if you spill your period on your sheets—don't put them in the basket. Just drop them in the machine and run a cycle. This is not a nursery. I expect you to take care of yourself. Understood?"

"Yes, M—Aunt Lyn."

"Those are the general housekeeping rules. Now, no sex in this house. None at all. And if I catch you, the consequences will be considerable. No boys when I am not here. And if you have friends over, they have to leave by eleven, okay? Oh, and no phone calls after eleven. And try not to give the phone number to people who will make crank calls. You think you can live with those rules?"

I don't think I have absorbed everything, but I nod anyway.

"When would be a good time for you to move in?"

"Aahm . . . I think—I think Uncle Hartley will give me a ride over here tomorrow."

"Okay, ma'am, I guess I will see you tomorrow. Let me give you some keys. This opens the front grille, this silver one is for the front door . . ."

I walk from Aunt Lyn's to Natalia's in a daze. I feel sort of giddy with freedom. I tell Natalia everything Aunt Lyn said.

She can barely contain herself. "Wow, you are lucky for real. It seems like you hit the jackpot with this one. How you feel about everything?"

"Okay, I guess."

"You guess? You know how many people would kill to have that kind of freedom? You can spend the night with your boyfriend and not get in trouble! You have the life that every teenager want to have, Stacey! Why you look like something is wrong?"

"I am happy to have all me freedom, but guess I feel sort of sad too, to know that I can do anything and nobody would care."

"I guess I understand that, but it must be cool to be able to do anything you want."

"I suppose so. But make us do our homework before Uncle Hartley come check on us."

That night in bed I lie listening to Natalia's even breathing. The sheets are clean and smell like lemon. The room is kept cool by a silver overhead fan. I wish this room were *my* room. The room at Aunt Lyn's is nice, and it is quite an unexpected luxury to have my own bathroom, but I know it is not really *my* room—not the way that this room is *Natalia's room*. Uncle Hartley took her to the paint store to pick out her own paint.

Even when she is married and living somewhere else, this room will still be her room.

I think of Elisha and Grace stretching out in the bed I used to sleep in. I know that Grace is glad to see the back of me. She will throw out the few clothes I left there. By next week there will be no sign of my having been there at all.

Heaven and Earth Will Pass Away, but My Words Will Not Pass Away

I am the only fifteen-year-old in the tenth grade who can do anything I want after school. But while everyone dreams of going dancing with boys, I choose to spend my evenings doing homework with Natalia.

I hardly see Uncle Desmond or April anymore. I no longer visit the furniture store. It feels strange to hear April tell people that we are cousins when my father maintains that I am not his daughter. At Junior Chin's house I am a charity case. I ring the bell, pick up the money, and say thank you and good-bye.

I don't even like to visit Delano. He and I hardly talk. We just sit there watching TV until it is time for me to leave. I only go when I have to ask Uncle Charlie for money. Everything in the tenth grade is about preparing for the eleventh-grade finals. These exams will mark the end of our lives as secondary school students. Uncle Hartley says that even though it does not feel like it, our big graduation is only a year away. Before we know it, summer will be gone, and so will everything we learned in the tenth grade. He insists that we take extra lessons during the summer to keep us sharp. "If you ladies are to do well, you have to work hard while others are at play."

When June comes, Aunt Lyn asks if I have any plans for the summer holidays. I tell her I will be at Natalia's for most of it, studying. Relief washes over her face and she blurts out, "Well, that is just as well, because my daughter is coming home from college for good in September and she needs her room." She sighs and looks away "Staceyann, I am sorry to drop this on you so, but you think you could find another room for the next school year?"

I nod and stuff my backpack with enough clothes to stay with Natalia for the rest of the week.

Sister Joan Claire finds me a new place with Miss Wellington, an old widow whose daughter just got married. Then in six months, Mrs. Wellington's daughter gets a divorce and she tells me I have to move. Sister Joan Claire finds me another room. In another house. With another old woman who wants me to call her Auntie.

I look at the freshly painted white walls of the new room and wonder if anything has changed with my old bedroom in Paradise. Elisha must be glad to have more space now that she is thirteen. This new house has a pool. I can swim at home if I want to. But I have no time to swim. I have to make notes and write up experiments and conjugate the verb *to be* in French. And make time to pick up money from everybody's fathers.

The Christmas holidays pass in a haze of algebraic calculations and Shakespearean tragedies. There is no time to think about my sixteenth birthday, only the scores we get on the mock exams.

Finally, the real exams begin.

At night Natalia and I cram and eat and cram and eat. In the morning we slip on our uniforms and spend the next three hours trying to remember formulas and facts in a quiet room filled with the nervous ambition of hundreds of hopeful teenage girls.

Natalia already knows she is heading to Miami for university. She wants to be a pilot. I am not sure what I want to be, but I know I want to get out of Montego Bay.

On the day after my last exam, Miss Tolloch, the graduation coordinator, calls me into her office. She sits behind her desk and clasps her hands together. I wonder what kind of trouble I am in. She leans into the desk and sighs. "Staceyann, I am not sure if you know this, but I cannot tell you how very proud we are of you. You have done so well despite the turbulent circumstances of your home life. We on the graduation committee feel it is appropriate that you make a speech at the graduation ball."

"Really? Me—I can make a speech? I can say anything I want?"

"Well, within reason, but yes, you can talk about how you feel about your successes. Perhaps say something to inspire your fellow graduates."

"Thank you, Miss Tolloch, thank you so much! I thought I was being called in here because I was in trouble! Thank you!"

"You are quite welcome, ma'am. It is nice to see you smiling!"

She stands and looks at my untidy hair. My tie has a big juice spot on it. She brushes at the spot and says, "Never mind what you look like today, now you have a reason to look extra nice on graduation night."

That night I call Annmarie and invite her to my graduation. She agrees to make the trip and though we have never been close, I am suddenly very grateful that Annmarie is my cousin. She will be my only family there. I know better than to invite Delano. He has never even come to visit me in any of the places I have lived. I ask about Grandma, but Annmarie says she doesn't see her much. Grandma now lives outside of Kingston with one of her sons and his wife. She gives me the phone number, but we both know that Grandma is deaf and cannot talk on the phone. I call anyway. A woman answers and tells me that my grandmother still begins each day praying for my brother and me. I wish Grandma could come to see me collect my diploma.

I know I should be spending the time writing down my thoughts, but I am more interested in finding the perfect dress to wear to stand in front of the whole eleventh-grade class on graduation night. I look at dresses in the stores on St. James Street, but everything looks the same to me. I want to wear something that makes me look better than everybody else.

When I go to pick up my money from my father, I tell Miss P. about the speech.

"Oh, my goodness! That is good to hear!" She pauses. Then she asks, "You have the time to come inside for a glass of orange juice?"

It takes me a while to make sense of the words. She puts the envelope on the table and opens the grille. I am so surprised, she has to ask me again.

"You not too busy to stop, are you? Don't look so surprised. This is a special occasion. You finished with school and graduating with a speech. Please come inside, man."

She gestures to the couch and I sit down. The house smells like cinnamon and sugar. She tells me to wait right there on the couch while she gets me some orange juice. The glass has tiny white stars on it and the juice tastes just like a real orange. She sits down beside me and exclaims, "Wow! But, Stacey, that is wonderful, man! That is wonderful news. Congratulations! So what you going to wear for the ball?"

"For the ceremony we are all wearing our uniforms under our gowns, but I don't have anything to wear to the ball, Miss P. I have no idea what I am going to do."

"Well . . . I have just taken up dressmaking. If you don't mind, I could see what I could rustle up for you."

"Oh, that would be wonderful, Miss P. It would be something different, not the same old, same old that everybody buys from the stores."

The next day I tell everyone that my *stepmother* is making my graduation dress. When Uncle Hartley drives me to my father's, I feel so normal. It is almost irrelevant that I have no mother. I am headed to my father's for the evening. I have Uncle Hartley drive me inside the yard. And I make sure to stand on the stairs and wave at Natalia as they drive away.

Miss P. hurries me in and calls the helper to get me some orange juice. Then she tells me to follow her. We walk down the hallways and into a big room with fancy curtains and a big bed with brown and beige sheets on it. She gestures toward the suitcase on the floor. "Stacey, you have to forgive the mess here. I just came back last night. The flight was delayed, so I didn't get to bed until late. I'm only just getting out of bed."

"It's okay, Miss P. You have a very nice bedroom."

It is the strangest feeling, to be standing next to the bed in which my father sleeps. There is a pair of shorts on his pillow. Miss P. pulls out a sheer peach roll of fabric from her suitcase. It shimmers when she moves it. "What you think of this?"

My heart is beating so fast I hardly hear myself answer. "Oh, it is very nice. I like it a lot."

"Okay, good. I am happy you like it. I am not quite sure what kind of dress you want, but I bought a couple of patterns that you can look at."

I choose something from the book of patterns that she shows me.

"Good choice, Stacey. What you prefer—Stacey, or Staceyann?"

"I prefer Staceyann, but it doesn't matter, you can call me whatever you want to call me."

"No, man, Staceyann. You have to tell people how to address you. You are at least in charge of your own name."

I peer down the hallway, looking for my father.

"Don't worry, he is not here now. He won't be back until later. But I told him about this and he was all right with it."

"Okay."

"So if I am making this thing for you, I want you to come by after school every other day for a fitting. I am not an expert, so I need lots of time with the model. Come make us take the measurements now."

My father walks in as she is measuring my waist.

"Hello, Junior." Miss P. does not look up from the task at hand.

"Hello, P., how's it going?"

"Okay. I am just trying to make sure Miss Staceyann here is properly outfitted for her big day."

"Hello, young lady."

"Hello, sir."

"Congratulations on your good fortune. I hope you make good use of it. Not everyone gets that sort of opportunity. I see I was not wrong to invest in you."

"Thank you, sir. I am very grateful that you did invest in me."

"Never mind the thanks. Remember what I told you? The only thanks I need is for you to succeed. Have you had dinner already?"

"No, sir."

"Would you like to eat with us?"

I try my best to sound casual saying yes.

The TV is on CNN while we eat. The pundits are dissecting the horror of the *Valdez* oil spill. Dawn dishwashing liquid is being used to save the tiny, dying, oil-soaked birds.

"Boy, P.! Them Americans is something, eh? Always something dramatic on them news stations. Look at how the people reacting! Them care more for them birds than them care about people in Africa who starving."

"That is why I would never live there," Miss P. answers. "America is the kind of paradox that I only use for shopping. Quick trip in, get what you need, and get out."

"So what do you think of all this, young lady?"

I finish chewing my mouthful of pork chop before I respond. I want to say something brilliant. "About America, or the oil spill, or about what you just said?"

"Isn't all the same thing? You stalling, man. Put your opinion on the table."

"Well, I—ah—I think that the oil spill only shows us how everything is big in America. Do you know how much oil it would take to create that kind of mess? But I think they are doing a good job with trying to clean it up. Uncle Hartley says he thinks it may have been some kind of terrorist act. I don't know. I am only sorry for the poor birds."

"The poor birds? What about all the people in China and Africa and India who is starving? What about them? Are you sorry for them?"

"Yes, but we are not talking about them. You ask me about the oil spill."

"And therein lies the greatest fiction about America. It is never about just anything. It is always about something else. Something big. When it comes to the USA, other seemingly unconnected things are always connected."

"Okay."

"You don't believe me?"

"Junior, leave the poor child alone. Come, Staceyann, let us finish the measurements."

I am sorry that Miss P. cut our conversation short. I wanted to hear what he was going to say. When we are finished with the measurements, Miss P. tells me that she is done for the day. As I descend the stairs, I promise myself that next time I am going to ask my father about my mother.

But he is not there the next time. So Miss P. and I sit silently in the room while she cuts and measures and figures out the right stitches to use.

The following week, however, he greets me at the door, ushers me in. "Miss P. won't be home for another hour or so. Just come in and make yourself at home."

When the answer to Final Jeopardy is given, and the winner is properly congratulated, I gather my courage. "Ah—can I talk to you for a second?"

"Sure. What is it?"

"Well, you said that you knew my mother when she was living in Jamaica, right?"

"I did not know her well, but I knew her."

"What was she like? I mean—what did she look like? Who were her friends? And how did you get to meet her?"

"Well, she was quite a looker, your mother. She was a very pretty girl. The first time I saw her, she was wearing a pair of red hot pants and she had these long, long legs."

I sit very still as he relaxes into the story.

"I was very taken with her. And I am only telling you these things because you asked. She used to come to a bar I frequented. I took her out a couple of times—and I am not proud of this, but I tried to have sex with her in the back seat of my car."

I pick at the dirt under my nails.

"But she wasn't willing. She said no and I backed off. I think she wanted a relationship and I already had a wife and a family. So I know that I couldn't be your father," he said, "because we really didn't have that kind of interaction. No sex, no baby."

"Okay. Thank you for answering."

"You know, you say thank you for the oddest things. But you are welcome."

"Another thing. I know you are Chinese. But were you born in Jamaica or China?"

"I was born right here on this island. I come from poor Chinese immigrants to Jamaica. They came here with nothing and worked like dogs just to feed their children. We had a very interesting life. Me and my brothers could tell you stories about this place."

He tells me that as a boy, he sold river shrimp to passersby in order to feed himself and his brothers. He knew he was different from the other boys around him, he said, always a little smarter, a little faster. I can't imagine him as a small boy begging people to buy anything.

"I believe that is why I have done so well. I did not begin life with all this." He gestures at the room.

I look around. There are giant painted vases with no flowers in them. And dark heavy drapes pulled back to let in the light. The dining table looks like it could seat a hundred people. And there are miles and miles of wooden floors—floors that would be perfect for playing Superman. Natalia's whole house is carpeted. But this wood is smooth and unstained. It looks like somebody spent eons sanding and varnishing it. I decide that when I have a house I am going to have unstained wooden floors.

As the days pass, the dress begins to take shape. It is two layers—peach/orange organza sewn over a shimmer of peach silk. Naked on one shoulder and narrow at the waist, the skirt flares outward like the dress on a princess. Dress in hand, Miss P. brandishes a pair of shiny white pumps with the tiniest of bows across the toes. They are the prettiest shoes I have ever seen. I try the whole outfit on and walk out into the living room.

My father stands up and applauds.

"Bravo, ladies, bravo! That is such a beautiful dress. Miss P., you did a splendid job! Not that you didn't have good material to start with."

As he leaves the room, the space inside my chest swells and swells and swells. Twice Miss P. has to tell me to relax my body as she makes the final adjustments. When the last orange thread is knotted, she smiles and tells me we are done with our project. She thanks me for trusting her novice sewing skills. "I really enjoyed spending the time with you, Staceyann. I think you will be just fine as you make your way in the world. Anyways, let me not take up the time that is left. Junior wants to see you in his office."

I walk to the back veranda and knock on his office door.

"Come, come."

I inch my way in and stand in front of the desk.

"Sit down, young lady, sit down." I sit and face him.

"Young lady, you are about to graduate from high school in a few days. You are really a young lady now. A woman, almost."

I have to work hard to keep the smile off my face.

"So have you finished your speech?"

"Sort of, sir. I'm still working on it."

"What do you plan to say to your fellow graduates?"

"I don't know exactly, but I guess I'll say something inspiring—something about our achievements and good wishes in their lives. Maybe I will quote the school motto: *ad astra per aspera*—to the stars through difficulties!"

"Inspiration is nice, but a bit of hard truth is good too. And a true personal story is always a bonus. Do a Michael Manley on them. Now, that man is an orator!"

"Well, I'm not finished yet, so I will definitely take your advice into consideration."

"Okay, then. Now you are almost out of high school, have you thought about what you might do directly after that?"

I tell him I am thinking of applying to the university. He asks how I intend to afford that. I'm not quite sure what he expects me to say, but I tell him that there are loans and government subsidies for tuition. And if I am careful, I can eat and pay for boarding with what he gives me.

"Listen, young lady, I cannot keep supporting you forever. And I think I have been more than generous to you."

It takes me a minute to understand what he is saying. University is very expensive, he continues, especially for someone who has no job. His sister-in-law works in the bursar's office at Shortwood Teachers' College. And she can get me a full scholarship with room and board there. He tells me I mustn't feel pressured by any of this. I can do whatever I want. If I don't take him up on his offer he won't hold it against me. I am finished with high school now. I am not a child anymore, so I can do exactly as I please.

On graduation day, my dress hangs in Natalia's room with the pretty white pumps beneath it. I promise myself that no matter what happens after this, I am going to enjoy this last day as a Mount Alvernian. Auntie Bamsey trims my hair and smoothes it onto big pink curlers. I sit under the dryer for two hours. While I wait, I reread my speech and make minor corrections.

Auntie Bamsey wraps my head with a silk scarf to keep it neat. I decide to take a bath so as not to get my hair wet from the shower. As I turn on the tap, a spray of warm water from the showerhead douses my four-hour graduation hairdo. I sit in the bath crying until Natalia comes looking for me. My face is red and swollen and my hair is a wet skullcap. Auntie Bamsey tries to fix it, but we don't have the time. It is graduation day and I look like a wet rat.

Not even seeing Annmarie, who has traveled all the way from Kingston to see me, can make me feel better. As I slip on my gown to join the line of graduates, she whispers that she cannot stay for the ball afterward, but she just wanted to come see me collect my diploma. "I hope you feel proud that you did it almost all by yourself. I know I am very proud of you. But who in God's name did your hair?"

When the commencement speech is over, we head to the ballroom. As the sea of ball gowns converge, Natalia asks, "You ready to leave your final words with us now?"

I pat my pockets. "Shit!"

"What?" Natalia grabs my hand. "What is it?"

"Shit! Shit! Shit, Natalia! I left the speech at the house."

"You sure you didn't leave it in the pocket of the graduation gown?"

"No. I left it on the back of the toilet. Shit! Oh, man! Oh, man! What am I going to say?"

"Is okay, Stace. You have a bigger vocabulary than anybody in the whole school and you are very good at talking in public. You will be just fine."

We get inside and Miss Tolloch asks me if I am ready.

My hand is shaking so hard the mike is making rustling sounds against my orange organza dress. I take a breath and begin.

"Ladies and gentlemen, fellow graduates, parents, well-wishers, and friends, this has been a difficult five years for many of us. As—as some of you may know, I myself have had great ch-challenges to endure—absent parents, poverty, and a-a-an—an unstable home life. And many times I have wished to be someone else, ah—perhaps even one of you. But today I stand here, in my own shoes, knowing that I have accomplished the first leg of my life's journey. Regardless—no, not regardless, but *especially* because of my difficult circumstances, the circumstances I mentioned before, I can be particularly proud that I have satisfactorily finished the course set before me . . . ."

I don't feel like I am making any sense, but I press on. "I am not a victim. No matter the beginning, I know that it is up to me to make a way for myself. And I have every confidence that I will!"

By this time I am speaking with my hands and bellowing the words into the microphone. The room is so quiet that the words are bouncing off the walls: ". . . to conclude, I would like to thank the members of the Grawley family, who have stood in for my own absent family, and the many women who have opened their homes to me—thank you, thank you for your generosity. And finally, on behalf of my fellow graduates, I extend a heartfelt thank-you to the parents, the friends, and the teachers. We would not be here tonight without your support. *Ad astra per aspera*— to the stars through difficulties! Thank you, thank you all, and good night!"

When the last word is out, the entire room is standing and cheering. Some of the girls are crying. Natalia hugs me and tells me she has never been more proud to be my friend. Miss Tolloch comes over to say she is happy to see that I have come into my own. "I knew you could do it, Staceyann Chin! I knew you had it in you."

I feel as though someone has lifted half my weight away. I promise myself that as long as I live I will never tell another lie again.

The next day I call my father to tell him that I have decided to enroll at the Shortwood Teachers' College. Saying good-bye to everyone feels good. I am glad I have time to visit friends and let them know I am leaving.

I save Delano for last.

Uncle Charlie greets me at the door and tells me that my brother has moved away to Germany. I am so shocked I don't know what to say. Delano has never even visited Miami. I can't imagine my silent brother living in a place as foreign as Germany. "You sure is Germany, Uncle Charlie? Who him have in Germany?"

"Stacey, I don't know him business, you know. That is all him tell me. Him never say anything to you?" I am ashamed to admit that he did not tell me anything. I want to lie, but I remember the promise I made to myself. I shake my head and say, "No, him never say anything, Uncle Charlie."

"So how is everything with you?"

I want to say how hurt I am that my only brother has moved away without so much as a by-your-leave, but I smile and say, "I am fine. I am going away to college in Kingston."

Uncle Charlie is genuinely pleased that I am doing well. "But that is very good, man! Congratulations! Me proud of you. Your father must be happy fi you, man."

I try to muster up some enthusiasm. "Yeah. Yeah, I guess that is good, Uncle Charlie."

"Well, I always tell you that if you ever need anything, you must come and ask me. I can see that you going to do big things with your life. And I am happy to help with whatever I can. Anything at all you need, just come right here and ask."

"As a matter of fact, I do need your help to go. I have to pay tuition and boarding and books and—"

"How much you need?"

"As much as you can give me. Only because c-college is a very expensive place."

"Yes, man. I know. I know these things. I never go to no college, but I know that these things is expensive." He goes to his room and comes back with a wad of cash. "You think it is enough?"

"Yes, man, Uncle Charlie! I think so. And if it is not enough, I will call and tell you."

He hands me the wad of money and hugs me awkwardly. "Put that in your pocket. For books and pens and so on."

I quickly extricate myself from his embrace. "Thank you, sir. And can you please tell my brother I said hello if he calls you from Germany?"

Part III

The Beginning of Knowledge

The rules at the Shortwood Teachers' College are simple enough. Don't leave the property without permission and treat your flatmates with the love and courtesy with which you treat members of your family. At first it is easy to smile and say good morning and listen politely about Jesus and all he has done for me. But after a while I just want to be left alone. I am tired of hearing about the Lord and his blessings. Having been the recipient of an equal number of curses and blessings, I feel I owe the Lord very little gratitude.

But I love that there are only girls in the bathroom, girls in the bedroom, in the living room, only girls. My roommate, Cynthia, is a devout Pentecostal Christian. She is a neat, pretty, early-childhood major who sits on the edge of her bed and reads her Bible every moment that she is not in class. I like Kayla, who lives in the room across the hall, because she is brave enough to wear her skirts shorter than the rules allow, and Judith, the resident cook, because she feeds those of us who are not inspired to use the kitchen. The double science group consists of seven devout Christians and me. It amazes me that we spend all day studying evolution, yet they still believe blindly in the creation story. I find myself biting my tongue in the most basic conversations with them.

My favorite class is philosophy, because I can argue about everything— including the existence of God—without being looked at like something is wrong with me. And I feel like I am doing well with my decision not to make up any more stories about my family. I am not telling everything about myself, but I am not lying either. When people ask why my parents never visit, my answers are vague: my mother is away and my father works a lot, "but nothing is interesting about a half-Chinese transplant from Montego Bay. Tell me about cool, cool Mandeville. I hear you guys have to wear sweaters almost all the time."

I wish everyone weren't so interested in me. But the less I say, the more questions people ask. Where in Montego Bay am I from? Where exactly is my mother? What does my father do? Every time someone asks me something, I quell the urge to tell a little lie. Finally, one day when my roommate asks me why I am so secretive about everything, I blurt out, "Well, Cynthia, I guess it's because my mother says that this Chinaman in Montego Bay is my father, and he told me he never did the nasty with my mother. So I'm not really sure which penis exactly is responsible for my existence. To tell you the truth, I suspect my mother was trying to trick him and he was just trying to screw her. All in all, my paternity is questionable. I am only able to be here at college because my father loaned me the money to come. And by the way, my mother left me as soon as she pushed me out of her body. So, yeah, that is why I am so secretive about my family. Any more questions?"

She never asks me anything again.

I begin to tell everybody everything about my life. I decide that if everyone knows everything about me, then I won't have to spend so much of my energy trying to hide anything. I soon learn that Christian girls do not like to know everything. I spend most of my time without company. The weekends are the most unbearable. With no classes to help pass the time, I lie in bed and stare at the ceiling until it is dark enough to go to sleep. Going to bed that early means that dawn finds me wide awake with a whole day of nothing stretching ahead of me.

One Saturday I call Annmarie, who invites me to spend the weekend at her apartment. She lives with Auntie Ella's Christian mentor, Desi, on the other side of Kingston. Desi's house has more rules than Shortwood. No swearing, no VH1 (on account of the demons in the music videos), and no talk of sex. I suggest we take the bus to visit Grandma, who lives in Braeton, about forty minutes outside of Kingston. The ride there is long and dusty, and the bus is full and noisy. I cannot imagine what Grandma's life is like in Braeton. I was glad when I heard that she had moved to Kingston to live with Auntie Ella. Now she is living somewhere else, with someone else. She must be so tired of moving. I wonder if she is happy.

We walk through the tiny streets, past little look-alike houses, until we find the address Annmarie has in her little red notebook. Grandma is as still as a rock on the veranda. And she doesn't move when we approach. It is not until we are almost right in front of her that she looks up. She looks older and smaller than the last time I saw her. She wrinkles her brow, trying to figure out who we are. When she recognizes me, she whoops, "Lord Jesus Christ in heaven! Stacey? Stacey, you going live long, you know. Me was just here wondering if me was ever going to lay eyes on you before me dead! Come in, come in out of the hot, hot sun."

Her hearing is much worse. And her eyes are so bad she can't read lips anymore, but she can still talk the same. She is happy to hear I am attending college. She hopes Annmarie's job is not too hard, that they pay her enough to buy food. She nods, and smiles, and pats my knee. But there is little for me to say. Her son and daughter-in-law are away at work, so she is at home alone. I ask her what she does all day. She reminds me that though she is too old for work, she has Jesus, so she can pray.

Annmarie and I sit on the veranda and watch her while she eats one of the beef patties we brought her. She hugs us both and cries when we leave. "This might be the last time me see oonu. We never know when Jesus go take the breath of life from me mouth. So take care and God bless oonu as oonu travel back to Kingston." Annmarie and I say nothing to each other on the ride home. I get the feeling that if we spoke, we would both start crying.

At school the weekends are one long stretch of solitary reading. Hot and miserable from the heat, one Friday night I dial Racquel's number. Auntie Pam answers and immediately invites me to come over. When I arrive, Racquel is waiting at the gate. She is tall and as lean as a bean-pole. And excited to see me. She still has the smile of that three-year-old runaway coming to save me from my tears.

Auntie Pam tells me that she is very happy to see that I have made it out of my *difficult circumstances* and to college. Chauntelle smiles tentatively at me and disappears into her room.

After dinner, Racquel and I head out to lie under the mango tree. Though she is five years younger than my almost-seventeen, I feel like I can tell her anything. I tell her about life at Shortwood. She listens quietly and rubs my back when I tell her how lonely I am on campus. At nightfall we shift to her bedroom with snacks. Before I know it, I have told her all about my father and Delano and how much I wish I could have stayed with Grandma after Mummy came and left.

We end up chatting for the whole night. It surprises me that after so much time we still have so much in common. But Racquel says she knew we were soul sisters from the very first moment she saw me. She confesses that that first summer I spent in Kingston she'd overheard her mother saying I had no family but Grandma. From way back then she's wanted to give me her family so I wouldn't have to be without people who loved me. And now she can. She offers me the use of her family for as long as I need it. I want to cry, but I laugh and ask what she would do without her family, after she had given everybody away. My throat tightens and my eyes fill up when she says that it doesn't matter, because I seem to need them more than she does.

Soon I am spending every weekend at the Bremmers'. Racquel and I do everything together and we tell everyone that we are sisters. When people ask why we look so different, we say we have different fathers. Auntie Pam tells her colleagues that I am her adopted daughter. Only, the tiniest things still remind me that I am an outsider. Auntie Pam buys socks for everyone when she goes shopping in Miami. The girls get a pack of six. I get a pair from each of the packs. And they both move in and out of the pantry all day. They eat what they want, whenever they want. I know that I can't just take anything I want from the pantry. I have to ask if it is okay. No one says so, but I *know* it is better for me to ask.

For the most part, life ambles pleasantly along in Kingston. Every now and then I wonder how Delano is finding life in Germany, but most days I don't think of him at all. Nothing of my old life in Montego Bay seems to have survived the transition to Kingston. I have no idea what is happening with Elisha and Auntie. They have no phone and I never go back to see them. I have not spoken to my father since I left. I hear nothing of him, until one day I read an article in the Montego Bay newspaper, the *Western Mirror*, reporting that his house has burnt to the ground.

I drop to the ground, shaking. There is a picture of the burnt-out brick shell that remains. The article says no one was in the house at the time, but nothing could be saved from the blackened ruins. A shock of glee courses through me; I am glad that Junior has lost his home. I laugh out loud. Then I think of Miss P.'s beautiful curtains and I feel guilty for laughing. The wicker chairs and the office windows and Junior's gym equipment are all gone. The book with my dated signatures to prove that the money Junior gave me was a loan is nothing but ashes. It's like I have never been there. I am sick to my belly. I want to throw up, but the walls of my stomach won't contract.

I don't even realize I am crying until I feel Racquel shaking me. "Stacey, what happened? Why are you crying? Are you all right?"

"Yeah, ah—I—I'm fine." I fold the paper in two. "I was just reading some stupid sob story in the paper. Nothing to even talk about."

"Okay. I am going downstairs to say hi to Michael. You want to come and meet him?"

I fold the newspaper again. "Okay. Who is Michael?"

Michael is the tenant who lives in the downstairs apartment. Racquel knocks on the door. "Michael! Michael! It's Racquel! You want to come out and meet my new-old sister, Stacey?" A handsome young man in a white dress shirt steps outside. He smiles at Racquel but doesn't say anything.

"Michael, this is my sister, Stacey. Stacey, this is Michael. He plays Scrabble with Mummy all the time. You should play with them sometimes."

"Yes, man, we playing later."

"Michael is a very good player; he beats Mummy all the time."

That evening, as I place the wooden tiles on the board, I am thinking of my father and Miss P. and my little brother, Ruel. Then I am angry with myself for being concerned about them. They have never really shown any concern for me. The feelings of guilt return, and I force myself to concentrate on the game at hand. I want to impress Michael by winning my first game, but both he and Auntie Pam are seasoned players. Scrabble is a game that requires a vocabulary of small, unusual words and a whole lot of bluffing. I keep a straight face and put down a word I know is misspelled. No one challenges me. And I win by a significant margin.

Michael looks at me and laughs accusingly. "I thought this was your first game! Where you learn to play like that?" His voice is gravelly but kind.

"What that supposed to mean? Can't I just be naturally talented?" I smile up at him. His face is serious, but I can see that he is trying not to smile.

The next weekend when we play alone he asks why I was so sad the week before. I am surprised and pleased that he noticed. I tell him about Miss P. and my father and the burnt-down house. While I am speaking he doesn't say anything. After a comfortable silence, he clears his throat. "Wow. That must be complicated."

"You don't know the half of it," I say.

"Well, maybe you should tell me about it while I whip you up the best cheesecake in the world," he says.

It's both strange and wonderful to sit on the floor of the kitchen and watch a man make a cake for me. He carefully adds eggs and sugar to the bowl of whipped cream cheese. He crumbles graham crackers for the crust. It's easy to tell him about Mummy and Delano and Grandma as he stirs and folds and tastes. He offers me a spoon of the sticky sweet mixture before he scrapes it into the crust. I know I would be the envy of every girl in school if they could see Michael with his hands covered in graham cracker crumbs.

When the pan is in the fridge he tells me about his mother, who is away in America, and his father, whom he says is unpredictable and distant. I tell him about living at Auntie's house in Paradise. His voice is low and angry when he tells me that men who want to do those things to little girls should be killed. If he could kill them and not go to jail, he would. I tell him that when I have children I would never leave them with anyone. I confess to him that I hate my mother and that some days I pray for the death of my father. It's scary to tell him everything, but he hugs me and tells me not to worry, that everything will be okay after I eat his magical cheesecake. I don't really believe that things are ever going to be okay, but it makes me feel good to hear him say it. I want him to kiss me, but he just holds me while we watch *Love Connection* on his nineteen-inch TV. I wish I could stay in his apartment with him forever.

After that I spend most of my free time at the Bremmers' playing scrabble with Michael. Auntie Pam teases us about spending so much time together. She says that we had better be careful of Cupid and his flying arrows. I get hot in the face and giggle when she asks if we have had our first kiss, but Michael gets serious and firmly denies that there is anything between us. He would never take advantage of me like that, he adds. One afternoon, in the heat of a close Scrabble game, she asks if he is scoring low because he is distracted by being so close to me. He snaps at her, saying it is time to stop making that stupid joke.

I am so tired of him denying there is something between us that I turn my rack of tiles over and walk away. When he follows me to the mango tree I ask, "Is that what you think of me? That I am stupid? That I am a joke? You couldn't be interested me?"

"Well, Staceyann, it's not that. You are just too young for me, and if not, then you are certainly too young for the law in some countries. Seventeen is almost illegal in Jamaica."

"So, you are attracted to me!"

"Yes, but—"

"But nothing—"

"Staceyann Marshree Chin! Do you know that in America, I could get arrested for being on the same block with you?"

I am so impressed that he remembers my middle name that I kiss him right smack on the mouth and say, "Well, is a good thing this is not America, eh?"

He collapses into laughter but doesn't say anything else, and I know that something has changed.

Michael tells the corniest jokes, but he is the first boy to make me really laugh. We spend hours and hours together. But I don't really know how to get him to ask me to be his girlfriend. Everybody else at school has a boyfriend or a fiancé. I want one too. But I know if I leave it up to Michael we will never do anything. So finally one night I tell him about the kiss I had with Troy. I place my lips on his, in an effort to reenact it. When he kisses me back I know I have something to tell the other girls when I get back on Sunday night.

We play game after game of Scrabble. And he tries to teach me to make cheesecake, but I have no talent for measuring. Eventually he gives up and just makes them himself. We watch CNN while we eat the whole cake in one sitting. When I am not at school, I am in his apartment. And while he goes to work, I spend the afternoon waiting for him to get home. I know Michael would be a good boyfriend; he picks me up from school every Friday and drives me back every Sunday.

Then one balmy Sunday afternoon, with less than three hours to go before curfew, we strip naked and make love. As he enters my body, I am strangely excited that I can finally say I have a serious boyfriend, one with whom I am having sex. Afterward we snuggle and sleep past nightfall. When we awaken, he whispers that he loves me, more than he has ever loved anyone else. And though I am not sure what that means, I sleepily whisper it back.

* * *

After five months, I tell Michael that I want to meet his family. His mother is his real family, but since she is all the way in Florida, he takes me to meet his father. I put on my nicest skirt and ask Michael what he thinks. He rolls his eyes and tells me I am taking this thing too seriously. His stepmother is a small, pretty woman who smiles and tells me she is glad to finally meet a special friend of Michael. His baby sister is almost eight years old. She climbs onto my lap and asks me if I am going to marry her big brother. His father, a tall, loud man who looks like an older version of Michael, laughs and asks us when the family can expect the sound of wedding bells. Michael turns copper red and brushes him off with a quick joke.

That night I run upstairs to recount every single detail of the evening to Racquel. I tell her that I'm not so sure that Michael really loves me. If he really loved me, he would not have been so casual when his family asked about our future. Racquel thinks I am overreacting. She says I have to give him time to make up his mind about something as big as forever. She points out that anybody with eyes can see how much Michael loves me, he was probably just nervous around his father. The red-faced joke grows and grows for months, until it becomes proof that he never had any intention to marry me.

I tell Racquel that I am going to break up with Michael if he does not propose to me soon. I tell her that I think he is only using me to pass time. That when he is really ready he will find someone with a real family to marry; someone with a mother, and father, and little sister that he can go home and sit to dinner with. I read all the articles I can find on why men marry. *Cosmopolitan* magazine reports that men are more likely to marry women when they have met their family. I decide I have to take Michael to meet Grandma.

On the ride to Braeton, when Michael makes silly jokes I remind him of how important my grandmother is to me. And when he begs me to relax, I tell him he has to take this meeting seriously. Finally he just sighs and stares out the window. I want to be calm and light, but I can't. We stop to get mints and Kentucky Fried Chicken for her, but they don't have the kind she likes. And I am afraid the chicken will be cold by the time we get there. I know that Grandma will be grateful no matter what I bring, but I want everything to be perfect. I begin to worry that he won't connect with her, that he will think her stupid or backward. His brooding silence does nothing to alleviate my anxiety.

By the time we arrive, we are both a bundle of twisted nerves and barely controlled annoyance. I stand aside while Grandma shakes his hand and pulls him close. "Pardon me, sir, me don't hear so good, sir. What you say him name is? Midol?"

"No, Grandma. Michael."

"Mynat?"

"Michael, like the angel. Mi-chael?"

"My-kill?"

I look over at Michael, who finds the whole thing hilarious.

"Yes, Grandma. That is right. Him name My-kill."

She reaches for his hand. "Pleased to meet you, Mr. My-kill." I relax when Michael kisses her and brandishes the fried chicken.

Grandma raises her hand to God. "Stacey, from you was a likkle girl, I tell you that Jesus will always provide for the poor and needy. That is why me have to praise him every day. Oonu go to church on Sunday?"

We look at each other and smile. She takes that as an affirmative. "Well, that is good to know. Is nice to meet you, sir. Thank you fi come visit the poor old woman. You want a drink of something cold?"

"No, ma'am."

She settles back into her chair and reaches for her mug of iced water. Her movements are slow and even. I ask her if she wants me to braid her hair before we go. "Thank you very much, me chile. I don't want to keep Mr. My-kill too late, but me was just thinking that it need fi comb. The white hairs them make the head so untidy. As soon as it comb—two-twos, me head start look like rasta."

Her hair is almost all white. But her shoulders feel like a child's beneath my hands. I have to tilt and turn and straighten her the way she straightened me years ago. Her scalp is very tender. I am gentle with the comb.

Michael sits on the veranda while Grandma fills me in on the gossip that has come to her through other visitors.

"You remember Miss Icy? You did hear she dead?"

I part the snowy fuzz into equal parts and weave them into sturdy plats.

"And Miss Cherry gone home to Jesus too—you don't remember Miss

Cherry? Me used to leave you with her when you was a baby and me had to run go Montego Bay?

"And you grandfather—him sick, you know. I hear that him low, low." I try not to think of the pride with which he walked away from me last. "Stacey, when him dead me have to ask your uncle to take me down for the funeral."

When we say good-bye, Grandma pauses dramatically and assures us that this will be the last time we see her alive. God is sure to take her before we visit again. I smile and kiss her forehead. She places her hand against my cheek and tells me that Michael is a good man, that I should try my best to do as he says. "Remember, now, Stacey, obedience is better than sacrifice."

Michael hugs her awkwardly while she begs him to take care of me. "She never have a easy life. And she have a quick mouth. But she good as gold, this one. She never forget her old granny. She always come, even when them others forget. She will come." Her eyes are filled with tears.

I step between them and hug her again.

On the ride back to Kingston we are silent. Occasionally I glance over at Michael, trying to figure out what he is thinking. I am angry with myself for caring what he thinks about Grandma. If Michael doesn't want me because of Grandma, then *he* does not deserve me. But even inside my head that argument sounds inadequate. I want him to tell me that she was wonderful, that she was sweet, that he wouldn't mind having her as a part of his family, but he quietly changes gears and presses the gas pedal without saying a word.

Three days later Elisha calls to say my grandfather is dead. I write one line about him in my journal.

My maternal grandfather died today and his funeral will be on Saturday.

On Saturday, the weatherman announces that it might rain. I wear my black school shoes. I won't ruin my good shoes for him. There are frequent and violent thunderstorms that darken the sky all along the way. The huge raindrops splatter against the glass windows and lightning and thunder make the passengers cringe. The bus ride takes longer because the roads are wet. But when I arrive in Montego Bay, the sky is blue and clear. There is just enough time to get to the church before the service begins. As the organist plays the opening hymn, I slip into the front pew beside my grandmother. She looks very nice in her purple dress with the lavender flowers around the neckline, but the dress is too festive for a funeral.

The ceremony drags on and the room smells like too many flowers. I hum a wordless tune under my breath when the preacher says, "Algie Jennings was a good man, a fine father, and a good soldier in the army of Christ!"

Although Grandma cannot hear the words, she cries silently as they lower the coffin into the ground. I do not understand why she is wasting her tears on this man, but I hold her shaking hand and cry with her. I wonder if my mother knows that her father is dead. I look around at the strangers who line the edges of the grave. None of them feel like family.

But the man is dead now. Perhaps this is the time to stop hating him. I lay a flower at the head of the coffin and gently take Grandma's hand, leading her away from the mouth of the grave, pointing out the people she hasn't seen in years and introducing the younger ones she has never met. A young girl, about sixteen years old, introduces herself as my grandfather's girlfriend. My fury returns, more venomous than before, as she rubs her protruding belly and proudly announces that she is carrying my grandfather's youngest child.

As a Man Sows

In my third semester the bursar pulls me out of class to say that my father's wife is very, very sick. "We don't know what will happen to her, Staceyann. I think you should at least call."

My father and I have not spoken for more than a year. As I dial, I wonder if the number is still the same. The phone rings only once. "Hello."

"Hello. It's me, Staceyann."

"Oh, hello. Hello, young lady, how are you?"

"I'm good. Just here on campus. And how is everything with you?"

"Fine. Fine," he says.

"And Miss P.?"

"Boy, Miss P. sick, you know. Very, very sick. The doctors say there is nothing else to do but make her comfortable."

"Really?"

"That is what them say. But she doing the best she can. She is always asking about you. She was very proud of that graduation dress she made for you. If you were down here, I know she would love to see you."

There is a lump in my throat. "Yes. It was a very nice dress. It was kind of her to make it—ahm, I wanted to ask you—is it possible for—you think it is okay if I come to see her this weekend?"

"Yes, man. I told you already that she would be very glad to see you."

I take the bus to Montego Bay. From downtown I catch a taxi to Leader Avenue. A woman in the back seat sticks her head out the window and asks, "This is Junior Chin house, eh? But wait—you are the daughter who used to live up at Paradise? After the way him treated you, is nice to see that you still come visit him. You are a blessed child."

"Listen, ma'am, I am not really coming to visit my father. I am here to see his wife. She is at the top of those stairs, dying. Death is the only reason that drawing me to this place."

"Well, me dear. Is still good that you visiting her. *Vengeance is mine, sayeth the Lord.* You never know why God allow sickness and death to happen to a person." I nod, but I cannot imagine Miss P. dead.

The new building is several stories higher than the old house. At the top of the stairs I rap my knuckles on the gate. Junior comes out with a towel over his shoulder. He opens the grille and beckons me in.

"As usual, you have to forgive my sweaty clothes. Just trying to keep the old body running. I did not want to make you wait while I change."

I smile and ask, "So how is Miss P. doing?"

He points toward a door and calls out her name. "Pat. Miss P. Patricia, you have a visitor here. Can she come in?"

Miss P. is many shades darker than she was before. Her face is puffy and shiny. I ask her how she's feeling.

"Not so good," she says. "Nobody knows what is wrong with me, I am here getting sicker every day."

I ask if she had had a couple of different doctors' opinions.

"Stacey, I'm so tired. I go everywhere—Miami, New York, Canada—yet nobody can tell me what is wrong with me."

I have no idea what to say.

She keeps nodding off to sleep. I sit with her for a while. Her nose and cheeks are twisted from swelling. She looks about sixty pounds heavier than her regular weight. It is as if someone has put a bicycle pump to her mouth and filled her with air.

Junior comes into the room with a picture of a small girl smiling.

"Look here, I have something I want to show you," he says. "Look at this mouth. This is my granddaughter, Mikey's daughter, Abby. Look at her mouth!" He is excited to share this bit of information. "All the children who come from my loins have this mouth. You don't have this mouth. That is how I know you are not my child—you do not have this mouth!"

I don't say anything, but Miss P. tries to sit up. "Junior, let bygones be bygones, nuh! She never come here to talk 'bout that. She come to visit me." Her voice is plaintive as she waves him away.

When he leaves the room, I ask, "Miss P., do you think Junior is my father?"

"I don't know, Staceyann. I really don't know."

"Okay. So how is Ruel?"

Her face lights up. "Oh, he's in Canada at school. He's okay, man. If I die tomorrow, I know I did a good job with that one. He is a fine young man. I am very proud of him."

She asks about Shortwood. I tell her it is very good.

"I am glad. I know you going to do something wonderful with your life. No matter if Junior is your father or not. I would tell you if I know. Especially now. I definitely don't want to carry something like that to my grave."

I thank her for her honesty and tell her I have to leave. She asks if I will come back to see her soon. I say that I will. She is asleep before I close the door.

I read about Miss P.'s death in the obituaries. I clip the notice from the paper and use it as a bookmark. For a week I attend classes and tell myself that nothing has changed. Then the weekend comes and Michael whispers that it is okay for me to cry.

For most of the night, he holds me while I cry. It is morning before I am able to say how I feel. He nods when I tell him that I feel stupid for crying when Miss P. could not even acknowledge me as her stepdaughter. His hands are steady on my back when I say that I hate my father. But I want him to talk it through with me. I want him to help me understand why I feel so sad about a woman who was not even that close to me. I want him to say that I shouldn't cry about Miss P. and Junior Chin, that they are not my family. I want him to say that he is my family and that he will never leave me.

The next weekend when he brings me dinner I ask him why he finds it so hard to talk to me about death and family and his feelings. He sighs heavily and closes his eyes. I ask him what he would do if I were to die. He says it would be hard, but he would do his best to move on with his life. I don't want him to move on. I tell him I expect him to be devastated. If he died, I know I would want to die too. I want him to promise me that if I died, he would never get over me. But he only says that it is getting late and he has to go soon.

I can't believe he is dismissing me like this. I grab his car keys and I tell him that he is nothing but a coward. He softly accuses me of being melodramatic. I wish he would show some passion. I tell him I feel like I am trapped in a relationship with a dead fish. Then I toss his car keys onto the lawn. He calmly retrieves them and comes back into the car. He asks me what I want from him. I say nothing and before I know what has happened we have broken off our almost-two-year relationship. I want to take back everything that was said, but I instead I say, "Okay, fine, Michael. Go. Just go and don't say anything more to me. And don't call me either. I don't need you to be okay. I don't need anybody. Just go and don't ever come back."

When Racquel asks, I tell her that Michael is selfish and has no idea how to love a woman. I tell her that I am also glad to be done with waiting for him to leave me, plus it's time I stop fooling around with romance and turn my attention to my studies. I pack away everything that reminds me of Michael and spend my waking moments reading about speed and velocity and electrons. I take on extra work so I am busy from dawn till night. Most evenings I am so tired I fall into bed without changing my clothes. In a few weeks, I don't even think of Michael as I go about my day.

Without any weekends with Michael, Shortwood becomes a cage. I like being in college, but I am bored with the pure sciences. When I tell my chemistry professor that I wish I had come in as an English literature or psychology major, she suggests that I apply to literature or psychology programs at the University of the West Indies.

When the acceptance letter arrives in the mail, I don't know what to do with myself. It all feels a little bizarre, like it's not really happening to me. One minute I am sitting in my physics class wanting to die from boredom, the next I am on my way to studying at the most prestigious institution in the Caribbean. Everybody is saying how lucky I am. Annmarie says that Auntie Ella is very proud of me, and Uncle Hartley says he never doubted that I could do it. But I am not quite sure what it is that I have done.

I visit Uncle Charlie to tell him my big news and to ask him for a contribution. His hair has turned gray and his arms and legs no longer fill out his clothes. He gladly agrees to give me the tuition for the first year. I am surprised he says yes, so I nod vigorously when he asks me if it is okay to give me a check. "This is a big amount, you know, Stacey. I don't want you walking around with this much cash."

Uncle Charlie has become a deacon in his church. His eyes light up when he talks about his belief in God. He asks if I go to a good church in Kingston. I want him to keep giving me money for school, so I do not tell him that I am not sure I believe in God anymore. I tell him that there is a beautiful chapel on the university campus. As I nod and watch him pull out his tattered checkbook, I realize I have nothing else to say to him. He squints and adjusts his glasses when he writes. I feel funny just sitting there waiting, so I ask about Delano. He lights up when he tells me that Delano is still living in Germany. "Yes, man. Him having a good time over there. Him speak the German language and everything. And I think him say your mother is living over there too."

"My mother? How come? She not living in Canada anymore?" It annoys me that I sound so eager, but I want him to tell me everything he knows about my mother. I want to know if Delano has seen her or talked to her, if she asked him anything about me. Suddenly I miss Delano. I ask Uncle Charlie what part of Germany he said he lived in and if we could call him there now.

"I don't really remember what part exactly. And I don't really have a telephone number for him. When him call again I will ask him for you."

"Okay, Uncle Charlie. And thanks again for the tuition money."

On the bus to Kingston, I think of my mother speaking German. I spent seven years studying French because Mummy spoke French in Montreal. Now she is not even living in Canada. Germany seems so far away from Jamaica. It makes me sick to my stomach to think that I may never see my mother again.

Gave Themselves Over
to Vile Affections

My rented flat is small, but it is nice and just five minutes' walk from the university. On the first day I arrive early. I spend the hour watching pretty girls jump from shiny cars dressed in long, loose skirts and very short shorts. I am very excited to be studying at the university, but by the end of my first class I am annoyed with the immaturity of the boys. I had expected them to be like Michael. But most of them act like eleven-year-olds, throwing paper missiles at each other and making farting noises when the professor's back is turned.

The girls impress me with their focus and intelligence, especially the rebels for whom the rules of normal conduct do not apply. These girls are not afraid to show their bodies. And most of them have strong opinions about sex and God and whether Jamaica is backward for having a law that prohibits homosexuals from having sex with each other, which they have no qualms about voicing.

In my Introduction to Philosophy class, Dr. McKenzie, with his bushy eyebrows and deliberate speech, allows us to argue and curse and challenge each other without boundaries. For most of the sessions, Annabella Andersen, a pretty girl with short curly hair, chews on her pen and listens intently. She doesn't say much, but when she does it is to challenge ideas of race, gender, or sexuality. I find myself wanting to be next to her.

One day Brandt, a Trinidadian boy, turns to me and whispers, "It's a pleasure to be in the presence of a woman who is striking in both intellect and aesthetics."

"I wouldn't put it as Victorian as that, but I know exactly what you mean. She is soooo sharp and sexy at the same time."

Brandt taps his pen against his forehead and raises his eyebrows. "I wasn't talking about her. I was talking about you."

I wave him away. "Oh, thank you very much, but you don't have to play those games with me. She is the prettiest girl in here and you and I both know it."

"I know you have very strong opinions, Miss Chin, but I think this is the arena where we are permitted to differ. Plus, Annabella is my buddy. We don't have any pheromones floating around between us."

Brandt invites me to eat lunch with him and Annabella. On the walk to the car they ask where I'm from, what my interests are, if I'm a fatalist or a determinist. Then Brandt jumps in with, "I saw you admiring our mutual friend here in class. Does that mean you're gay and you want to jump her bones?"

"What!" My heart is trying to squeeze itself through my throat. I can't tell if he is joking. I tell myself he has no right to ask me that, but I am not offended that he did. I try to look everywhere but at Annabella. But my eyes keep landing on her open wine-red mouth.

"No need to be shy," he continues, "we are all intellectuals here. You are what you are and to us it is only relevant if we intend to move in on you ourselves."

Annabella is dying with laughter. There is something beautiful about the way she lets herself go when she laughs. I quickly look away before she notices me watching her. Brandt narrows his eyes at her until she quiets down. "But seriously," he continues, "is there room for a lone academic from the eastern Caribbean, or are you solely enamored with the half-Swede, half-Jamaican beauty Miss Andersen, here?"

Annabella kicks him with the longest leg in the world. "Brandt, could you please leave her alone? Anyways, Staceyann, if you can stand this idiot, we could meet this weekend?"

"Oh, he's no problem, and funny as hell." My face is hot, and my voice sounds high. "And I am completely available on the weekends."

"Okay, I'll pick up both of you. Brandt is just at Hope Pastures. Where are you?"

I don't trust myself to speak again, so I write down my address and hand it to her. I am not sure what is wrong with me. Every time I am around Annabella I start feeling funny in my stomach.

Brandt is relentless. "But seriously, are you one of those men-hating lesbians? Or are you a freaky bisexual who can't make up your mind? Because the Bible (which I don't happen to always follow) tells you, *You cannot serve two masters.* You are either gay or straight! Everybody has to choose."

Anna chews on the poor pencil and wrinkles her brow. "I think it is so much more complex than that. She could be attracted to both sexes. Should she deny one of them just because . . ." I am no longer listening, but watching her mouth work its way around the wooden pencil.

"Staceyann, you still have not answered my question."

Brandt's voice jolts me from my reverie. "What? I'm sorry. I was . . ."

"Well—"

I jump in, "I don't think I am anything." Anna looks at me dubiously. "I mean, I think that these questions are interesting, but who can say what you are, really? You are only a product of your environment. Who can say what we would be without these artificial social constructs?"

"But, Staceyann"—Annabella's fingers are gentle on my arm—"those social constructs do exist, so you have to be *something.*"

"True—true, hmm, but—but . . ." I move away from Annabella's touch and clear my throat. "*Because* I can't distinguish what is constructed and what is not, I would rather not try to say. I believe what I am is as elusive as what I could have been if I . . ." I am rambling, but I can't help myself. I wish Brandt would just go away and leave Annabella and me alone.

Annabella is serious as she responds, "Well, I believe you can choose an identity, but I am fully aware that it is not entirely a matter of choice. I am what I am in terms of biology and experience. But I still have the capacity to change my allegiances or to be influenced by society or religion or even desire."

Something about the way she says the word desire makes my stomach flip. I am suddenly afraid that one of them will notice me looking at Anna's mouth. I get up so quickly my books and pencils fall to the floor.

"You okay, Staceyann?" Annabella looks at me.

"Yeah, man, I am fine—it's just that we don't seem to be getting anywhere and I am getting hungry. Can we pursue this line of argument when my stomach is full?"

"Okay, but, guys, I have to confess I am running a little short on cash, so can we eat lunch at my house today?" Her bottom brushes against me as she bends to pick up her backpack.

Annabella's house is the most elegant I have ever seen. There are large wooden chests and armoires and carved furniture everywhere. The dining room is a giant hall with the long table set formally for dinner. The maid, silent and uniformed, anticipates your need and meets it before you ask. The bedrooms upstairs are spacious and comfortable. Standing in Annabella's room, looking out over the garden, I know that when I have a home I want it to be every bit as grand as this.

"Hey, Staceyann, you wanna spend the night here tonight? My mom says it's cool."

I turn around, startled. I thought I was alone. "Oh, ah—I didn't—"

"If you have plans it's okay."

"No—no, no plans. I just don't have any clothes with me."

"I can take you to get clothes, or you could borrow some from me. Just wash your undies and sleep without. They should be dry in the morning."

I quietly take a deep breath to conceal my excitement.

After dinner we read Lorna Goodison. I know half her poems by heart. I can't stop talking about how the poems make you feel.

"I really, really love her work. She just makes the women jump off the page. This poem about her mother reminds me of the grandma I knew as a little girl. I always cry at the part when her mother breaks down. I can feel her passion and her loneliness and her joy in every line."

"Yeah. I know what you mean. She makes Jamaica seem like paradise. Sometimes I read a line and I just feel so lucky to be Jamaican."

"I don't know if I feel lucky to be Jamaican, Anna. It really depends on what side of Paradise you're from."

"I suppose."

"I mean, you can't imagine that your helper feels lucky to be Jamaican."

"So you think money is all that matters? What about her children? I think we can't make the assumption that she is unhappy because she is poor."

I think about the people who live in Paradise Crescent. Life would have been different there if we hadn't been so poor. But I don't say anything to Anna. Those memories have no place here. She looks too beautiful sitting by the window with her feet tucked under her bottom.

"I have to tell you that I think you are the most beautiful girl I have ever seen." I can't believe I just said that.

Annabella chews her pencil and sighs. "Thank you, but I am not sure what to say to that."

"You don't have to say anything else. I was just paying you a simple compliment. All you have to do is say thank you."

"Yes, but that is not all you are saying when you say that. And it's not like I am not flattered. If Jamaica was a different place, I might feel differently, but I don't think I have the freedom to even consider that as an option."

"Annabella, I did not ask you to consider anything. I just said that I thought you were beautiful. And you are. So just accept the compliment and let us move on. I am going to get some juice, do you want some?"

"That would be nice, thank you."

As class provocateur, I read ahead and take notes so I can pick arguments with the girls I find attractive. Most of them ignore me—except for Tanya, who giggles when I tell her I'm not sure that she's as smart as she is pretty. One evening after class she invites me back to her dorm room. The walk across campus is tense, with neither of us saying much.

When we get to her room, she locks the door behind her and asks me what I want to do. I don't know what to say, so I tell her whatever she wants to do is fine with me. I sit on her bed and watch her change into a T-shirt and shorts. I get the feeling that she is flirting with me, but I'm not sure. Then she sits next to me and puts her hand on my leg. I pull her to me and place my lips against hers.

I spend two hours in Tanya's room. I want to make love to her, but she tells me that she is not a lesbian. When I try to tell her how much I like her, she laughs and says, "I'm just curious, Stacey. This is an experiment. I chose you because people say that you are that way, but please, don't get too attached."

During class I fantasize about having sex with Tanya. I keep hoping she will invite me to her room again. But she doesn't, and I spend the nights crying and writing love letters I will never send. Then I wonder if I am just curious also. Maybe I just want to sleep with a girl so I can say I tried it. But I'm not so convinced when I spend the days hoping that

Tanya or Belinda or Francine will take a chance and invite me up to the dorms to "experiment." But everyone seems a little afraid or disgusted, even the ones who start out flirting with me.

When Brandt catches me watching the pretty English major Seranna, he pokes me with his pencil. "I see you have transferred your ardor again, Miss Chin. It's a good thing I am not too attached to you, you are so disloyal in love!"

"Oh, shut up, Brandt Benetton!" I'm much harsher than I intend.

"I'm just teasing, Stace. No need to get your knickers in a bunch."

"I know. I'm sorry, Brandt. But you are not the only one saying things."

"It's okay. I know, but you are only acting like an adolescent boy because you are frustrated."

"Frustrated is not the word! I am going stark raving mad here. Everybody wants to flirt, but nobody wants to deliver the goods."

"So you are really considering this lesbian thing, eh?"

"Not lesbian. Bisexual."

"If you so bisexual, how come you aren't attracted to boys?"

"I have been. I am just not attracted to any right now! And I don't even know if this bisexual thing is serious, but I am interested in exploring it. I thought that that was what university is all about. Exploration."

"What about Tanya? I thought you were *exploring* that. What happened?"

"Same thing that happen with Annabella and Lesley and Kemora and all those girls who would jump to sleep with another girl if their boyfriends wanted it but won't even let themselves admit that they might like it without him. I suppose it is hard to ignore the fact that you could get jumped or raped or killed if somebody suspect you could be serious about a woman. Maybe I might have to leave Jamaica."

"Where would you go, though?"

"New York, I guess. I like how James Baldwin describes New York in *Another Country*. I can't imagine being in a place where you can just be everything that you want to be. Imagine, Brandt, having the freedom to bleed and obsess and be concerned with the tragedy of your life, *your chosen life!*"

"But didn't the guy in the book kill himself?"

"Yes, but that is not the point. There is a line in the book—you read it?"

"I fully intended to, but—"

"Well, there is this line in it. *The train shot into the darkness with phallic abandon.* I had to read the line again. Brandt, I want to see the train shoot into the dark with phallic abandon!"

"Well, for a lesbian, you are very impressed with that phallic reference."

"Brandt, I am not—"

"I know, I know. I'm just teasing. New York sounds cool. And I am sure you would have some kind of lesbian—I mean, *bisexual* experience in New York. I hear that if you throw a stone into a crowd in the Village, you are bound to hit at least three lesbians."

"Very funny, Brandt. But this is serious, I really want to go somewhere for the summer."

"So don't think about it anymore. Just apply for a visa and go visit your New York."

Love as I Have Loved You

When the plane lands, the New York City lights blink in code, as if they are welcoming me to the city. I am staying with my mother's older brother, David, in the projects of Red Hook in Brooklyn. The dim hallway reeks of urine, and the noise of boys fighting and sirens outside the window is unbearable.

One night, when I am taking the garbage to the incinerator, a tall fat man with a runny nose offers me twenty dollars to give him a blow job. I drop the garbage in the hallway and scream for Uncle David, who comes barreling out the front door with a knife. The fat man ambles away before I can find the words to say what happened. Uncle David hugs me and warns me to avoid the people who live in the other apartments.

I spend the hot and humid days roaming the city. A dollar twenty-five takes me anywhere on the subway. And I love to stand on the platform and watch the gigantic metal structure squeal to a halt. Then I hop into the middle car and attempt small talk with the other passengers. "Hey, there. My name is Staceyann Chin. What is your name?"

People look at me like I am crazy. Only other tourists talk to me. In Union Square, I meet a man who was born in South Africa of Dutch parents and raised in London. His wife is Somalian and they are both moving to Italy after their summer vacation in New York and Toronto. I feel quite cosmopolitan just talking to him. The chic Asian girls in Banana Republic jackets rush quickly by me. Caribbean restaurants, slim dark men in leather suits, pornographic bookstores, Black girls with Afro-Mohawks, and white girls with pink hair line the streets.

One afternoon I venture into a bar called Stonewall. A white man dressed in a blond wig and women's clothing offers to buy me a drink.

"So where are you from, honey?"

His voice is husky and his mascara is running, so he looks like a raccoon in sequined eveningwear. I sip my ginger ale and whisper, "Jamaica."

"Oh, I had a Jamaican lover once. He had the biggest dick I had ever seen. I always had to stay in bed after we fucked. I couldn't walk. You shoulda seen me, honey, I would be laid out like a dead body *for days*! I finally had to leave him when it got ridiculous. He wanted to fuck every day. I think I would be in a wheelchair if I had kept on with that big ole Jamaican dick." He turns his rheumy eyes to the side and runs his finger down his cheek. "Now me? My dick is the most itty-bitty thing in the whole wide world. Not that you would care—aren't you a lesbian?"

"Ah—I—I—really don't know. I think I am. I know I like girls, but—I—I don't—"

"Sweetie, you ain't gotta know just yet. You young, you'll figure it out. Whatever it is, just go with it. Fuck, this is New York City! You can be anything you goddamned wanna be. Now run along, little maybe-dyke, I see a nice little tidbit I need to go swallow up."

There is something thrilling about the way he said fuck and dick out loud in public. In Jamaica I could get killed for talking about the things I want to do with women.

I am almost halfway through my trip when I discover the bookstores: A DIFFERENT LIGHT, OSCAR WILDE, THE REVOLUTIONARY BOOKSTORE, THE PEOPLE'S REPUBLIC OF ANTI-IMPERIALIST LITERATURE—the names on the signs draw me in. I find a volume of short stories with true lesbian love stories. I read and reread the stories. I am fascinated with people *coming out of the closet*. They describe how good it feels to be proud of their sexuality. I suddenly want to *come out* to my friends as a lesbian. Now I want everyone to know exactly what I am.

I buy psychology books about homosexuality and highlight sections I think will help with my coming-out process. I pack my books and head off to the airport.

I lift my overweight suitcase and hand my passport to the woman checking me in.

"What is it that you have in this bag? A body?"

"No, just books. Just books I picked up in the hundreds of little bookstores in New York City." I smile and watch her struggle to heave the suitcase onto the conveyor belt.

* * *

I decide to come out to Racquel first. Not just because she is my oldest friend, but because she may be the only person in my life who could
accept this about me and still love me the same.

Racquel is set to begin her first year at the university this semester, so
we arrange to meet the first day right after classes. That morning I wear
my favorite sarong and pull my hair back into a tight ponytail. One of the
coming-out books says that it is best to look as becoming and as "normal"
as possible when delivering the news to family and friends. Looking good
makes it harder for people you love to reject you. So I add perfume and
put on some lip gloss. If she tells me she doesn't want to be my friend, it
won't be because I look shabby.

I am happy that she is an English major because we get to see each
other every day. Then I worry that that won't be so good if she no longer
wants to be my friend. Losing Racquel would be like losing my only sister. I hope she won't think I suddenly want to convert her so I can have
wild, crazy sex with her. In my heart of hearts I believe that Racquel
will remain my friend, but all the nasty comments I grew up hearing
about the sinful residents of Sodom and Gomorrah make me doubt my
instincts. Maybe I should wait. Maybe I should tell her later on in the
semester. But I am afraid that someone will say something to her before
I do. It has to be now.

I spend the day searching the library for newspaper articles about
homosexuality. All I find are stories about women who are caught having sex with their children or men raping little boys. The articles say that
homosexuality is the most unforgivable sin. Almost all the reported incidents involve mobs. Many end in violence and sometimes, for the alleged
homosexual, or batty man, death. I tell myself I have to stop reading these
horrible stories, but hours later I have to drag myself away to go meet
Racquel. I dash across the campus and arrive sweaty and on edge.

I can hardly concentrate on what Racquel is saying. "Staceyann, it
just seems like the work is so much, and nobody seems to help you with
anything. And every paper wants to know how I feel about this and that
and whatnot! I am so tired of examining morality!"

I laugh nervously and tell her that she has many more years to go
before she is done with arguments about morality. I wonder if a good

segue is to ask what her moral stance is on homosexuality. I try to open my mouth to ask, but the words are stuck in my throat.

When Racquel confesses that she thought the boys would be more mature at the university I see my opening. I gather my courage and blurt out, "Racquel, I think I have something I should tell you."

She looks up from her rice and peas and pushes her plate aside. "What's up, big sis?"

"Well, I—I think I know what you mean. Yeah, I think the boys are immature too—and I think—no—I *know*—"

"Staceyann, I think I am a lesbian."

"What! What did you say, Racquel Antoinette Bremmer?"

"Just what I said—I think I might be homosexual."

"Well I guess that makes two of us on the island."

"No—no! You are pulling my leg! You cannot be serious! Really?"

The silence is long and filled with all our questions. I sip on my Pepsi and wait for her to put her ginger beer down.

Racquel takes a deep breath and leans in to me. "Stace, what exactly are you saying to me?"

"Racquel, are you deaf? I like girls. I think that they are sexy. I—I haven't really had sex with anybody yet, but I sure as hell want to."

"Wow! Wow! So why you just telling me now?"

"Well, I never wanted to influence you—and I thought you were going to stop talking to me . . ."

"You should know better than that. And don't think I didn't have my suspicions—but I bet you never even *suspect* anything with me."

"Not at all. Wow! You're not joking? You really like women?"

"More than I care to say out loud." Racquel lowers her voice and confesses that she has had those feelings for years. "I have had crushes on my friends since prep school, but you know how it go in Jamaica . . ."

"Tell me about it! You think things would be different on the campus, eh?"

"Yes, but you learn quick that them not. Listen, when I came in for registration, a construction worker was cussing out a boy because he had in an earring—about how the university is the reason why *battymanism* is taking over the island. How this kind free thinking is why the dollar not worth anything—and everybody was just nodding, telling him that him is right."

"Yeah, but I don't care what them say. This is how I am and I am not going to feel ashamed of it. But seriously, when did you know that you were, you know . . ."

I beg her to tell me every single detail about every girl she has ever liked. We make a list of the girls in Kingston that we think are cute. When we discover common crushes, we fall over ourselves laughing. I am relieved and happy that I told her. Now I'm not alone. I tell her about my crush on Seranna, my Shakespeare study partner. Racquel urges me to make a move on her. When I ask her if she has ever made a move on anyone, she tells me that she has already kissed the girl she likes. She describes it as the single most amazing event of her life. I decide it is time to do something about Seranna.

Seranna and I are only study partners because I asked her before anyone else did. We meet in her room because the air conditioner in the library is always turned up too high. The following week when she mentions that her neck hurts, I offer to massage it for her. Her skin is warm under my hands, and I let my fingers slip beneath the collar of her white silk blouse. When I unsnap her bra, she does not resist. Twenty minutes later we are both naked from the waist up and kissing. Though I do not have the courage to reach below her belt, making out with Seranna is the most exciting thing I have ever done.

As I am leaving, she leans her body against the closed door and asks what can I give her in exchange for my passage out. I offer her my next study session. She accepts and we kiss long and hard to seal the deal. On my way home, I inhale the scent of her perfume on my hands, reliving the evening and counting the hours till I see her next.

Racquel and I have an emergency meeting to discuss how things went with Seranna. When I tell her we took our shirts off, she high-fives me and points out that being a lesbian in Jamaica may not be so bad for me. "If women are taking off their clothes on the first date, our little island may be not be as *homophobic* as you think."

She encourages me to tell Annabella and Brandt that I am not bisexual but lesbian. Annabella blushes and giggles and tells me that she knew all along. Brandt says he is proud of me for finally admitting it. I am so relieved I decide to have a real talk with Seranna about my sexuality. I wait until we are half-naked and snuggling to lean in to her neck and tell her that the rumors about my being a lesbian are true. She pushes me away and reaches for her shirt. When she is dressed, she tells me to get out of her room. "You disgust me with your nastiness, Staceyann Chin! I can't imagine why I let you in my room! I never, ever want to see you again."

I move toward her, to hug her, to beg her not to speak to me like that, but she quickly opens the door and tosses my books out into the hallway. The girl who lives in the room next door pokes her head out to ask if everything is all right. I tell her to mind her own business. When Seranna tries to shut the door, I stick my foot inside and ask, "What do you think we were doing, Seranna? We were participating in lesbian sexual activity! You might be bisexual, but you were rolling around with a lesbian."

"Staceyann, lower your voice! And if you ever speak to me again, I will tell everyone that today you came into my room and tried to put your hand up my skirt when I was sleeping. If I were you, I would forget you ever knew a girl called Seranna Laine Parker."

I spend the days longing for Seranna. Until I notice that Cheryl, from my African Literature tutorial, is making eyes at me. I say hello after class and she invites me to spend the night in her room. Cheryl's boyfriend has gone to Miami for the weekend, and she has always been curious about kissing women, she says. We spend the night groping at each other fully clothed. The following week, when she tells me her boyfriend wants to watch, I tell her I cannot see her again. Then Tanya, from social sciences, admits to me that she prefers women to men. After nights and nights of kissing, I ask her if she could ever partner exclusively with a woman. She points out that that kind of life is an abomination. We never see each other again. There are plenty of girls who allow for some sexual intimacy under the guise of exploration, but they stop talking to me when they find out that I want to be exclusive. The more it happens, the angrier I become.

Every day I complain to Racquel. "We really do live in a community of the most vile type of hypocrites! Imagine, all those intellectuals who talk about homosexuality in class—Racquel, I have heard them myself— they talk about freedom and progress and all that crap! Some of them have *friends* that everybody know for sure that them gay. Some of those girls have been in bed with me! And now they are acting as if I am some sort of pariah!"

"Yes, Stace, but I think people are just uncomfortable with you announcing it so loudly."

"You mean to tell me that them don't mind if I am a lesbian, but them vex with me for saying it?"

Racquel cautions, "Well, you can say it as much as you want, but changes like these take time. You can't expect people to just accept your coming out so easily. Give them a few weeks, a week even."

"No, Racquel—they are all hypocrites. If my friends cannot accept me now, them can kiss my ass! I don't need any of their halfway friendships. And none of them can tell me how to act. I will say it as much as I want. I intend to tell every one of my friends so I can see exactly what they are made of!"

The girls are generally very clear about how they feel. One girl in my African Philosophy class threatens to pay somebody to kill me if I ever come near her again. Another retracts an invitation to her birthday party. Animated conversations end when I approach. And when I attempt to speak to anyone, the crowd disperses. Angry and defiant, one day I walk into the center of the hush and extend my right hand to the girl who sits behind me in Shakespeare. As she takes it I say, "Hi there, Kendra, I know you know I'm Staceyann, but I don't think it's been confirmed for you that I eat pussy and not dick." I grin when she withdraws her hand and quickly shoves it in her pocket.

The boys, however, are caught somewhere between livid and fascinated. My classmate Martin approaches me after class. "So, Stacey, since you say you are a lesbian, I have a friend who would do a little thing with you. I can hook you up if I can watch."

"No, thank you, Martin. If and when I have sex with any woman, no man will be watching. This is not *Playboy*. It is a relationship between me and my girl. Would you like it if Allan were to watch you have sex with Cherise?"

"Stacey, I was just trying to help you. You don't have to be so crude."

"Martin, I am only being crude because you were being crude just now. How you going to invite yourself into my sex life? You think every time a woman have sex it have to include you and your little shrimp dick?"

"You know, Stacey, if I were you I would be careful how you move on this campus. One of these days that mouth of yours is going to get you into some real trouble."

"Thank you for the advice, Martin. As from today I will refrain from telling people that I am a lesbian." I raise my voice and gesture to Martin. "You hear this, everybody? Because of Martin's expert advice, I am never going to tell any of you that I am a lesbian, that I am choosing not to have sex with men—because of this lone cowboy I will now conduct myself in a manner that will keep me safe from the vigilante homophobes on this island."

Martin pulls his cap down over his eyes and whispers, "Staceyann Chin, it looks like you just want something to happen to you. If I were you I would watch my step." He bumps me with his shoulder as he walks away.

A tiny worry that I am in danger niggles at me. I become aware of the boys who watch me as I move across the campus. I comb the newspapers for incidents of violent homophobia. I become obsessed with the stories I read of gay men and lesbians who are attacked by mobs in rural Jamaica. Now that I am out, it feels like there are more of them happening. But I count the incidents and the numbers haven't changed.

I remind myself that the University of the West Indies is the place where the intellectuals are. People like Martin may have their narrow-minded opinions, but this is a place of scholarship. People are not attacked here. I am definitely spooking myself. Nobody would be so stupid as to attack me here, I think. I laugh at myself for being so skittish. I tell myself that there is no reason to be so scared.

That night I decide to show everybody that I am not afraid. I sift through the lesbian magazines I bought in New York, fascinated with the women with very, very short hair. The shorter the hair, the more confident they seem. The next day I walk into the barbershop and tell the barber to take it all off. He slowly changes the head of his electronic clippers and asks, "You sure that is what you want?"

"Yes. Yes, I am very sure. Just shave it off clean."

"Now, why you want to go and do that? You want to look like you have cancer?"

"You going to shave it or you going to question me? There's another barbershop just down the street. My money is just as good there."

The clippers are cold at the back of my neck. He hesitates for only a moment before he flips the switch. At first there is a buzzing sensation, then there is a rush of cool air tickling my naked scalp as he removes the hair. Halfway through the process I catch a glimpse of myself in the mirror. I look like a punk rocker. Then he spins the chair and the rest of the hair falls to the floor around me. When he is finished, there is a complete stranger staring back at me. I never realized how much my hair pulled focus away from my eyes, my cheekbones, my mouth—every feature looks more present, fuller on my face. I look more honest to myself.

"Now you look like a dyke," I tell myself.

"What you say? You talking to me?" asks the barber.

"No. I was just saying that I finally look like myself."

"All right, if you say so. You can pay the guy at the front."

Everyone is shocked. Seranna asks loudly, "Why you do that to your hair? Why on earth would you want to look like a man?"

"No, Seranna, I want to look like a dyke. So I am wearing a dyke hairstyle. You have a problem with that?" She buttons her lips and looks away.

Racquel is worried that I am putting myself in danger unnecessarily. I tell her I won't allow myself to be cowed back into the closet. She tells me that people are saying I sleep with a different girl every night and that I have sex with little girls and dogs too. She points out that it doesn't take long for rumors about my close friends to join the circuit too. I tell her that if she feels like she is in any danger, I would understand if she wanted to conduct our relationship in private. She tells me that she is not really worried. "I am okay. Plus, people know that you and I are like sisters. And nobody suspects anything about me because I wear heels and lipstick. I just want *you* to be more careful. You never know what these idiots will do to you if they get the chance."

In the climate of the nasty rumors, Annabella and Brandt begin to avoid me. Annabella explains that she doesn't care that I am a lesbian, but she thinks I am being overly offensive. "Some of the things you say to people are really uncalled for. Gay or straight, Staceyann, in these last weeks, being around you has been very unpleasant." Brandt nods in agreement.

The tears sting my eyes, but I take a breath and will them away. I say that I am disappointed and angry, that I had expected some people to move away from me, but not them. "You guys have known about me from the very beginning. In a funny kind of way, you knew before I did."

Brandt looks away, but I can see that he is still siding with Annabella, who has her mouth set in a way that lets me know she has already made up her mind. I decide right then that I don't need them. I tell them they no longer have to worry about what I say to people. "I'd really appreciate it if you guys started pretending that I'm dead." I push past Annabella and swat Brandt's hand from my shoulder.

Lisa, my study partner in philosophy, slips me a note explaining that she really, really likes me as a person, but people in her dorm are asking what we do together when we study in her room. She wants to stop studying together. I read the note, crush it, and toss it back to her. It feels like I am losing everybody. I button my lips and look away, taking deep, even breaths and clenching my teeth to keep the tears from starting. Lisa looks nervously around, leans in toward my desk, and whispers, "Staceyann, you have to understand, I don't have anything against your business, but somebody wrote the word *lesbian* on my door last night!"

"Are you a lesbian?" I ask out loud.

"What?"

"Are you a lesbian?" I repeat.

"No! What kind of question is that?"

"Lisa, if you are not a lesbian, then it doesn't matter what a stupid backward-thinking bigot writes on your door, now, does it?"

"Is not as easy as that, Stacey."

"It never is, Lisa. Some people will stand up for friendship and some people won't. But since we were never friends, I guess none of that is relevant, now, is it?"

"Staceyann—"

"You know, Lisa, I really would like to hear what the teacher is saying. I would appreciate it if you would let me."

Pretty soon, the boys make a game of trying to guess which of my friends I have already had sex with. That makes the girls avoid me altogether. I tell myself that I do not care. I simply put on my headphones and crank up the volume on Melissa Etheridge's *Yes I Am,* trying my best to look like it doesn't bother me that I have lost all my friends.

One evening, the West Indian drama lecturer, Miss Archer, beckons me into her office. "Staceyann, you seem to have a lot of time on your hands, you want to help me with a theater production?"

I am so grateful to have something to do with my evenings. Miss Archer is mounting *Passages,* a theatrical interpretation of Kamau Braithwaite's poems from *The Arrivants.* My job is to run lines with the players while they learn them. The cast is loud and jovial and no one seems to care about who is dating whom. Everyone talks passionately about *the work*. Emette Hicklingworth, a heavyset, effeminate boy, says that he only began *living* after he discovered the stage. "I was a corpse before that, a walking, talking, depressed corpse. The Creative Arts Center changed my life. Here there is no Black and white, no rich and poor, no outcast or member—here there is only the show!"

And it does seem as if the center is a home for misfits. The more outrageous characters seem to be indulged by everyone. People sing at the top of their voices on the steps of the center, and all throughout rehearsals they mutter and scream lines at each other. There is no room for self-consciousness on the stage. For the first time since I came out, I feel like I belong. I am ecstatic to discover that Racquel is also in the cast. Because of the production I can see her every day without people gossiping about us.

I work at pleasing Miss Archer. I throw myself into the process. Often I step into the part and explore it with the players in order to find better ways to express the lines. One day I am working with Racquel when Miss Archer walks in. "Oh, Staceyann, I didn't know that you were such an actress. You look like you should be starring in this production, man."

At first I protest and say I am not an actor, but she insists that I will be a wonderful addition to the cast. She says she will not take no for an answer. Miss Archer does a little dance and says how delighted she is to have me on board. "You really seem to have a knack for the stage, Staceyann. I think it is a good idea for you to try it."

To conceal my swelling pride, I open the script and shout to the cast, "All right, everybody! Run the lines again, from the top—and absolutely no mistakes this time."

Ye Without Sin Cast the First Stone

After rehearsals I walk across the campus to visit Anya, who pretends she does not know I have a crush on her. Nobody knows that we are friends yet, and I am working very hard to keep it that way.

My headphones are blasting Sarah McLachlan's *Fumbling Towards Ecstasy* into my ears. So immersed am I in the music, I do not hear the boys until they have circled me. By the time I look up, they have herded me through the open door of the bathroom. I take off my headphones and stuff them into my pocket.

My heart hammers a hole through my chest. I try to calm my nerves by counting.

One.

Two.

Three. I can't remember what number comes after three.

The lock clicks comfortably into place as the handsome boy in the red shirt turns around to face me. "You don't have no mouth now, eh?" His voice is raspy. Almost sexy. It makes me think of ginger cookies to hear him speak. But I am disappointed by his diction.

"Pussy have you tongue under lockdown, eh?" The circle of boys all grin.

The question confuses me. This strange pink mouth shouldn't be whispering those words against the side of my face. The bouts of laughter are melding and separating, melding and separating—I can hear the air in their lungs. They are excited. If I look at them with my eyes squinted, they are all a blur of eyes and teeth. All laughing. I am so distracted by the moving faces I can't count straight.

Focus, Staceyann.

You can escape. But there are too many of them for me to get away. No matter, escape is in the mind. But I'm only one hundred and five pounds. Maybe one hundred six . . .

Focus.

How many? Count them! Count, and stop being so afraid! And focus. Think. Think and count! Count!

One by one, look into their faces and count them.

Okay, first the one with the shaved head. His scalp is darker than mine. My head is shaped better. No bumps in sight as the clippers glide uninterrupted over the smooth yellow of my scalp. I have a better head. I am certain of it. Bumpy-head, number one.

Big pink lips. Number two. I prefer such thick lips on the smile of a woman; on the rugged face of a man, fleshy lips seem vulgar. Was that number three? No, still number two.

Blue shirt with gray buttons, number three.

Red shirt with a butterflylike collar, number four.

White T-shirt, needs bleach, number five.

Facial. Features. Particular.

"We nah promote your kinda slackness 'pon de campus, you know." Blue Shirt. Dirty fingernails digging into his armpits as he speaks.

"No, man, all Sodomite fi dead. Nuff fire fi bun fi dem, yes." Red Shirt.

White Shirt grabs his protruding crotch and pushes his pelvis in my direction. "Unless, of course, them come to the Holy Temple of the Royal Wood to repent and worship."

His lack of taste disgusts me. His language is coarse. Some people should not be allowed to speak. His eyes narrow at my scornful expression. "And who is you to look down on me? You who commit the worst sin that can be committed against God!" He suddenly throws back his head, grabs his crotch, and laughs.

The harsh laughter unsettles me. Andy and Shappy had that laugh. The raucous rush of sound scares me even more in this moment because number six, the large copper-colored boy in a bright yellow shirt, stands between my body and the only door.

"Is why you don't want no man? Why you 'fraid o' the rod of correction, eh, baby?" Blue Shirt's tone attempts the seduction of Red's. If I weren't here, it would be hilarious to watch.

"Yes, why you so frighten a de big bamboo? You think it goin' hurt you? It not goin hurt you, you know. Just make you get better quick. Come feel it, nuh." White Shirt moves closer to me. Blue Shirt follows him. The circle moves in.

I tell myself to stay focused.

How many times have you negotiated men in this scenario?

Not like this, though, not like this!

This is real, this is real—oh, my God! These boys are going to—oh, my God! They are really going to rape me! Oh, God! I haven't had sex with a man in—I don't even know how long. Oh, God! What am I going to—But pay attention to the faces! And features, now. Features. Particular. Facial. Features.

Okay, Red Shirt has a cleft in his chin. No—that's the boy in the blue shirt. What if they take off their shirts? How will I remember? And what color is the shirt directly behind me? And how many shirts are there in all? Count them again, Staceyann. Two, four, six—

One large-muscled arm wraps itself around my middle. The unexpected intimacy spreads nausea throughout my entire body. Another pair of hands pulls at my navy blue tank. The gentle fingers deftly unsnap the slender bra strap. These fingers have to be Red's. The left breast drops lower than the right. His hand snakes into my tank top. The surprising smoothness of his palm is silky on the loose breast. I can *hear* my heart jumping under his hand.

I lean my lower half away from the bulge pressing against my hip. Blue Shirt licks on my left shoulder. Red's chest is beating urgently against my face. His sharp cologne tickles my nose. I recognize the sharp smell of Cool Water by Davidoff.

Start over, stupid. You will need the exact number later. Later when all of this is over.

One, two, three, four, five—oh, my God! Red's fleshy tongue is deep in my mouth; the sharp taste of Red Stripe stings bitter on his breath. Why was he drinking beer at two in the afternoon? He was probably playing dominoes before he came in here.

I like dominoes. The full lips are behind my ear. I used to play dominoes with Glen and Elisha in Montego Bay. The rough stubble prickles my neck. We always played . . . cutthroat. Every man for himself. Cutthroat, we called it. I watch, body strangely relaxed, as they push and pull at my breasts, my belly, the back of my neck. They are not doing this to me, I am thinking. It must be some other girl collapsed and silent against them. This is not me. Not me at all, at all, at all.

"Why you cut off all you long, long hair, eh, baby love?" Red mutters the question, petulant, against the nape of my neck. I am surprised at his even breathing.

"It was too long," I mouth back, soundless and apologetic.

"Answer me, you little raas-claat cunt!" He did not hear me. His fingers rake forward over the shaved crown, down over my face, down to cup my chin and tilt my head back against his shoulders. His fingernails bruise my face. He should be more careful, I think. If he wants to get away with this, he shouldn't leave any marks.

The ceiling is white and flawless. They must have painted it recently. I can smell the acrid tobacco on his breath. Craven A. Legal ganja, the foreigners call it.

"Answer me when me talk to you. You must try and make things easier for yourself, you hear me?" He pulls my head all the way back. His face is now touching mine but upside down. "I will break you neck, you know. Now, why the fuck you cut you hair?"

"It was too long!" I shout back. "Jesus Christ! It was too long, it was too long, it was too much to deal with . . ." The warm tears mark a trail from right eye to right ear. Why the fuck am I crying?

His chin rests easy against my pounding jugular. He licks the salty tears seeping slowly into my cochlea. I wonder what color his undershirt is. I can't see it, but I can feel the thick seam lines pressing against my scapular.

Red's manicured fingers struggle with the simple knot at my waist. He has the most beautiful hands. "Is what happen to this bloodclaat skirt?"

"Bus it off, man," Blue prompts.

"No, man, she go need to put it on back." Red turns my body around to face him. Why am I so grateful to this monster?

He fumbles again with the knot. Surer fingers reach out and undo the flame-colored sarong. The folds fall caressingly at my feet. Why can't I match the faces to the shirts? What if I can't remember any of the faces? I can imagine me telling the police officer that it was a red shirt, and a blue shirt, and a white . . .

The perfect hands slide down into my panties. I pull up one knee and slam it into his crotch. The fingers suddenly become a fist. I am thrown against the wall.

"What kind of nastiness you a promote over 'pon Seacole Hall?" The flat of his palm connects with my left jawbone. The sound of it is miles away. The pain slowly extends to the inside of my lip. I savor the trickle of blood spreading over my tongue.

Red is now pressing his pelvis into mine.

I swallow hard. I have no idea what he or I will do next. I can see the reflection of my body in the shiny square above the sink. *I look slimmer in this mirror,* I am thinking, *not so chunky in the waist.*

But why can't I look at their faces?

Someone slides a hand between my legs again. I stand up on my tippy-toes and look away. I do not want to know whose hand is kneading away at my vagina. I jump when Red moves his body even closer. The familiar cackle of men hunting game fills the room.

"Shut up, you fuckers," Red commands. The room is immediately silent.

His large hand explores the medium-sized mound that is my loose breast. He roughly throws my body against the wet porcelain sink. The cheering starts again. The rough red fabric itches my nose. His crotch is pushing—

The metal lock of the bathroom door clicks as it opens. Everything goes completely still.

A tall slender boy steps into the bathroom. His piano fingers hold on to the silver door handle, unsure of what he has walked into. His unblemished brow wrinkles his confusion.

I am so relieved I start sobbing.

I know him! I am saved! I know him! I know him! His name is Orville Duhaney!

My chest dances its recognition as I sum him up in memory. I can't remember how I know him, but I know he likes Broadway musicals and soap operas. I know he is gay. So I know he would not let these boys rape me. That means it is over now. It is over. *Oh, my God! It is over now. Thank you, Jesus! Thank you, Jesus. It is over.*

Nothing happened and it is over. The muscles in my gut loosen as I stoop to pick up my sarong. I am so tired. I just want to go home and sleep. All I want now is a long—

"Ease up, there, baby love, don't go nowhere." Red grabs my right arm and pats my back. "We soon come back to you."

He then turns to face Orville. "All right, my youth. If you not for the cause, you must be against it. What you sayin? You leaving, or you coming? You with us or against us?" He poses the question quietly, as if it is the most logical query in the world.

Orville's hips swivel as if to exit, and the rage rises up hot and white through the cistern of my constricted throat. I can't believe the little faggot is going to leave me!

I find my voice and lunge toward him. "Yow, Orville, if you leave me here with them I will make sure you won't live to see another sunrise!"

The sound surprises me and Red's fingers tighten around my arm. He laughs and jerks my body back to his. The movement jiggles the loose breast. I am now looking straight into Orville's eyes. He meets my stare for a second. Then his gaze drops to the floor.

It's now or never.

"Listen to me, Orville, I want you understand what me sayin to you, now—listen to me, and listen good." The words spill from me without forethought or reason. "If you leave me here with them—I do things, say things to make sure you will never be safe in this country!"

I shouldn't be so angry with him. He is only scared of what they would do to him if they knew that he liked boys. The boys around me shift. Red is still behind me, one hand on my right arm, the other holding my left elbow. I can feel his erect penis pressing against me through his jeans. The little fuck is not going to leave me here! He is going to help me.

Red laughs again. He is not even worried about Orville's presence in the room. I have to do something to make him help me. "Orville, you want me to tell you how I will do it?" I push my ass against Red—to remind me that this is necessary. "I will tell everybody everything I know about you. I will tell everybody what you do when—"

"What you want me to do?" he cuts me off. "You think me one can fight all of them?" He stands straight and faces me. "And furthermore, this is really none of my business."

How can the little prick be so spineless?

"I really don't give a fuck, Orville. You have to—you can't leave—you don't see what they going do to me?" I raise the crushed sarong in testament.

"What I going do, Stacey? I really can't do nuttin."

Red is no longer amused by our conversation. He points a finger at Orville's nose. "Hey, pussyhole, you can talk to her after we done with her. Right now big man have business fi deal wid. So get the raas outta here—before we start beat you fi the foreplay!" His armpits are dark red from sweat.

"I am sorry, Stacey, I really don't think I can do anything . . ." Orville steps away from the raised arms. "What I must do?"

My response leaves little room for negotiation. "If you leave me now, I going fuck you up later."

I am sorry for him. But I need his consideration more than he needs mine. He hangs his head again.

"Orville, if you leave me . . ."

"All right, all right, Stacey! I hear you the first time. I hear you the first time."

Orville is almost crying as he turns his body from the door and toward the rainbow of schoolboy shirts. He begins with a painfully feeble attempt. "All right—All right, now—make us look at the situation—make us see what exactly we can—"

I almost laugh out loud at his ineptitude.

"Why you don't want to join in? You is a batty bwoy or what?" asks Red Shirt.

Blue steps forward and pushes Orville in the chest. "Yeah, what is that? Free pussy and you refusin—you must be a sodomite or a priest—and I don't see no Bible in you hand. Sonny bwoy, we beat faggot just fi fun, you know." He pushes him again. "Is mus bloodclaat batty you love! Is that why you don't want to fuck her? Because you prefer to fuck man?"

Orville is almost hyperventilating.

Blue addresses the group. "Yow, bredren, we just might have fi deal with a faggot situation when we done with this lesbian."

Orville finally finds his voice. "No man—just listen to me, nuh—I like pussy—I like pussy, man—the same as—" I hold my breath and pray for his eloquence. "No, man, trust me, I love pussy just like the next man, but I don't like kill my own meat. I like it prepare and ready fi eat—I mean ready fi fuck."

"What that supposed to mean?" He finally has their attention.

"Well, we all civilized people, right?" Silence clips the edge off his question.

"We a big man now, right? Right. And we all get pussy all the time. It come to we—we no need fi run it down like ice-cream truck. Right?"

Blue steps forward. "Yow, don't feel is desperation make we have her in here, you know. We nah go fuck her because we can't get pussy—we trying to curb this lesbian business we hear 'bout her. We can't have sodomite mongst we, free fi do all them nastiness. Make them feel is all good and well fi disrespect the way God put we down here fi live. Something have to be done 'bout this way of thinking that creeping on this island!"

His cronies nod their conviction.

Red runs his hands down my right hip and thigh. "Yes, we going fuck her to bring her back to the right way of thinking. We fucking her to save her from herself and from hellfire."

The group nods again.

I wish I could speak, but I am too afraid of how they would respond to anything I would say.

"All right, forget all o' that. What if somebody find out?" A slight pause interrupts the nodding.

"What if the police find out? Her family might have money, you know." He is better than I thought. They are still listening to him.

"Who going tell them? You?" Red Shirt narrows his eyes in question.

"No, man, but just like I walk in here, somebody else can walk in too."

Doubt settles over the congregation. And Orville forges ahead. "Anybody can just walk in, the cleaning man, the plumber—anybody. And oonu say she a sodomite? What if she have some kinda fuck-up disease? What if she have AIDS?"

"The woman them get AIDS too?" Blue Shirt's tone is unsure.

No one is holding me now. And I am five feet from the door. Five small steps. Three medium ones. One carefully planned lunge and then the door.

"Yes, man, the whole a them fuck each other in them batty and do all kinda nastiness—you never know, and some of them have disease that worse than AIDS." Orville is on a roll.

Four and a half tiny feet to the door. Four and a quarter. Four. No one is looking at me. All eyes are on Orville.

"And, you know, it quicker fi a man get AIDS from a woman than the other way around. Who in here did know that?" He indicts their lack of knowledge.

Three and a half feet. Skirt wrapped around my hips. Left hand holding the ends together. Three feet.

My right hand is inches from the door.

"And from what I hear, more woman have AIDS than man and some disease you can get just by touching one of them—"

Red's voice cuts into Orville's. "Where the bloodclaat you think you going? Oonu hold her, nuh!"

But everyone is afraid of touching me. And that split second is all I need to swing the door back and run. And run I do. Across the grass and toward the parking lot. Through the red cars, the blue cars, the white cars. Down the seductive curve of Ring Road. Across the Arts parking lot. Blue cars. Red cars. White cars. Green grass under my bare feet again. Through the Nat Sci parking lot. Over the wide expanse of grass again between Soc Sci and Mona, through the wire gate. Hot asphalt slapping the soles of my feet. Violet Avenue, Begonia Drive, Carnation Avenue. And then home.

I Will Make a Way

Once I am inside my apartment, I can barely move. My shoulders feel as if they are working hard not to close in on themselves. My heart refuses to stop racing and my eyes won't close for more than a few minutes at a time. And my body begins to shake when I think about going outside. I am completely and utterly disgusted with myself.

The events of the afternoon play over and over in my head. I want to go back there and scream at them, fight them, do anything but stand there paralyzed, unable to defend myself. I can't believe that I just let them pull off my clothes and touch me without saying one word.

For four days I remain in my house. I don't want to go back on campus and bump into one of them in the corridors or in the cafeteria. The printed sarong is draped guiltily across my bed. I want to throw it away, but I wonder if I should keep it as evidence.

"Evidence of what, Staceyann Chin? Nothing happened. There was no penile penetration. No rape. Nothing happened to you." The face in the bathroom mirror does even not look like mine anymore. "Who are you, Staceyann Chin? Who are you but a coward and a farce? Why do you need fucking evidence? Who will you tell and whatever will you say? Nobody *raped* you! A couple of stupid homophobic college boys *roughed you up a little*. There is nothing to tell! You just have to stop being dramatic, and shower and get dressed and take your ass to class!"

The bruise on my cheek has almost faded. But the warm stream of tears stings the cut that keeps reopening on my lip. I have to lie down again. I wipe my face with the sarong. It still smells like sweat and the walls of that bathroom. I wish I could just go straight to the police and report it. But I can never tell anyone how silent the brave Staceyann Chin was in that room.

I carefully fold the sarong and place it in my bottom drawer. It was once my favorite. Now I cry every time I look at it. I examine the almost-invisible bruise again. I wish I lived in a big city, far, far away. That way I could go outside without the likelihood of my almost-rapists seeing me. Maybe I could move to Germany, find my sorry excuse for a mother. I would like to ask her what the hell she was thinking when she left two small children with a poor, deaf, illiterate woman. But I don't even know where in Germany she lives. Maybe I should go to Canada, practice this irrelevant French. But Canada is really the dream of that little girl waiting for someone to come back and save her. I am a big girl now. I am not waiting for anyone to come back for me. I can go anywhere by myself. I should go to America. I should go to New York.

"I am going to America!"

I say it out loud. The woman in the mirror looks excited. "Yes, I am going to migrate to America!"

In New York I wouldn't have to sneak around and live like something is wrong with me. I could go on dates with women and hold hands and act like I am a normal person. I could forget my father's denial of me, my mother leaving. America seems like the kind of place where people go when they want to leave everything behind. Sometimes it's good to leave everything behind. So you can make room for new and better things. I yank the sarong out of my special drawer, cut the fringed rectangle to pieces, and toss them one by one into the garbage can.

I strike a match and let it fall into the can. The fabric sizzles and the flames blaze higher and higher. Bending over the black smoke makes me cough and I get scared the apartment will catch fire. In my hurry to get water, I overturn the bin and the flames fizzle to nothing on the smooth tiles. I pour the water over the charred bits of sarong anyway. The blackened water looks like ink on the white tiles. I wipe the floor and wash out the garbage can. Only the faint smell of Lysol lingers in the air. If anyone walked in, they would never guess that moments before something important had been burnt to ash.

I walk the long way to rehearsal at lightning speed across the campus. As I cross the Arts parking lot Brandt calls out to me, but do I not want any company, so I pretend not to hear. I play Melissa Etheridge for all she is worth. I keep my favorite song on repeat and belt the words out to the empty sky.

I travel from agency to agency hunting for the least expensive ticket to New York. I sell my computer for enough money to buy the ticket with seven hundred U.S. dollars left over. Then I start selling my books. I am so focused on leaving that I barely attend classes. My professors want to know what is going on with me. But I say nothing to anyone.

The only place I feel present is in rehearsals. I run my lines over and over, getting angrier as I stomp around on the stage. It feels good to scream Braithwaite's poem out loud. It feels good to say the words *fuck* and *raas* and "*Down, down, white man!*"

On the night of the performance I fill the theater with my voice. I think of Red's hands in my panties and I whisper,

> *Ever seen*
> *a man*
> *travel more*
> *seen more*
> *lands*
> *than this poor*
> *land-*
> *less, harbour-*
> *less spade?*

I think about how I let those hands touch me—how I did not say anything while they did what they wanted to me.

> *To hell / with Af- / rica / to hell / with Eu- / rope too, / just call my blue /*
> *black bloody spade / a spade and kiss / my ass. O- / kay? So / let's begin.*

The audience applauds every time I speak. I want to stop my lines and start shouting that I am a lesbian. To tell them they are clapping their heterosexual hands in appreciation of a lesbian in performance. I want to run out into the crowd and tell them what I am. But the scripted words keep forcing themselves out of me with an anger I do not recognize:

> *But bes' leh we get to rass / o' this place; out o' this / asshole, out o' the stink o' this / hell. To rass o' this . . .*

At the end of the night the audience is on its feet. One girl corners me after the performance and tells me, "Boy, Staceyann, you were so electrifying when you were shouting at the audience. You looked so angry! It was wonderful! You looked so sexy and powerful up there!"

I cough and nod my thanks.

"You are quite welcome, Miss Chin." Then she kisses me on the cheek and walks away.

The girl has never spoken to me before. And I am confused by the kiss. Does that mean she likes me? That she is a lesbian? That I am to speak to her when I next see her?

The next day I pick up my ticket to travel to New York on August 20. Now all I have to do is finish my thesis and fly far, far away.

My head of department, Dr. Chang, asks me to house-sit for the two months before I leave. In the morning I head to the library. I walk with a book of poems and a novel in case I lose the urge to work. In the afternoon I sit on the grass. I do not feel so alone when I can see the sky.

One evening I come home to find an invitation to a party. The square card, slipped under the door, is glossy and has a phone number where the invitee has to RSVP. The host, Sunflower, is throwing a party and I am invited. I am shocked to see that the card says *Gays and lesbians only.*

I show Racquel the invitation "Can you believe this? A real live invitation?"

"Of course! This is the first one you ever see?"

"What you mean by the first one? You have seen one of these before?"

"Yes. There are lots of us on campus. But you are so *out* that everybody is afraid to talk to you. There's even a club."

"A club? A *gay* club? In Jamaica?"

"Yes. It's called Entourage. And it's in New Kingston."

Entourage is really the living room of a man named Brian Williamson. One wall of the room has been converted to a bar of sorts. There are mirrors behind a shelf with various bottles of alcohol and a cleared space in the middle of the room for dancing. On the other side of the room a DJ spins while one dark slim boy in cut-off shorts wiggles provocatively on the lap of another. A muscular girl wearing a white T-shirt and a black tie winks at me. Everyone else stirs colored drinks and looks around nervously.

The girl from the *Passages* audience, Marlene is her name, is also there. She kisses me on the lips and asks me if I got the invitation to the party in the hills. I tell her I can't go because I don't have a ride. She offers me a lift if I promise not to tell her father where she will be taking his car.

The ride is long and the directions aren't clear, but Marlene knows exactly where she is going. She tells me that the instructions are intentionally misleading to discourage straight people and their dangerous curiosity about who goes to these parties. Old Stony Hill Road is dark, and it is raining, but when we get there I am not disappointed. I never imagined that there were this many lesbians in Jamaica. There are scores of girls dressed in suits and slinky ball gowns, and jeans and shorts. The gay men are out too, dressed in drag—men sporting muscled glutes in batty-riders and lots of heavy, heavy security at the gate.

I recognize a few people from school. Orville is there, but we both pretend that we do not see each other. Seranna is there in a beautiful white dress that makes me want to take it off her. When I try to say hello she turns her back, lights a cigarette, and leans in to the beautiful woman standing next to her. I tap her on the shoulder and Marlene elbows me and quickly pulls me away. Generally, she says, people don't speak to each other unless they come in together. I explain to her that I already know Seranna, but she says it does not matter. Occasionally, she says, if there is a mutual crush, you can ask a common friend for her number later, but the rule is you leave people alone to have a good time at the parties. You just listen to the music and stand around and thank God that you are with people who are like you.

I watch Seranna dance with her friends. I really want to just walk over to her and tell her about my decision to move to America, but every time I meet her gaze she seems to look right through me. I count at least ten people from the English Department and five from Philosophy, but no one even looks in my direction. I feel as if I am in a film. We all have the balls to come out to a big secret party, but we are all too scared to actually talk to each other.

Two weeks later I get another invitation. The day after that Marlene shows up waving a note she says was sent by the pretty woman who was standing next to Seranna at the last party. Kimberly is a final-year medical student who identifies as bisexual. Her note is short and to the point.

You looked really good in that little dress you wore at the last party. If you promise to wear something equally fetching, I will give you a ride in my pretty car to the next one.

Kimberly makes me laugh. And she has the most beautiful legs. And she quotes verses and verses of poetry while she kisses my feet. She spends most nights in my apartment. We stay up till dawn, talking about everything from politics to babies to religion to sex. But one day I bump into her at the library and she passes me, barely nodding hello. That night when she knocks I do not answer the door. She begs and begs, but I tell her I refuse to speak to her unless she promises that that will never happen again. She tells me I am being unfair, that I want her to risk her life for my crazy politics. I tell her I would rather die honest than live the deceitful life she has planned for herself. I turn up the television and close the windows. I don't even know when she leaves.

Days later she shows up with flowers and a poem written on rice paper. She admits that I am right and promises to introduce me to her friends. After a while I realize that even when she admits that she knows me, I am still only her literature-major *friend.* By the first week of August we are back to sneaking into her apartment by day and out of mine late at night. I know I cannot live my life like this. I refuse to grow old kissing the woman I love under the cover of night and pretending I don't know her the next day.

I finish my thesis on the sixteenth. My bags are packed by the morning of the seventeenth. When the last bag is zipped, I lie on the floor and stare at the ceiling. The list of people I have to see is short. Racquel, Grandma—I wonder how Delano is doing all the way in Germany. I still have no number for him. It hurts my chest to think I may never see him again.

Racquel and I plan to have our last lunch together on the eighteenth— the day before I leave. I get there half an hour before we are to meet so I can journal. I write two lines before she arrives.

August 18, 1997
I leave Jamaica tomorrow. Lots of emotions.
   I can't believe I am really doing this!

She is quiet as she hugs me. And when I pull away there are tears in her eyes. I beg her not to cry. "Please, please, please. I'm not sure if I can handle that, Racquel."

"I'm sorry, Stace. But you must expect that I am going to miss you."

"I know that. I know that. It's funny, though, a few days ago I was so happy to be leaving. Today I am wishing I had another month to be here—I don't even know what I would do with another month, I just wish I wasn't leaving tomorrow."

"What is funny is that I wish it were me going."

"You could still come with me . . ."

"No—that journey is yours. You are the wild, crazy one that everybody expects to go and conquer new horizons and all that jazz. Go on and do your thing. I am staying right here. Come hell or high water."

I had hoped she would want to leave too. But I know she has two more years of school, and I know she would not just up and leave her family. Maybe later she will change her mind. Still, I can't imagine my life without Racquel close by. Who will I call to complain to or argue with—or just sit with?

"Racquel, for most of my life you have been such a good friend. And even though I'm not crying, I will miss you—very, very much. Everything is so complicated, and I don't know if I really feel sad about leaving, but I know I will never find a better friend than you. Please be careful here. And I hope you and your girl stay together for a very long time." My heart is a rock inside my chest as I whisper good-bye to my oldest friend.

She holds me and mutters that I could still change my mind. There must be another way around this. I wrap my arms around her and squeeze. It isn't fair. In my heart of hearts I don't want to leave either, but I don't see a way I can stay. Plus the wheels have been set to turning and I am already on my way.

When I go to see Grandma, the lump in my throat almost makes me call the travel agent to cancel my ticket. When I tell her I am leaving for America, she wipes her eyes with her handkerchief and nods. Her hands are gentle on my shoulder as she begs me to be careful. "America is a very big place, and you was never very big. But me will be here praying for you. Every day that God send I am going to put you safety before the Lord—God bless the day that you was born . . ." She buries her face into her hands and sobs.

I put my arms around her and hold her until she stops shaking. I remember how easily I left her crying at that tiny bus stop in Bethel Town. I wish I could tell her how sorry I am about that, how wrong I was to think we would have been better off without her. I want to be nine again so I can hug her, say how grateful I am that she looked after Delano and me for all those years. I want to explain to her that I am not my mother, that I will come back. But I am twenty-four years old and I know better than to make promises I'm not sure I can keep. So I just rub her face and tell her that as soon as I get a job I will send her some money. She makes me promise that if she dies I will come home for the funeral. I promise, though I am not certain I will ever see Jamaica again. I need to be far away from the things that have happened to me here.

As I board the plane, the attendant accidentally drops my passport on the floor. "Oh, I'm sorry, dear. Looks like somebody doesn't want you to go today. How long will you be gone?"

I smile as she hands me my boarding pass. It takes all my willpower not to say that I intend to be away until it is safe for Jamaicans to be openly gay. I try not to think of how long that might be. From my window seat on the plane the world seems small, manageable. And as the ground falls away, a feeling of excitement wells up inside me. Suddenly it dawns on me that, though leaving is hard, this is something I want to do. The choice to go is *my* decision. For the first time in my life my leaving is something I *want* to be happening to me.

Epilogue

Today my relationship with most of my family remains somewhat estranged. But now there exists an odd symbiosis of phone calls and very short visits dictated by scheduling and distance. In the effort to connect them to each other, I pass photographs and messages and facilitate three-way calls between people who have not seen each other in decades. Delano has settled in a valley somewhere between the snowy mountains in the Alps. My mother, who also remained in Europe, has become an interesting character. Her third and youngest child is sixteen years my junior, and already my sister has given the family a berth wide enough for all of us to drown in.

Over the years Grandma changed very little. Except for getting older and older and more fascinated with predicting her own death, she was the same old woman who told me stories of my past and encouraged me to lay my troubles at the feet of Jesus to make everything all right. Every time I went home to see her, she would say the same things. "Remember, now, Stacey, God save you from that pit toilet for a reason. No matter what worries you have, don't forget, you have many blessings too. Make good use of the breath of life. Time is passing, and the Heavenly Father soon call all of us home. I tell you, you might not come back and see the old lady sitting here again."

Having heard this speech a million times before, I would nod and snap photographs of her as she got warmed up. "Look at me, look how me old—Stacey, you know that me nearly a hundred year old now?"

"Me know, Grandma, me know."

"Me know you know, but me still telling you. The Bible only promise us three score years and ten—I wouldn't have a thing to complain about if the good Lord decide to take me home tonight."

But when she passed away in September 2007 I was still unprepared for her leaving. I felt as if I had suddenly become an orphan. Her physical absence from Jamaica has forced me to examine the ways in which Jamaica is still my home. And when I bump up against seemingly insurmountable obstacles she remains the voice of encouragement in my head, urging me to at least *attempt* the impossible, to let the record show that I did not shy away from any task simply because I was afraid. Her life stands as the example of how much one can do with so little.

Junior Chin and I still speak occasionally. When I ring, our talk is of economy and politics. *Yes, Obama's victory is historical. No, McCain is not as good-looking. Or as smart as Hillary. I know, I know, but it's a real shame about the foreclosures, eh? Jamaica is bound to bear the brunt of the recessional aftershock.* He still maintains that I am not his biological daughter and he refuses to do a DNA test. But for better or worse, he is the only father to which I can lay any claim. And outside of a mild curiosity (to know for sure), I am not certain that such scientific knowledge is necessary. Perhaps I am only in denial, but there is something wonderful in the muddy gray that informs our spirited interaction.

I am learning that one never really puts a turbulent childhood completely to rest. As an adult, I have been very lucky. As soon as I got to New York City I discovered the culture of performance poetry. From the very first moment I stepped to the microphone, I have been telling bits of this story in verse, in prose, and, later on, more fully in autobiographical one-person Off-Broadway plays. The constant examination of the life I have lived has made it clear to me that the events of those early years were not my fault; I did nothing to deserve being abandoned or assaulted or otherwise abused. After that I began the business of managing my defense mechanisms, neuroses, and general feelings of worthlessness.

More than ten years and thousands of dollars and countless romances later, I am mostly proud of the path I have taken. A few regrets linger among these pages. I wish I had found a way to remain closer to my brother. And I wish I hadn't been as hard on my friends when I came out in Jamaica. I also ache for my mother to find a place where she feels at rest. I have yet to find a way to let her know that I understand that she was young and under the siege of poverty when she left us. In a way, she saw a choice between trying to save us and saving herself. The fallout was massive, but I cannot say that under similar circumstances I would have done differently. These days, she spends our phone calls lamenting that she does not deserve my kindnesses. I am hoping that if and when I have a child, she will have the room to be a doddering and doting old grandmother. Perhaps she can find forgiveness for herself in an easy relationship with a child who wears my face.

In some ways, the tools I developed as a child have served me well in my career. I go from place to place spouting the gospel of courage and survival. I encourage victims to take hold of destiny and chart it for themselves. But I know that not all of us have the emotional or financial resources right at our fingertips. Some people will have to work much harder than I did; others will suffer more permanent scars. Many of the characters in the early part of this tale remain impoverished and without any discernible escape from that poverty. And when I visit them in Jamaica, I am often caught between anger at the suffering I endured in the years I spent with them and understanding that, more often than not, people did the best they could under remarkably difficult and pressing circumstances.

My friends say I am mellowing. And at the risk of proving such a statement true, I must admit that, these days, I am more inclined to kindness than rage. Most mornings I become conscious at dawn, with my cat stepping on my head as if I am not there. But if I want to enjoy a moment of stillness before being pounced on, I keep my eyes closed, pretending I am still asleep. For when I eventually stir, my dogs, London and Kingston, will come sailing at me missile-like through the air, excited and insisting that I get up and fill their empty bowls.

New York City has been good to me. It has been everything I needed and more. Between Broadway and Brooklyn, Far Rockaway and the Bronx, I have kept pace with its teeming, changing, grueling skyline. I continue to be grateful for the friends who consistently show up at Thanksgiving and Christmas and Kwanzaa and Hanukkah and Easter and all the other holidays when biological families usually gather. Sitting with them over smothered chicken and stuffing and fried plantains and sushi, I can safely say I did more than just survive.

Acknowledgments

As it reads, this story would not have been possible without my friend and editor, Alexis Gargagliano. A believer in my awkward poems and my self-indulgent, multicultural identity, she followed my career and waited till it was possible and prudent to bid on this memoir. She has read draft after draft and navigated my doubts and neuroses, my sorrows and my small triumphs for three years. She has cooked for me and cried with me. And when my grandmother passed away, she was patient and sometimes far gentler than was required as she encouraged me to stay with the process. I had no idea how well I was choosing when I decided to trust her, and Scribner, with the disconnected patchwork of narratives that has become this version of my survival.

The other hands that stirred the pot of this story have been many and varied.

Frances Goldin, my agent and friend, finds time to kiss my face, read unfinished drafts, travel to see Mumia on death row, do yoga, cook soups for sick friends, and tell all her clients how lucky she feels to represent them. I know that it was my good fortune to have met you and your trusty sidekick, Ellen Geiger.

I tip my hat to my friend and mentor, Walter Mosley, who mandated that I *write for two hours every day*. Thank you for listening to my fears and giving me the best advice in the business.

I could not proceed without saying thanks to those who gave me permission to write my story, even when they were not sure how kind my pen would be. I remain grateful in that trust for my sister/friend, Racquel

Bremmer, my mother, Hazel, my brother, Delano, my cousins Elisha and Annmarie, my Auntie Olga, and the others who, out of respect for their privacy, I have decided to keep anonymous.

My Jamaican cheering squad remains undaunted by those who would rather I keep my counsel. To them I extend my most heartfelt gratitude: Kerry-Jo Lyn, Camara Brown, Maziki Thame, Vivette Miller, Karl Williams, Dane Lewis, June Lewis, Deean Fontaine, Lana Ho-Shing, Colin Channer, Natalie Bennett, Aliya Leslie, Sandra Mullings, Lisa Mullings, Natasha Gracey, Nkromo Ross, Ysanne Latchman, and the sea of others who would speak alongside me if they could.

Then there are those who first encouraged the story through poetry and theater: Kamau Brathwaite, Roger Bonair-Agard, Lynne Procope, Eric Guerrieri, Guy Gonzalez, Allan Buchman, Ira Pittleman, Carolyn Allen, Ruby Sales, CC Carter, Soyini Dyson, Jackie Anderson, Greg Polvere, the late Peter James Conti, his mother Carole Conti, and the plethora of activists and artists I have met and worked with since happening upon New York life. I don't think I would have had the courage to write this book without those early years of being onstage.

Others who do not fall so easily into neat categories but have been invaluable to my process as a writer and a functional human being include Michael, Dionne Brand, Leleti Russell, Asha Punnett, Andrea Barrow, Angela Williams, Gloria Bigelow, Shontina Vernon, Kalamu Ya Salaam, Laini Madhubuti, Tiona McClodden, Bernadette "Ebony" Brown, Alana Proctor, Asha Bandele, Carmen Grau, Mark Chung, Michelle Hampton, Shawn Carter, Lisa Schwinghammer, and Larah Mills-Moller. To you and the host of hands who have kept me sane and smiling, I owe my best self.

And finally, to the voices who have been listening from afar and waiting for this story, thank you for waiting and making me feel like there would be palms open enough to receive this tale. I hope I have done the telling justice. I hope it rings clear with pieces of your own truths, your own stories, your yearning for the other side of your very own paradise.